DICK JENNINGS
661-831-9459

MOSCOW MADNESS

[Moscow Madness]

Crime, Corruption, and
One Man's Pursuit of Profit
in the New Russia

TIMOTHY HARPER

McGRAW-HILL

New York San Francisco Washington, D.C. Auckland Bogotá Caracas
Lisbon London Madrid Mexico City Milan Montreal New Delhi
San Juan Singapore Sydney Tokyo Toronto

Library of Congress Cataloging-in-Publication Data

Harper, Timothy.
    Moscow madness : crime, corruption, and one man's pursuit of
profit in the new Russia / Timothy Harper.
        p.   cm.
    Includes index.
    ISBN 0-07-026700-6 (alk. paper)
    1. Grajirena, Rick. 2. Businessmen—United States—Biography.
3. Businessmen—Russia (Federation)—Biography. 4. Business ethics—
Russia (Federation) 5. Russia (Federation)—Commerce. 6. Beer
industry—Russia (Federation) I. Title.
HC102.5.G715H37 1999
338'.04'092—dc21
    [B]   99-11347
                                                                    CIP

McGraw-Hill

A Division of The **McGraw·Hill** Companies

1 2 3 4 5 6 7 8 9 0   AGM/AGM   9 0 3 2 1 0 9 8

ISBN 0-07-026700-6

Book design by Tina Thompson

Printed and bound by Quebecor/Martinsburg.

McGraw-Hill books are available at special quantity discounts to use as
premiums and sales promotions, or for use in corporate training programs.
For more information, please write to Director of Special Sales,
McGraw-Hill, 11 West 19th Street, New York, NY 10011. Or contact your
local bookstore.

 This book is printed on recycled, acid-free paper containing a
minimum of 50% recycled, de-inked fiber.

To the memory of
John N. Hazard

Contents

PART 2: HANGOVER HELPERS

PREFACE

In early 1995, cruising through writers' forums on CompuServe and America Online, I came across a cryptic but intriguing message. An American entrepreneur doing business in Russia thought he had a story to tell. He was looking for a writer to help him tell it. Curious, I replied and told him a little about myself. The entrepreneur responded and identified himself as Rick Grajirena. He liked the fact that I had international experience, that I had written several previous books, that I had spent some time in and written about Russia, and that I was involved in a marginal way in the beer business. (I was one of the Brooklyn Brewery's founding investors, and two of my books were about beer.) He was in the beer business in Moscow, Grajirena told me, doing all sorts of things no businessperson had ever tried to do in Russia, and coping with all sorts of crazy things that happened to him and his associates. Doing a little research, I also found out that Grajirena had been a world-class sailor and was still well known in yachting circles. We exchanged e-mail and faxes, talked on the phone, and got together in New York. He agreed to tell me his story. Over the next three-plus years, we spent a considerable amount of time together, much of it in Russia, as his prospects and fortunes ebbed and flowed.

Since this is one man's story, it unfolds largely from his own perspective, and from the perspective of those around him—including, at times, myself. Other people who were part of his story may view things differently. I am sorry I could not include every point of view, and that some events or incidents were not explored as completely as they might have been or were left out entirely. It should be pointed out that several names were changed or identities obscured at Grajirena's request.

This book is Rick Grajirena's story, but in some ways it is the story of many other American business pioneers who braved the frontier of the new

Russia. It is also, in some ways, the story of future American entrepreneurs who no doubt will try to do their part in other emerging nations, as Rick Grajirena and others have tried to do in Russia: to open free markets, to establish reliable business cultures, and to institute the rule of law. And, of course, to make themselves rich.

———————

This book is dedicated to the memory of John N. Hazard, the eminent Columbia University law professor who knew more about the Russian legal system than perhaps anyone, including anyone in Russia. He was a scholar and a gentleman who eagerly shared his fascination with Russia and Russians. I was fortunate to make my first two trips to Russia and the Soviet Union with Professor Hazard.

There are many other people to thank, beginning with my research associate, Terri Mierswa, and my agent, Chris Crane of Authors Alliance. I'm grateful for the encouragement from my editor at McGraw-Hill, Susan Barry, who urged me to focus on the humanity in this story of business, and her assistant, Griffin Hansbury. Thanks to my friend Drew Von Glahn, a banker who knows more about international business than I could ever hope to know, for reading the manuscript and making many valuable suggestions. Also, thanks for the continuing support in so many ways, on this and other writing projects, to my editors at *Sky* magazine and Pace Communications, especially Duncan Christy but also David Bailey, Mickey McLean, and their colleagues.

Among the many sources and interviewees, I must single out Robert Greco, Chris Mitchell, Geoffrey Farrar, and especially, of course, Rick Grajirena. Remarkable were his generosity, his memory, his openness, his humor, his honest if sometimes painful look at his mistakes, his grilled pastrami sandwiches, and particularly his patience with a thousand questions. This is his book as much as it is mine. I also must thank the Grajirena family: Rick's wife, Valerie, their sons Rob and Anthony, and their chocolate lab, Murphy Brown. They all provided much help and hospitality, particularly in welcoming nine-year-old Jonathan, my sidekick on trips to Florida, when Rick and I spent long days locked in his office.

I'd like to thank my mother and father, Bud and Eleanor Harper, who always made sure I had all the books I wanted when I was growing up. They also nurtured the seeds of curiosity and wanderlust, and convinced me from an early age that reading and writing could take me anywhere, including Russia.

Finally, thanks as always to my own family. To Jonny, thanks for making those research trips more fun. (I'm flattered that you want to be a writer, son, but I feel obliged to warn you that journalism isn't all video games, barbecues, and splashing in a pool with a friendly dog.) To my daughter, Lizzie, thanks for all the work as an underpaid but efficient office assistant. And, as always, I appreciate all the support from their mother, Nancy, during those long months of research and writing, and for holding things together while I was in Russia and elsewhere. Nancy, who has considerable international business experience herself, deserves special thanks for invaluable advice in sharpening the manuscript. In our house, writing a book, like just about everything else, is a family project.

PART 1

RUSSIA ON TAP

[Russia on Tap]

CHAPTER 1

August 1994

Rick Grajirena eyed the two beefy Russians. One was wearing a cheap, ill-fitting suit. The other had on blue jeans, a black T-shirt, and a heavy leather jacket, despite the August heat in Moscow. Were they carrying guns? Grajirena couldn't really tell. Could they speak English? He couldn't really tell that, either, given that their only responses—to his greetings in English, and then in rudimentary Russian—were nods and grunts. No matter. They were Grajirena's bodyguards, hired for $25 a day each to keep him alive before, during, and after the meeting at which he intended to fire the manager of his company's Moscow operations. He had been told that the bodyguards understood that he had received death threats, and that the previous evening someone had broken into the apartment where he was staying. He scrutinized the two bullet-headed Russians. They might be brothers.

Grajirena wondered about their commitment to their work. They looked stupid, but were they stupid enough to risk their own lives to save his? For $25? He knew other American businesspeople, especially bankers, who used bodyguards routinely in Moscow. But he himself didn't know anything about bodyguards. Was he paying them too much? Too little? How much did other Americans trust their bodyguards? He consoled himself: at least Americans were not regular targets in the same way as successful Russian businesspeople were, particularly bankers. Two dozen Russian bankers had been assassinated on the streets of Moscow in previous months. Fortunately, no American businesspeople had been killed by the so-called *mafiya*—yet. (Though that would happen soon enough.) All Grajirena knew was that he didn't want to be the first.

As he often did, he pondered the wisdom of trying to do business in the "new" Russia, which had become the high-risk, high-reward frontier for adventuresome American entrepreneurs since the breakup of the Soviet Union less than three years before. Maybe he should have stayed home with his wife and two young kids in Clearwater, Florida, working as a yacht salesman and sailmaker, and hiring on as the unofficial weekend skipper for rich guys who wanted to race their sleek sailboats. But this wasn't the time to think about that. Grajirena swallowed hard, said, "Let's go," and walked out of his office, one bodyguard in front, the other trailing, toward the car that would take him to meet and fire the manager.

Richard A. Grajirena was founder and chief executive officer of First Republic Inc., a Tampa-based company that imported and distributed Miller beer to Moscow. It was a small but high-profile company that was proving that an American distribution network could work in the new Russia, and that Russians would respond enthusiastically to American-style marketing and promotions.

Grajirena and his investors formed First Republic to provide what he jokingly called his "grown-up" job after a long career as an international yachtsman. Over the years he had been involved in several sailing ventures with Russians, including making sails for the Russian Olympic yachting team. Traveling back and forth to Russia on sailing business in the early 1990s, after the fall of the Berlin Wall, he could see the coming economic changes in Eastern Europe, Russia, and the other former Soviet republics.

He could also recognize his own need for change. He was almost fifty years old, and every nickel he ever earned had somehow come from sailing. While sailing provided a simple but comfortable life, he was looking for something that would give him the kind of money he needed to send his kids, now in grade school, to college in a few years. He also had started thinking for the first time about a decent retirement for himself and the younger wife he had found after a long and happy bachelorhood. Grajirena (it is a Basque name, pronounced graj-uh-REE-nuh) formed First Republic in 1992, in hopes of using his Russian contacts—from factory managers to government officials to popular sports figures—as the platform for an import-export business that would take advantage of the fall of Communism and the opening of Russian markets to Western capitalism. Russian people were free for the first time to buy whatever they could afford instead of what their government told them to buy, and they were eager for all manner of American products, from food and drink to cars and television programs. Russian companies were free to make and sell whatever they wanted for whatever price they wanted, instead of relying on government production orders, subsidies, and quotas. They were eager to exploit their technical expertise and cheap labor to sell products to the West. Grajirena reckoned that with trade set to explode in both directions, to and from Russia, there was room for him to serve as the middleman for somebody. Anybody.

It was not difficult for Grajirena to find prospective partners and possible deals. Indeed, when it became known that he was an American looking to buy and sell in Russia, all sorts of characters—some seemingly reputable, many obviously not—came forward with one scheme after another. The propositions covered a broad range, but all had one common element: a commission or finder's fee or percentage of the deal for the person bringing it to Grajirena. More difficult for Grajirena, and for many other American entrepreneurs in Russia, was settling on the right import-export products, and the right partners. He had literally hundreds of meetings with anyone and everyone, on both sides of the Atlantic. Countless meetings were held over drinks, and countless business proposals, many of them outlandish, blurred together in a haze of vodka.

Through it all, Grajirena got an education about Russia and Russians. He was astounded at how the decades of central state planning had stunted the work ethic and dimmed the ability of many Russians, even top managers, to grasp the most basic realities of free-market economics. Many Russians had difficulty understanding the simple profit-and-loss principles of the bottom line. People in the street, who had been clamoring for decades for what the government derided as Western decadence, had difficulty deciding which laundry detergent to buy when a couple of new brands suddenly appeared on supermarket shelves. "How do we decide?" one well-educated Russian woman wailed to Grajirena at a party. "Before, there was only one kind of soap powder, made by the state factory, and that's what we bought."

Grajirena was astonished and frightened by the reach of the *mafiya* and the gang lords relying on thugs who were happy to commit casual mayhem for a few American dollars. They used violence and intimidation to turn central Moscow into a version of gangland Chicago in the Capone era. The *mafiya* gangs—they had no Italian connections; the Russians merely adapted the Sicilian word—tried to get a cut of businesses springing up in the post-Communist free-market economy, and they paid special attention to hard-currency operations. Now, in 1994, two years after he first got the idea to import American beer into Russia, Grajirena again studied the two body-guards. If they weren't part of a *mafiya* gang, they probably were on the fringes. They were probably small-time hoods, independent contractors, who were eager to undertake any sort of dirty work at the behest of any *mafiya* leader who hired them for a job, in the same way that Grajirena, through an old Russian sailing buddy, had hired them to protect his life.

The firing of the Russian manager of First Republic's office in Moscow was the latest in a series of crises that began before the company opened its doors. Grajirena had encountered myriad other problems, with both Russians and Americans, both inside and outside the company—problems with Miller Brewing, problems with customs, problems with taxes, problems with the weather, problems with landlords, problems with investors, accounting problems, and problems with employees on both sides of the Atlantic. The current problem was Misha, the Moscow office manager who only a few months before had been First Republic's golden boy. Misha was young, well dressed, and good looking, and he spoke English reasonably well. He seemed passably educated but also street smart. He certainly knew his way around Moscow. When he first hired Misha, in the autumn of 1992, as one of the company's first three salesmen, Grajirena suspected he at least knew some *mafiya*.

However, Grajirena reasoned, *mafiya* connections weren't necessarily a bad thing, as many other Western businesspeople in Moscow had discovered. Maybe Misha could deflect some of the inevitable *mafiya* attention and persuade the gang bosses to leave First Republic alone. If he had connections, maybe he could help get things done when First Republic encountered the inevitable problems with Moscow's mind-numbing web of ever-changing rules, regulations, and requirements. Certainly Misha made a big impression in his first two days as manager of First Republic's Moscow distribution operation. That was after Grajirena had had to fire First Republic's first Moscow manager, an American. It was one of Grajirena's first encounters with "Moscow Madness," a common syndrome among Americans working in Russia. Businesspeople came to Moscow and lost their professional and personal moorings.

Immediately after Grajirena fired the American manager, Misha stepped in. His quick thinking saved the company from a financial and public relations debacle. Grajirena was grateful to him. In recent months, however, Grajirena began to realize that Misha was taking advantage of his position. He was spending company money lavishly and hiring friends and relatives for questionable jobs. Beer and promotional items, such as T-shirts, were disappearing. Moreover, Misha made several serious management mistakes.

He borrowed money for the company from a loan shark. And he "sold" a large shipment of beer to an apparent *mafiya* gang that was now refusing to pay.

When Grajirena arrived in Moscow, he called the office and found that Misha was out of town. He had gone on vacation in Greece. Perhaps Misha hoped he could save his job by avoiding a confrontation with Grajirena. Perhaps he figured his job was lost anyway, and he wanted to squeeze in one more paid vacation before he was canned. The people in the First Republic office were tense. One of the Americans pulled Grajirena aside and said that one of Misha's recently hired buddies, a tough-looking Russian known to the other staffers only as Igor, had made a not-so-veiled threat. Igor had said he knew people who, for a mere $500, would relish the chance to kill a visiting American businessman, particularly one who was intent on firing Russian workers. Grajirena was not dissuaded, but he resolved to be even more careful. He didn't want to fire Misha in the office, so he looked around for a neutral spot.

He called Jack Robinson, First Republic's lawyer in Moscow. Robinson, however, was away, back home in Canada. He himself had made the mistake of trying to fire a Russian employee, his chauffeur. The fired chauffeur had shown up at Robinson's apartment one evening, demanding $200 in back pay. He pushed his way inside the apartment, stole all the money he could find, and gave Robinson a savage beating. Striking him repeatedly with the blunt edge of an antique sword, he broke both Robinson's arms in several places, and left his bleeding and unconscious former employer handcuffed to the kitchen stove. The chauffeur positioned Robinson's head near the oven door, opened it, turned on the gas, and left. Fortunately, Robinson woke up before being overcome and was able to shout for help. A neighbor called the police. The next day, after colleagues in Robinson's law office tracked him down in a Russian hospital, Canadian authorities arranged a special flight home for him.

In the aftermath, Robinson's law office was decidedly cool to Grajirena's request for help in firing a Russian employee. Grajirena asked one of Robinson's partners to handle the voluminous paperwork required by the government, a hangover from the Soviet era, when it was all but impossible to fire anyone. Grajirena also asked to use the law firm's conference room for the meeting to fire Misha, and for the partner to serve as a witness to the dismissal. The partner said he would do the paperwork, but that was all. He wouldn't allow Grajirena to use the office, and he wouldn't serve as a witness. He wouldn't use his firm's letterhead or his name in any of the documents. The partner wanted to stay as far away from Misha as possible. "Be careful," he urged Grajirena. "Get some security in your offices. And get some security for yourself." A Russian friend in the nearby Canadian consulate agreed to lend Grajirena a conference room. He set the meeting for the day Misha was due back at First Republic after his vacation. The day before the meeting, Grajirena left word in the First Republic office that Misha should be sent to meet him at ten o'clock the next morning.

The arrangements all made, Grajirena returned to the apartment that First Republic had rented in Moscow to save on hotel bills. Recently, he had begun to suspect that someone was entering the apartment while he was out. Somebody apparently had a key, and he didn't like it. He started positioning a small piece of paper in the door, near the lower hinge, every time he locked it and went out. If the paper was on the floor, that would mean someone had opened the door. So far, each time Grajirena returned to the apartment, the paper was still in the door. Each time, Grajirena felt a little foolish, as if he were playing spy. This time, however, the scrap of paper was on the floor. Someone had been in the apartment. Grajirena opened the door cautiously and looked around. No one was there. He quickly gathered his bags, caught a taxi, and checked into a hotel under a different name. He asked the desk to block all calls. Around midnight the phone woke him up. Grajirena could tell someone was listening on the other end. But whoever it was never said anything. He hung up. An hour later it happened again. And an hour after that. At three o'clock he finally took the phone off the hook.

Grajirena was tired and nervous as he walked into the meeting with Misha. He wasn't comfortable with these bodyguards, or with the very idea of having bodyguards in the first place. But he was glad they were with him when the door of the borrowed office at the Canadian consulate opened, and Misha, looked tanned and relaxed, walked in a few minutes after ten o'clock.

CHAPTER 2

Grajirena

Rick Grajirena hadn't grown up thinking he would be an international entrepreneur. He didn't grow up thinking he would be much of anything. Until he was well into middle age, his mid-to-late forties, he never knew or cared much about Russia. Certainly he never anticipated being a pioneer among Americans doing business in the new post-Communist Russia. Looking back, his tumultuous childhood may have had a lot to do with his ability to do business in a place as strange and far away as Russia.

He was born in 1943 in New Hyde Park, New York, a crowded part of Long Island near New York City, not far from the Queens border. The Grajirena household was not a happy one. His father was a steward for Pan Am and was often away. When his father was home, his parents fought. The family moved frequently. In addition to various American cities, they lived for a time in Portugal and later Brazil. His father left home for good when Rick was seven. His mother and grandmother moved with Rick and his brother to the Miami area. In Coral Gables his mother got a job as a secretary, and the family lived a simple lower-middle-class lifestyle. They never had a car and never took vacations. Grajirena occasionally heard that his father had landed a new job, usually in hotel management, and then that he had lost the job, usually because of drinking. He heard rumors that his father was involved in smuggling. Eventually his father committed suicide without ever reconciling with the family.

Rick was a terrible student and flunked both third and fifth grades. After a teacher noticed that he needed glasses, his schoolwork improved. In high school he was a natural athlete but was too embarrassed to go out for football or any other team sport because he was two years older than most of his classmates. One of his few friends came from a family that was fairly well off and belonged to a yacht club. The friend's family took an interest in young Rick—who was cheerful and had an outgoing personality that adults seemed to like—and invited him sailing. For the first time, out on the water, he felt he belonged. He was calm and comfortable. He joined the Sea Scouts, a marine version of the Boy Scouts, and learned to sail eight-foot prams. He took small jobs around various yacht clubs, doing errands for members. He offered to crew for anyone and everyone and sailed all manner of boats large and small, from dinghies to yachts. It quickly became clear to him, and to everyone on the water with him, that he was good at it. Yacht club members began asking him to sail with them as a crew member, especially for weekend races. Grajirena recognized that sailing for speed, and beating other boats, was a complex tactical exercise and that he had an intuitive gift for it. When he was fourteen, the Coconut Grove Sailing Club gave him a junior membership in exchange for cleaning up the grounds. He spent all his free time there, either patrolling the walkways and docks for any scrap of litter, or teaching himself to sail different boats in different conditions. He picked up part-time and summer jobs at clubs, marinas, and resorts and saved his money for a boat. The summer he was fifteen, he bought a $600 kit and built a sixteen-foot, two-sail Southeaster. He used that boat to win many races, including his first Florida state sailing championship. It was an extraordinary accomplishment for a high school kid, and all the trophies and newspaper clippings and handshakes from rich weekend sailors—"yachties," they called themselves—made young Rick Grajirena feel like a rock star. A few envious older sailors scoffed that it was beginner's luck. Experienced sailors with their sleek, varnished boats and pristine sails laughed at him when he showed up with his boat made from a kit and sails that he literally patched together himself. Then he won the state championship again. His sailing club entered him in the Mallory Cup, a national competition. He won the quarterfinals and finished second in the semifinals while still in high school.

For decades sailing was all Grajirena wanted to do. And for decades it was pretty much all he did. After he graduated from Coral Gables High in 1962, he went to Miami-Dade Junior College, but mostly because his friends were going. It was a wasted year. He was captain of the school sailing team and chased girls. He spent more time and energy winning races in borrowed boats—the sixteen-foot kit boat had rotted out because he didn't know how to take care of it—than he did in class. He was too undisciplined for college. He enrolled in a trade school to study electronics, but he didn't like that either. Late in 1963 he enlisted in the U.S. Navy, took an aptitude test, and was sent to communications school. "Here today, Guam tomorrow, Grajirena," his instructor warned him. "Flunk out of here, and the next stop is riverboat duty in Vietnam." Grajirena finished in the top five percent of his class and shipped out of Norfolk on a supply ship that delivered toilet paper and hamburger to the Seventh Fleet in the Mediterranean. In charge of shipboard movies, he showed classics rather than cowboy or action films, much to the consternation of many enlisted men. But several officers noticed him and got to know him. When they learned that Grajirena knew how to sail, they arranged to enter him in the 1965 all-Navy sailing championships. He was the only enlisted man competing, and he beat an admiral in the finals. "You know, we could use a guy like you at the Naval Academy," the admiral said at the awards ceremony. "You could coach our sailing team." Grajirena was posted to Annapolis, first as a security guard who carried a gun—"But no bullets, like Barney Fife," Grajirena recalled—and then as a personnel assistant who had little to do with personnel. His real job was sailing coach, under a lieutenant who held the formal title of coach. It wouldn't do, Grajirena was told, for the midshipmen to be officially coached by a common seaman. His navy sailing team did well, and Grajirena himself was invited to the 1968 Olympic trials in the twenty-foot Flying Dutchman class. At the trial in San Diego, he tore a stomach muscle during a race and had to quit. He returned to Annapolis, underwent surgery, and waited to be mustered out of the service in late 1968.

Back in Miami, he took the first and only job offered to him, at a small sailmaking company. He showed a knack for making sails and, just as important, for helping customers use those sails to win races. Within a few months he was hired away by North Sail Company, one of the nation's biggest sailmakers. He packed up his old Volkswagen Beetle and drove cross-country to Seal Beach, California. At North Sail he moved up the ladder quickly. By the end of 1969, Grajirena was head of one of North Sail's divisions, making sails for big ocean-racing yachts. California was like paradise to him. He had a steady job he liked, and the perks included racing everything from fourteen-foot singles to seventy-foot yachts in regattas up and down the Pacific Coast. At a regatta in Canada, he met Peter Harken, who was designing some of the world's best small sailboats. Harken, based in Wisconsin, was building boats in the 470 class, a two-person, seventeen-foot boat that was regarded as one of the best tests of true sail-racing ability. He asked Grajirena to race his boats. In 1970–71 Grajirena won many races in Harken's 470 boats. He also made and sold hundreds of sets of 470 sails for North Sail. At work, Mary Griffith, a pretty young secretary who was a junior at the University of Southern California, asked Grajirena to work on racing tactics with her. She proved to be an excellent sailor and ended up beating him in several races. They were married in 1971.

As good as things were in California, Grajirena found himself homesick for Florida. In 1972 he and Mary and one coworker from North Sail moved to Clearwater, on the Gulf Coast, to take over a small sailmaking company that was being sold cheap because the owner was retiring. Their goal was to make high-quality sails and to win as many races as possible. Sailing alone in single-handed races, and with Mary as his crew in two-man boats, Grajirena won a number of big races. He was a finalist for the coveted Martini & Rossi "Yachtsman of the Year" award in 1973. Business boomed, and Grajirena merged his company with Murphy & Nye, at the time one of the largest sailmakers in the world. With Murphy & Nye, Grajirena worked not only on sails but also on sailing accessories. One of his projects was making "soft" luggage for sailing: small, light canvas duffel bags, easily stuffed and stored. Nothing much happened with the luggage, however, and Grajirena turned his attention elsewhere. It turned out he was simply ahead of his time. A small company he had been working with didn't give up on the idea of canvas luggage and continued to develop various designs, including soft briefcases. Within a few years the boom in soft luggage helped that small company, Lands' End, become one of the giants in mail-order retailing.

While at Murphy & Nye, Grajirena met his first Russian at a regatta in Canada. Viktor Potapov was a good sailor, but his equipment was terrible, especially the sails. Grajirena realized that if he helped Potapov get better sails, Potapov would do better on the water. But that was true for a lot of sailors. Why did Grajirena help Potapov? Initially it was probably because Potapov was a Russian. Like most Americans, Grajirena always regarded Russia as America's enemy, and Russians as evil Communists who, in Khrushchev's words, wanted to "bury" capitalist America. But Potapov was a good guy, a good sailor. He was an officer in the Soviet navy, but he didn't seem to have any particular ideology other than to get the most out of his boat, the water, and the wind—just like any other sailor. His English was limited, but he nonetheless managed to participate in the camaraderie on the docks—what little camaraderie was allowed, that is, by his KGB minders. Grajirena marveled that the only time the Russian ever seemed to be without a KGB shadow was when he was sailing. Out on the water, when there was dead time between races, Grajirena and Potapov often pulled their boats side by side and talked, using Potapov's crewman as an interpreter.

Grajirena gave Potapov some new sails, and Potapov won his class at the regatta. Potapov said he had an idea for how he could return Grajirena's favor but didn't offer any details. Grajirena smiled, said good-bye, and figured it would be the last time he ever heard from the Russian.

The following year, the FBI called Grajirena and asked for an appointment. The Soviet Olympic team wanted to order sails from Grajirena, he was told, and it was routine procedure for the FBI to check out any Americans doing business with the Russians. Grajirena must not have been a big national security risk, because he made sails for Soviet national sailing teams for several years, through the 1970s. Meanwhile he continued to race various classes of boats across the globe. Grajirena and an assortment of new crew members—Mary Grajirena had bowed amicably out of both the marriage and the sailing partnership by then—won many more races. In the early-to-mid-1970s Grajirena won three national championships, six North American championships, and one world championship. By 1976, however, he felt stale. He was looking for new challenges. He left Murphy & Nye to spend a year as the project manager for Gulfstar Yachts, in charge of building *Southern Star,* a forty-eight-foot ocean racer-cruiser designed to show how new technology could enhance both comfort and performance. He won some big races with *Southern Star,* then left Gulfstar in 1978 to coach the U.S. team to victory in the 470 class at the world championships in Sweden. Back home he borrowed $5,000 and started another sailmaking company, this one geared toward ocean racing. By the early 1980s, he employed thirty workers and was doing more than $1.2 million worth of business a year. He made sails for boats forty feet and bigger, fulfilling orders for $60,000 to $80,000. Those big orders typically obliged him to help the customer race the boat. Usually Grajirena was the driver. During the race he was in charge. But before and after the race, on the docks, in the bars, at the awards ceremony, the RO—rich owner—was always officially the captain, the skipper. Grajirena was just another crew member in the background.

During those years of making sails and racing, Grajirena was admittedly a cad in relationships with women. Young women, all tanned in short-shorts and bare shoulders, were always hanging around yacht clubs hoping to meet an RO. Or when a rich yachtie wasn't available, they might latch on to a good-looking sailmaker and boat driver who was happy to have a fling and then dump them. A few times Grajirena got into a relationship that lasted a month or two. Three or four times he got engaged, but each time he backed out. He got a reputation as a womanizer, as a guy who couldn't or wouldn't settle down. After one race in 1981, there was a particularly pretty blonde in the bar. He noticed her, not just because she was tall, but because she looked familiar. He couldn't remember where he had seen her. Someone said she was a cheerleader for the Tampa Bay Rowdies, a North American Soccer League team. That's where he had seen her, months before, at a soccer match. "I like that tallest one," he remembered telling a friend when his attention strayed from the soccer to the sidelines and the "Wowdies."

In the bar Grajirena started talking to the woman. Her name was Valerie, and she worked as a paralegal for a judge. She didn't seem to fancy him, especially after finding out he was a sailor. She wasn't interested in sailing bums, she told him. But she was thinking too that he wasn't a bad-looking guy. He was in his mid-thirties, ten years older than she was. He was just under six feet tall, strongly built, with dark hair starting to go gray, a deep tan, and the slightly bowlegged, rolling gait of someone who spent a lot of time on slanting decks. She liked his easy manner, and the big white smile that cracked his permanently tanned face. She hadn't come to this bar looking for a serious romance. She never went out with guys who tried to chat her up in bars. But she told herself that if this guy Rick could make her laugh, she'd go out with him. "So you're not interested in sailors," he said. "Well, if you marry me, I'll go back to school and become a doctor." She laughed and agreed to go out with him. They were married a few months later.

The early 1980s was not a good time, business-wise, for the sailing world. The worldwide recession and high interest rates meant that fewer yachties had money to spend on boats, sails, and racing. Grajirena's company was still doing well, but nonetheless when he received a good offer he had no qualms about selling it. He became a yacht broker and worked for a couple of different brokerages over the next few years. As the economy improved in the mid-1980s, so did yacht sales. Grajirena made good money, in part because he could offer something that most yacht brokers could not. "Buy from me," he told customers, "and I'll sail with you. You'll win races." And they did. He was a good yacht salesman.

But Grajirena missed having his own company, and he missed sailmaking. He started another sailmaking company, the third he had owned and the second he had founded. He kept this one small, with only a handful of clients who were willing to pay top dollar for his sails and for his expertise at the wheel during races. The company did well, but Grajirena realized within a couple of years that he had made a mistake. He wanted to be his own boss, but he found himself at the beck and call of the ROs. One night an owner fired him for giving an interview to a reporter who had telephoned Grajirena instead of the RO for some quotes and a photo. Fine, Grajirena said, find yourself someone else to drive the boat. The owner reconsidered during the evening, however, and woke up Grajirena with a one A.M. phone call. "Be on the dock at five A.M. or else," the owner growled. "We have a race to win." It was just one of many times that Grajirena would have liked to tell an RO to forget it, but instead he kept quiet and went out and won the race. He and Valerie had two little boys by then, and he was in no position to say "Shove it" to anyone who could help put food on the table.

One day in 1990, he got a call from a freelance sail salesman in Fort Lauderdale. The yachts sailing in the Whitbread round-the-world race, widely regarded as the pinnacle of yachting competition, were in Fort Lauderdale for their scheduled layover for rest and repairs. *Fasizi,* the first boat from the Soviet Union ever to compete, needed sails. The Russian sailors knew Grajirena had made sails for the Soviet national teams, and they now wanted him to make the sails for *Fasizi.* Would he help? *Fasizi* wasn't a very good boat—the Italian-Russian sponsors hadn't put enough money into it—and it didn't have a prayer of finishing anywhere in the Whitbread except at the back of the pack. But Grajirena had always enjoyed his dealings with Russians in the past, and he recognized that there might be some promotional value in helping this boat now. He invited the crew to his house for pizza—the Russians were astounded that pizza could be ordered over the phone and delivered—and agreed to help the Russians raise money for sails. He offered to make the sails for $65,000, a steep discount, in exchange for whatever publicity the Russians could provide for Grajirena Sail Company.

In working with the Russians on the specifications for their sails, Grajirena became friends with a number of the *Fasizi* crew, particularly one sweet-dispositioned, fun-loving Russian whose full name was Vladimir Kulinichenko but whom everyone called Kuli, pronounced "coolie." In Fort Lauderdale during their month-long layover, Kuli and his Russian mates, with Grajirena's help, became local celebrities. Grajirena and others helped the Russians raise the money for their sails by arranging for them to appear at numerous cocktail parties, barbecues, and other functions, where people might want to meet them and contribute to the cause. And people did want to meet them. They were Russians, after all, and it wasn't all that long ago that President Reagan had called their country the "evil empire." Here was an opportunity, with little fuss and no danger, to talk to real live Russians and find out just what made them so evil. Or not. Kuli and the crew became popular fixtures on the waterside party scene. Hosts and hostesses wanted to have "the Russians" at their parties, and bar owners loved to see them show up because it was sure to be a lively and liquid party. The Russians were invited to serve as celebrity judges for bar beauty contests such as "Miss Hot Bod." By the end of their stay, bar owners were coming up with Russian-themed beauty contests for them to judge, such as "The Hunt for Miss October." When the *Fasizi* sailed from Fort Lauderdale in July 1990, Grajirena was on the pier waving good-bye to his new Russian friends—and expecting that he would never see or hear from them again.

———

Just after Christmas 1990, Grajirena's phone rang. It was Pan Am with a lost bag. When could it be delivered to Grajirena? The passenger had given the airline his home address in Clearwater. The passenger was Vladimir Kulinichenko. Kuli. "There must be some misunderstanding," Grajirena told the airline. "He left months ago." He gave the airline Kuli's address in Moscow and asked them to ship the bag there. The next day the phone rang again, and it was Kuli. He was in New York. "Didn't you get our letters?" he asked. "Don't you have my bag?" He and other crew members had been embarrassed by their poor showing in *Fasizi* in the Whitbread round-the-world race. They were better sailors than that and wanted to prove it. Anatoly Verba, one of the crew, was spearheading a syndicate for an entry in the next Whitbread race in 1993–94. This time the Russians wanted to do it right, first class all the way, no cutting corners the way they had with *Fasizi*. But they couldn't do it alone, and they couldn't do it solely in the Soviet Union. Would Grajirena help them line up American sponsors? "Well, come on down, Kuli, and we'll talk about it. Where are you staying?" Grajirena said. Kuli explained that he didn't have enough money for a hotel. Moreover, his cut-rate Pan Am ticket was only for Moscow to New York. He didn't have enough money to fly to Florida. Grajirena talked it over briefly with Valerie, then sent Kuli the money to fly down. The Russian sailor moved into their small den, borrowing Grajirena's clothes for the first month until his bag made its way back to Clearwater.

Grajirena, who was in the process of selling his sailmaking company and was casting about for what to do next, found what he thought would be a short-term diversion. He became head of a loosely organized committee devoted to raising money to build a high-tech round-the-world racer that would give the Russians a chance to win the Whitbread. The idea was that

Grajirena would oversee the marketing and promotion of the fundraising effort in the United States, and take a modest commission. Grajirena flew to London and met Anatoly Verba at the Whitbread headquarters. Verba told Grajirena that he already had raised 1.5 million rubles—$1.5 million at the official exchange rate—but he figured the syndicate ultimately would need at least $4 million. "If you think right now that you're going to need $4 million, you'd better try to raise $5 million," Grajirena advised. Verba had lined up several impressive sponsors and commissioned a factory in Gorky to build the boat. The factory was part of Volga Buran, an arm of the Soviet space program. It was taking on private contracts as a part of *perestroika*, Soviet leader Mikhail Gorbachev's program to promote private industry. The hull would be built in the Volga Buran factory, where the Soviet space shuttle had been built. The electronics and other fittings would be added later in Odessa, the Black Sea port in the Ukraine, where city officials promised Verba a large chunk of the sponsorship money to name the boat *Odessa 200* to help celebrate the city's second centennial.

Grajirena saw many marketing possibilities for the Odessa 200 project. He also saw many possibilities for opening up a new career for himself. Why should the marketing end when the boat sailed? He laid out plans to start a sports marketing company that would specialize in doing business with the Soviet Union. After all, this was the spring of 1991, the height of the era of *perestroika* and *glasnost* ("openness") under Gorbachev, and the Iron Curtain was being lifted to the West. Since the turn of the century, there had not been a better time for Americans to do business with Russians. Grajirena planned to set up seminars in Tampa that would serve several purposes. They would introduce Americans to the notion of doing business in the Soviet Union, both exporting products from the United States to Russia and importing products from Russia to the United States. The seminars would also explain Russian business and banking, and put Americans in contact with facilitators who could help open doors for them—including Rick Grajirena. At the same time the seminars would help the Odessa 200 project find American sponsors. Anatoly Verba liked the idea, and so did several of Grajirena's wealthy yachting friends who kicked in a few thousand dollars in seed money. Grajirena also lined up a number of sponsors who agreed to donate in-kind goods or services. A marine engine manufacturer offered to provide the diesels for the boat. An electronics firm contributed the navigational system. One of the Big Six accounting firms offered accounting and auditing services.

It was time to set up the first seminar. Grajirena needed speakers. The accounting firm offered an international consultant. Grajirena recruited a yachtie who worked as an international insurance broker, a lawyer who had clients doing business in Eastern Europe, and a man who had done some import and export with a couple of the Soviet republics. But he didn't have a banker, a finance specialist. Someone gave him the name of Geoffrey Farrar, who apparently worked at Barclays Bank Canada and had helped the Canadian arm of the McDonald's empire establish the first American-style fast-food restaurant in Moscow. That first McDonald's in Moscow had been a big news story, and its immediate success—it quickly became the busiest and most profitable McDonald's in the world—was regarded as one of the prime examples of how and why Westerners should consider doing business in Russia.

Grajirena hadn't known that the Moscow McDonald's was started by Canadians, rather than the U.S. headquarters, and he hadn't known that the Canadian branch of the British-based Barclays Bank was involved in the financing. He had never heard of Geoffrey Farrar. But he called directory assistance for the bank's main number in Toronto, rang the number, asked for Mr. Farrar, and then told a secretary why he wanted to talk to him. Farrar came on the line, and Grajirena explained again that he was trying to organize a seminar for Americans on doing business in Russia, and he needed a keynote speaker. The two men talked a bit, feeling each other out. Farrar, who happened to be a yachtie, was impressed with Grajirena's sailing credentials. Grajirena was impressed with Farrar's name-dropping in some of the deals he had helped finance in Canada, the United States, and elsewhere. Farrar was, for example, one of the bankers for the Reichmanns, the family that put together some of the biggest commercial development projects ever undertaken in North America and Europe. Eventually Grajirena brought the conversation back to the little seminar he wanted to hold in Tampa sometime that summer.

"I'd like to help," Farrar said, "but it depends on the schedule. The only time I can make it is July twenty-sixth."

"Well," Grajirena said, "that just so happens to be when we're going to have it."

He paused as both men scribbled diary entries. Finally Grajirena spoke again.

"Excuse me, Mr. Farrar, for my ignorance, but I've got to ask you one question. Uh, just what is your job there at Barclays Bank?"

"My boy," Farrar said with obvious satisfaction, "you are talking to the man. I'm the CEO and president of this bank."

CHAPTER 3

Ludmilla

By July 1991, Kuli had been living in the Grajirenas' den for seven months. He was a lovely guy, Valerie agreed, but he was getting on her nerves. Rick reluctantly went along with her. With Kuli around, he and Val had to go for a walk if they wanted to have an argument. It was too hard for the family, which included rambunctious boys now ages eight and six, to live and work around a lodger. "He's like a giant teenager," Val complained good-naturedly. "His stuff is all over. He eats like a horse. He hangs around watching TV. Even when he goes out, he can't drive, so I have to take him." Kuli was a good baby-sitter, she acknowledged, but after seven months she wanted the den back, and she wanted the family intact again. So Grajirena used some of the Odessa 200 contributions to rent a small apartment nearby for Kuli. It was a good investment, everyone connected with the project agreed. Kuli was a rainmaker, the "real-live Russian" who smiled and nodded and shook hands and exchanged pleasantries in heavily accented English and generally helped charm potential contributors out of their cash. The tension in the Grajirena household over Kuli's long encampment seemed like the only minor speed bump on what appeared to be a fast track for the Odessa 200 project and for Grajirena's hopes of building a company that would do business with Russians.

Grajirena's first seminar on doing business in Russia was held on July 26 and was a huge success. The *Tampa Tribune* became a sponsor and gave the event a tremendous buildup in its news pages. The former mayor of Tampa volunteered to give a welcome address. The Tampa Yacht and Country Club arranged for a black-tie cocktail party the night before, and a formal-wear store loaned tuxedos to Kuli and Anatoly Verba, who flew in to add his presence as "the Russian captain." A resort condo complex offered lodging for speakers. A car rental agency offered them cars while they were in town. A printer did the programs for free. Both the kickoff cocktail party and the seminar itself the following day were covered by the newspaper and by local television stations. Scores of people wanted to shake Grajirena's hand, talk about doing business with him in Russia, and contribute to the Odessa 200 project. Among the 150 people who paid $110 each to attend the seminar were two dentists from Missouri, John Hayhurst and Dale McElwee. Hayhurst was a good friend of Grajirena, an old sailing buddy. He was the orthodontist in McElwee's clinic in Camdenton, Missouri. They told Grajirena they wanted to be involved with him in Russia, and they were willing to put up some money to get started if and when he found a hot business prospect.

Others attending the seminar included a broad range of Tampa businesspeople, a few of whom actually had done some business with Russians, or at least had some ideas about how they might. Most, however, were only flirting with the notion. The seminar was an easy way to learn more. One of the Russian speakers was Ludmilla Danilova, a banker whose bank was one of the major sponsors of the Odessa 200 project. She was a large woman who wore loud clothes, jangling jewelry, and lots of makeup. She chain-smoked cigarettes with an oddly dainty flair, holding them up with her thumb and forefinger between frequent puffs. She was purported to have heavy government connections. Ludmilla qualified as a hot prospect, an actual Russian with whom Americans seemingly could do business, or perhaps use as a contact to meet other Russians with whom they could.

Grajirena made a point of sitting down with her for a quiet, earnest conversation. What was she looking for? Was there any way he could help? She smiled with those heavy red lips. Yes, perhaps he could help. She happened to have an export license, and she happened to have some friends who had some oil for sale. A large quantity of oil. She produced a stack of documents that appeared to be export licensing permits. Grajirena borrowed them and showed them to a consultant from one of the big accounting firms who had flown in from New York to be one of the speakers. The consultant said the licenses looked legitimate. Grajirena mentioned the potential oil deal to Dale McElwee and John Hayhurst, the Missouri dentists. They knew a man who worked for Bass Oil in Houston. Maybe he would want to buy Ludmilla's oil. Maybe Grajirena, McElwee, and Hayhurst could get a small commission for making it happen. It could be the foundation for their Russian import-export business.

That brief conversation was notable for several reasons. For one, it brought together the three men, the would-be entrepreneur from Florida and the two would-be investors from Missouri, for their first business venture. But not their last. It was also the first time—but hardly the last—that Grajirena put a potential Russian-American business deal together through nothing more than networking and gladhanding, telling somebody about somebody who knew somebody else who wanted to buy or sell something. And it was the first time—again, hardly the last—that Grajirena, and others around him, found their emotions swept up in the possibilities of doing business in Russia. This deal really could happen, Grajirena and the dentists told themselves. And they really could make money from it, probably some sort of commission or finder's fee. They agreed to form a company, with the three of them as partners, to do business with Russia. They could work out all the details later, like the name of the company, their roles, and exactly what business the company would do. For now, they felt like celebrating. They had nightcaps to toast the start of what they thought would be a long and profitable three-way partnership. They were partly right.

In the wake of the seminar, money poured into the small Odessa 200 office that Grajirena rented on Gandy Boulevard in Tampa, across the bay from his house in Clearwater. A flyer used for mass mailings urged, "Join The Crew Of The *Odessa 200* On A Round The World Adventure." For $5,000 donors could become Platinum Patrons and get their names, or their companies' names, permanently painted on the side of the yacht. They also would get a model of the boat mounted on teak; an invitation to sail on the yacht and attend the christening in Tampa Bay in 1992; a limited-edition poster signed by the captain and crew; a "crew member" certificate suitable for framing; invitations to Odessa 200 social events, such as a VIP cocktail party during the Fort Lauderdale break in the race; a polo shirt bearing the Odessa 200 logo; a crew-member duffel bag; and a subscription to the Odessa 200 newsletter through 1994. Donors who became Gold, Silver, and Bronze crew members would receive portions of the list of benefits and souvenirs, on a diminishing basis, for contributions of $1,000, $500, and $200, respectively. The brochure did not mention that the boat would be built in the Soviet Union, or that construction had not started. Indeed, anyone looking at the small drawing of the sleek boat in the brochure could easily have assumed that it was a photograph of the actual boat. The brochure did say the project was "a joint U.S./U.S.S.R. international yacht racing effort," but it neglected to say that the only American contribution was to put up the money so the Russians could build and sail the boat. Not that any of that mattered. The Tampa Bay area seemed eager to put up money to help Odessa 200, even if the promised souvenirs and keepsakes were no closer to reality at that point than the boat was. Eventually, Odessa 200, Inc., raised nearly $150,000 toward building and outfitting the boat.

Since childhood, Rick Grajirena had always gone to bed early. Even in his most devoted days as a dockside party animal, he was usually the first one to call it a night. It wasn't unusual for him to be asleep by ten o'clock, particularly if he was sailing the next day. He was also an early riser. So it was no great hardship for him to answer the phone when it rang shortly before four thirty one morning in August 1991, a few weeks after the seminar. It was the anchorman for the morning news program on one of the Tampa Bay television stations that had covered the seminar. The anchorman's tone was urgent. He wanted to know what Grajirena thought about the coup attempt, and whether he could come on the air and talk about it. "Coup?" Grajirena asked. "What coup?" The newsman explained that Gorbachev had been put under house arrest by a group of Communist Party conservative hardliners who thought *glasnost* and *perestroika* were undermining the foundations of the state. Would Grajirena come down to the station and provide some live commentary? Sure. He pulled on his clothes and drove to the station. They gave him a cup of coffee and put him on the air. He was introduced as a Tampa Bay area businessman who was heading the Odessa 200 project and who had numerous business and sports contacts in the Soviet Union. Grajirena answered questions on-air for almost four minutes. He started by saying he wasn't an expert or an authority. He went on to say that from what little he knew of Russians, they had no interest in going back to the old days of Communism. He predicted that the coup would fail. He spoke sincerely, with authority and gravity, as if he knew as much about the Soviet Union as anybody. In fact, he probably did know as much as or more than anybody else who happened to be in a Tampa Bay television studio at that moment. But another fact was that he had not yet even been to Russia.

Grajirena finally got to Russia a few weeks later. He and Dale McElwee and John Hayhurst had planned to go in August, but they delayed their trip because of the coup attempt. The coup ultimately failed, of course, but

Gorbachev's political career went down the drain with it. He was history, literally, from the moment that Boris Yeltsin, then the mayor of Moscow, climbed onto a tank and seemingly single-handedly rallied the Soviet army to follow him instead of the hardline plotters who were trying to overthrow Gorbachev. The plotters were arrested. Gorbachev was released from house arrest and returned to Moscow a chastened, subdued man, his power obviously diminished. In stunningly quick succession, the Soviet Union fell apart. There was talk that the Communist Party might be stripped of its official control, not only in Russia but in all the Soviet republics. The republics that had been sovereign nations three-quarters of a century earlier—Russia, Belarus, Ukraine, and a dozen others—became independent nations once more. They aligned themselves into the Commonwealth of Independent States (CIS) to present a united front to the world, but the CIS never looked like it could fill the power vacuum left by the demise of the Soviet Union. No, the biggest changes in Russia were not in politics or diplomacy or boundaries. The biggest changes were in attitude. Russia was open for business. Western business. Russians wanted the Western lifestyle. They had had a taste of McDonald's, and now they wanted MTV, Gap, and Procter & Gamble. They wanted to get rich.

Rick Grajirena and his partners wanted to get rich, too. He, McElwee, and Hayhurst got on a plane in New York with two representatives of Bass Oil from Houston. Ludmilla had made arrangements for all five men in Russia. Grajirena, McElwee, and Hayhurst had little interest in the nuts and bolts of the oil deal, however. They hoped things would work out, and that either Ludmilla or Bass Oil or both would pay them commissions for putting the deal together. They had no idea how much the commission might be, and they never discussed it with either Ludmilla or the men from Houston.

Grajirena and the dentists from Missouri had other priorities for their first trip to Russia. First, they wanted to check on the Odessa 200 project on the Russian side. The Tampa fundraising had been going extremely well up until the coup, then abruptly dried up. Not only were there no new pledges, but some promised contributions were not coming in. Sponsors who had made promises got cold feet, waiting to see what was going to happen in Russia. Grajirena hoped to go to Gorky, where the boat was being finished in one of the old Soviet rocket factories, and then return to the States with a glowing report. He wanted to be able to tell contributors that the boat looked good, Russia seemed stable, and the Odessa 200 project was right on track. There were difficulties, however, in arranging a visit to Gorky. For much of the Soviet era it had been a closed city, largely to keep outsiders

away from the secrets of the space center. Restrictions were eased some-
what by then, but Anatoly Verba said he was having trouble getting permission for Grajirena to visit the factory and inspect the boat. Verba said even
he, as the organizer of the syndicate and skipper of the boat, was unable to
visit. But he promised to keep working on it. Even if he could not get his
American fundraisers to Gorky, Verba said, he had scheduled meetings for
Grajirena, McElwee, and Hayhurst in Odessa with city officials and other
sponsors of the Odessa 200 project. He also said he was working on putting
together an Odessa version of the seminar that had been so successful in
Tampa the previous summer. Grajirena's other priority for that first trip was
to meet a relative of Kuli, the Odessa crewman who had lived in Grajirena's
den for the first half of that year. Kuli said Grajirena and the dentists had to
meet his uncle, Valery Gadgi, whom Kuli described as an important Russian
biznesman. Through Kuli, arrangements were made to meet Gadgi and talk
about potential business deals. Titanium, oil, and more—Gadgi was a big
player, Kuli promised.

They flew from New York to Frankfurt to Moscow on the German airline
Lufthansa, which was an Odessa 200 sponsor and offered them cheap tickets.
Grajirena's initial impression of Russia was a common one among Americans. The plane landed in mid-evening at Sheremetevo airport outside
Moscow, but it was already eerily dark. Few lights were visible from Grajirena's window seat as the plane approached. Even tiny airports serving small
American cities were better lit than this, he thought. Taxiing toward the ter-
minal, he saw row after row of Aeroflot planes, all emblazoned with the
hammer and sickle symbol of the old Soviet Union. The airport itself was
even more intimidating—all dark marble and cheap aluminum, put together in an imposing design that seemed to satisfy neither form nor function.
Walking down the vast but deserted aisles toward passport control, the only
Russians in sight were soldiers with guns. Machine guns. No one greeted the
tired travelers. No one smiled. There was no sign of welcome. The immigration and customs agents were grim and brusque, directing the passengers
with gestures rather than words. Why did it take so long—five minutes, at
least—for the immigration agent to approve a passport and visa? Was there
something wrong? No, this was normal.

Once through the formalities, Grajirena's party of five emerged to find
several of Ludmilla's staff waiting for them. Smiles and handshakes were
exchanged, and they piled into a bus that could have carried six times as

many people. The forty-minute drive into Moscow was dark, too—no streetlights, no signs, no billboards. Even as the bus came into the center of the city, Grajirena was struck by the absence of light and color. The buildings were large, heavy stone structures. Some had street-level windows that could have been for stores of some sort, but it was hard to tell. The town looked like one nondescript office building after another, and all were buttoned up tight and dark. There were few cars on the streets, and even fewer people. It wasn't even ten o'clock at night. "This," Grajirena wondered to himself, "is a world capital? The seat of the powerful evil empire?"

Ludmilla had arranged for them to stay at a central Moscow hotel owned by the Komsomol, the youth wing of the Communist Party. There were numerous such government hotels in Moscow and elsewhere in Russia that served, with varying degrees of accommodation and service, the specific groups or ministries that controlled them. When they could, they rented rooms to Westerners at exorbitant prices in order to collect hard currency. This hotel was typical. The lobby was worn and grim. A variety of bad, mostly musty smells pervaded the hotel, from the lobby to the elevators to the hallways to the rooms themselves. There were phones, but it was difficult to make a local call and impossible to make a long-distance call. The bar never seemed to be open, and when it was the only drinks available were sweet soda pop and Russian champagne, which was almost as sweet as the soda pop. Vodka? *Nyet.* Each floor of the hotel had a stern, blocky "key lady," often with bright henna hair, positioned near the elevators to monitor comings and goings, and to collect and hand out keys. She always seemed to be angry about something and muttered suspiciously at the Americans every time they asked for their room keys. The short, narrow single beds sagged, and the thick, stiff duvets were too short to cover the feet of anyone over five foot nine. The water from the bathroom taps ran brown before turning to a pale beige. The hotel restaurant had a printed menu, but ordering from it was hopeless. Nothing the Americans wanted to eat was available. The kitchen seemed to make one basic meal for each seating, and that was what everybody ate. Hard-to-chew sausage, leeks, tomatoes, and cabbage appeared to be the standard, in one form or another, for pretty much every meal. Cockroaches skittered across the tables, especially at breakfast. Even the coffee was black, nasty stuff, as if it came from the bottom of an urn that had never been rinsed out, much less cleaned.

Grajirena and his four traveling companions checked in and were greeted by the hotel manager. He was a bulky man who wore a dark chalkstripe suit and swept his gray hair straight back. He usually left work at five P.M., he said, but had waited to greet them because they were the first Americans ever to stay at his hotel. Would they care to join him for a nightcap? Grajirena said he was too tired and begged off, but the two Houston oilmen and the two dentists from Missouri said sure. They each had a glass of Russian champagne and were surprised at how syrupy it was—nothing at all like real French champagne, or even sweeter Italian sparkling wines. This stuff was absolutely cloying. One of the four reached into his carry-on bag and pulled out a bottle of scotch. The four Americans and the Russian hotel manager then did what Americans and Russians always seemed to do when they met in social situations during the Cold War era. They compared lives, got drunk, solved the world's problems, and decided that the tensions between their countries were due to the governments, not the people. By the time the informal welcoming party broke up at three A.M., after the bottle of scotch was gone, each of the Americans had invited the Russian and his family to come and stay at his home, and they had promised him that they would help him get his children enrolled in U.S. universities—good ones, with football teams that played on TV.

Ludmilla showed up the next morning with her bus and her entourage, including the tallest woman Grajirena had ever seen, at least six foot seven. For the next several days the tall woman and several other of Ludmilla's assistants squired the Americans around Moscow. They went sightseeing at Red Square, walked through the walled complex of government buildings known as the Kremlin, went to the Moscow State Circus, attended a Bolshoi ballet, and dined at a quaint old monastery. Meanwhile, Grajirena felt terrible. What little of the food he could eat, he couldn't seem to digest. The other four laughed at him and told him he had to tough it out, this was Russia. He went to the hotel manager and asked whether the new McDonald's would deliver. The hotel manager said that McDonald's did deliver in central Moscow, but only if the order was for more than $50. Grajirena gave him the money and asked him to place an order for as many Big Macs, fries, and shakes as $50 would buy. The dentists and the oilmen had laughed at him, but they didn't turn down Grajirena's invitation to join him for a McDonald's feast that evening. Every crumb of food was devoured—except for one Big Mac that Grajirena stuck in a drawer, out of sight, to save for breakfast the next morning. It seemed like nothing at the time, but getting those Big Macs was an important first step for Grajirena. He had made something happen in Russia, the land where "It is impossible" had been the unofficial national motto for decades.

CHAPTER 4

Autumn 1991

In the autumn of 1991, while Grajirena, Hayhurst, McElwee, and the Houston oilmen were in Moscow during that first trip to Russia, the Communist Party was formally disbanded. Over dinner that evening, the Americans could hear Komsomol officials in an adjacent room, making loud sorrowful toasts and singing their old anthems glorifying the youth of the movement. The Americans knew they were witnessing history. But a few days of up-close-and-personal history at the Komsomol hotel was enough. It didn't make the hotel's mystery meat any less mysterious. Emboldened by his success at acquiring fast food, Grajirena told his fellow Americans he was going to press Ludmilla to move them out of their hotel. Again, they scoffed. Again, they told him not to make waves. We're the guests in this country, they pleaded. Grajirena ignored them. He told Ludmilla the hotel was unsatisfactory. They wanted to stay someplace better. She didn't like it, but nonetheless she moved them to the Metropol, a landmark hotel from czarist times that recently had been restored to the standards of a Western business hotel, the first in Moscow. The rooms were clean and comfortable, the food was great, there was cold beer at the bar all evening, and it was possible to use the telephones in the rooms to dial directly to the States.

Ludmilla may have been miffed about the hotel change, but that didn't stop her from parading her American guests to one government office after another, where they smiled and shook hands with one mid-level ministry official after another. "We're not getting anywhere," Grajirena grumbled to his companions. "We're here to do business." It seemed as if they were Ludmilla's pet Americans, and they were being trotted around so she could impress people. The oilmen were particularly perturbed because Grajirena and the dentists were about to leave for Odessa, and they wanted some assurances that Ludmilla actually would get around to presenting the oil deal while they stayed behind in Moscow. Grajirena, as the group's unelected leader, had her promise that she would present the details to the oilmen after he and the dentists departed for Odessa.

The Aeroflot flight to Ukraine was bumpy, and the plane seemed cheap. Grajirena had been told that the seats on all Aeroflot jetliners had been installed in the Soviet era in such a way that they could be removed in minutes if the plane needed to be converted to a troop carrier. It seemed entirely possible, judging from his cramped, rattling seat. He and McElwee and Hayhurst steeled themselves for Odessa to be worse than Moscow. Instead, they were welcomed in sunshine at the small, pleasant airport by Anatoly Verba, the Russian skipper, and a clutch of smiling city officials. They were whisked in limos to an incredible little seven-room hotel that formerly had been reserved for top party officials. When Brezhnev had come to Odessa, this was where he had stayed. Up a beautiful spiral staircase, on the top floor, were two giant suites. Grajirena took one, and the dentists shared the other. Downstairs were five smaller bedrooms normally used by aides and bodyguards. There was also an elegant dining room and a plush billiard room with an outsize billiard table that must have been twelve feet long. Even the balls and pockets were larger than standard. Instead of key ladies, a pleasant housekeeper greeted them warmly in English.

"What would you like for dinner, gentlemen?" she asked.

"I'd kill for a steak," Grajirena said, joking. The woman smiled, disappeared, and Grajirena reckoned that at best they would get a typical pounded-down chunk of beef from some unidentifiable part of a cow. He didn't think anything more of it. But when the three Americans came down for dinner that evening, each was served a thick, juicy broiled filet mignon with a fried egg on top, sunny side up. After all that sausage and leeks, it seemed like the best meal they had ever eaten.

They spent two days in Odessa. They met the mayor and other city officials and were the subject of speeches praising their work with the Odessa 200 project. The city officials seemed to view the Whitbread sailboat not only as a promotional vehicle for their town but also as an integral cog in the machinery of world peace. A bemused Grajirena was called on several times to make remarks, and by the second day he had a set of pleasant platitudes he could recite in timing with the interpreter, who was translating his words, phrase by phrase, into Russian for the Ukrainian listeners.

The second day in Odessa, city officials took the Americans to a luncheon attended by what was described as a group of influential local people who were interested in doing business with Americans. Grajirena was asked to make a speech, and was told he and the dentists would be expected to chat with the guests. Grajirena spoke for ten minutes about the fundamentals of capitalism and explained how a free-market economy differs from a centrally planned state economy. "When you start a private business, the state doesn't make sure that you get customers or orders," he said. "You must offer a product or a service that people want, and you must let them know about it so they can find you. If somebody offers a better service or a better product, customers will go there, and you won't make any money. It's not like the old days, when there was no competition. Capitalism means competition." He talked about quality in production, about providing good service, about warranties and guarantees, about productivity, efficiency, and economies of scale. He talked about the bottom line. The Odessa audience sat around thirty little tables, four or five people to a table. They listened attentively, but Grajirena had the uneasy feeling that they really didn't understand or appreciate anything he was saying. When he finished, they applauded politely and all but sat up to attention behind their little tables, preparing for their audience with the Americans. City officials led Grajirena, the dentists, and their translator down the rows, from table to table, listening to each person describe his or her scheme for doing business with Americans.

One Ukrainian was convinced that all he needed was some investment money—for vineyards, for processing equipment, for a bottling plant, for advertising, for distribution—to produce wines that would rival anything from France, at a fraction of the price. Wouldn't Americans prefer a burgundy from Ukraine, he wondered innocently, if they could get it for a dollar or two less than a burgundy from France? Someone else wanted to export cars made in Ukraine. Another offered a run-down Soviet hotel and wanted to refurbish it in grand style but had no idea how much it would cost. One guy had some property on the Black Sea and the idea that all it needed was a few million dollars of investment to turn it into a Club Med–style resort that would draw jet-setters from all over the world. Another was confident that he had discovered a milk by-product that could "rejuvenate" the brain; all he needed was American money to produce and package it.

A factory manager brought in a stack of old American boating magazines that told him, he said, that one of the best-selling boats was the Boston Whaler, a fiberglass runabout that could be used for anything from fishing to waterskiing. He wanted an American partner who would ship him a Boston Whaler so that he could make identical copies of it. He figured that if a seventeen-foot Boston Whaler sold for $15,000 in America, he could make a copy for $2,000, ship it back and sell it for $4,000. He showed the Americans pictures of his factory and of other products he made of fiberglass. "This guy could never understand why this wouldn't work," Grajirena told McElwee. "Even if there weren't legal problems, what American is going to buy a boat like that with a 'Made in Russia' sticker on it? No matter how good his copy is, he's still not making a Boston Whaler."

One attractive middle-aged woman and her husband had a plan for a private school where they could charge young women for lessons on how to use and sell cosmetics, then take a cut of the cosmetics they sold at private parties. Grajirena wondered where the "students" would get the money for tuition; the couple explained that on the side, when the girls were not studying cosmetology, they would be part of an "escort service" and collect fees from foreign businessmen who enjoyed their company. "They want us to help them set up a whorehouse," Grajirena murmured to Hayhurst.

The Americans did not hear one business proposal worth considering. None of the Ukrainians had any real clue as to how they would market their product or service. Whenever the Americans asked about quality, or how the idea could be positioned in marketing terms, or whether there would be any warranties, the Ukrainians looked at them blankly. They had no understanding of the concepts. Grajirena, McElwee, and Hayhurst tried to be polite. These people, sitting at their little tables, so anxious, so hopeful, talking earnestly in broken English and through the translator, were desperate. They thrust stacks of crudely worded proposals, photos, blueprints, and clumsy business plans into Grajirena's hands. After four hours of smiling and nodding and trying not to show what he was thinking, Grajirena walked out with more than twenty pounds of the stuff. He threw all of it away except for a couple proposals to show people back home. Otherwise he was afraid no one would believe him.

On the Aeroflot flight from Odessa back to Moscow, Grajirena reflected on that first trip. He hadn't been allowed to see the boat. Despite the warm welcome in Odessa, he came away neither with any concrete assurances that the Odessa 200 project was in good shape, nor with any viable business prospects for the company that he wanted to form with McElwee and Hayhurst. It did not appear that the Odessa 200 project, even if it happened, was going to be a springboard for a private company doing business with Russia. It was depressing.

Back at the Metropol, Grajirena's mood lifted slightly when he found that Ludmilla had been busy proving to the two men from Bass Oil that her oil deal was real. They were in the process of touring facilities and talking to her associates about prices and logistics. Ludmilla wanted Grajirena and the dentists to join the tours and meetings. They declined, saying they weren't interested in the particulars of the oil deal. Well, Ludmilla said, she was happy to have her aides, led by the towering woman, set up some more sightseeing and cultural events for them. At this point Grajirena was forced to tell Ludmilla about Kuli's uncle, Valery Gadgi. He had been afraid she would be unhappy about it. He was right. She wanted Grajirena and the dentists to be her private Americans. She didn't want them going off and making deals with someone else. But there wasn't much she could do about it.

Valery Gadgi came to the hotel to introduce himself. He pulled up in a long black Mercedes, one of the few Western cars Grajirena and the dentists saw during that first trip. Gadgi was short, stocky, and balding and wore good Russian clothes—good by Russian standards, but still obviously Russian-made. His beautiful blond wife, who had worked as a nurse before marrying Gadgi, stayed in the car during that first meeting at the hotel. Two bodyguards emerged, however, and stayed constantly at Gadgi's side. Grajirena saw Gadgi several times over the coming months, and the Russian was never without at least one bodyguard. Gadgi's English was only fair, but he had a certain energy and a twinkle in his eye. He was a charming guy who liked to give the impression of being a rogue, the epitome of a wheeler-dealer.

He sat down in the hotel bar with the three Americans, ordered single-malt whisky, and got to the point. "I can facilitate all sorts of things in Russia," he said. "If I don't have what you need, I can get it for you. If I can't do what you need, I can have it done." Meanwhile he offered an immediate proposition. He had a contract to sell $10 million worth of heavy equipment to Syria. "Just trucks," he said with a wink. "No tanks." But he needed to run the money through an offshore bank account. How about if the Americans bought the equipment from him, and then sold it to the Syrians? They'd just have to do some paperwork and make some banking arrangements to earn a six-figure commission.

Grajirena and the dentists exchanged wary glances, and Grajirena spoke for all of them. "We're very flattered that you want to do business with us, and that you would offer us this opportunity," he said. "But I'm afraid we'll have to pass. We're not experts on American diplomacy or foreign relations or international law, but we do know that the U.S. government has restrictions on doing business with Syria. We're not in a position to take on something like that." Gadgi was insistent. No one needed to know, he said. The whole deal could be kept offshore. The American government would never find out. It would be easy money.

Finally Grajirena flatly said, "Look, we don't want to end up in jail. We're not going to do it." Gadgi gave up, at least for the moment. He smiled and started talking about other deals. He was confident he could find a way to work with these Americans. When were they returning to Russia? Not sure, Grajirena said, in three or four months perhaps, maybe in January or February. Fine, Gadgi said. They must let him know the exact dates and schedule a trip to come and visit him in Ulyanovsk. They would do business then.

After Gadgi swept away in his Mercedes, Grajirena, McElwee, and Hayhurst did a postmortem. Was Gadgi *mafiya*? He didn't fit the profile of the sleek, sneering, flashy young Georgian gangsters running Capone-style smuggling operations, prostitution rings, and protection rackets. Maybe he was a legitimate "new Russian," capitalizing on the opportunities of limited capitalism to get rich. The Americans preferred to believe the latter. And they agreed that it wouldn't hurt to go see Gadgi in Ulyanovsk next time.

The two Bass Oil men returned to the hotel from their final round of meetings with Ludmilla's contacts. It was the Americans' last night in Moscow. They were all beat. It had been a long ten days, and they needed to get up at four A.M. to catch their flight home. Grajirena said he was going to have another fast-food dinner and turn in early. The others said they were going out to dinner. Pizza Hut recently had opened its first restaurant in Moscow, so Grajirena asked the hotel to order a large pizza and a six-pack of beer for delivery. The hotel said the order wasn't big enough. Pizza Hut had the same rule as McDonald's, a fifty-dollar minimum for delivery. Okay, Grajirena said, make it two pizzas. Still not enough, Pizza Hut said. How about two pizzas and a case of beer? That did it. Grajirena ate most of one of the pizzas, drank a couple of weak Russian beers, and was asleep by ten o'clock.

He was awakened by one of the Bass Oil guys pounding on his door at two A.M. They had hooked up with Ludmilla's assistants, including the six-foot-seven woman, and were partying downstairs in the bar. But the bar had closed. Grajirena gave him the rest of the beer and went back to sleep. A couple of hours later, he rolled out of bed with his four o'clock wake-up call, did the last little bit of packing, and went down to the lobby to meet the other Americans. They were there all right, sprawled with five of Ludmilla's assistants, passed out in and on the lobby's leather chairs and, in the case of the six-foot-seven woman, across an entire couch. Grajirena woke the Americans, who moaned and groaned as they scrambled upstairs to throw their things together. They made their plane, but there was not a lot of conversation on the long flight home.

CHAPTER 5

"A Little War"

Rick Grajirena never found out what happened with Ludmilla and the Bass Oil deal. He never saw or heard from her again. On the plane back from that first trip, the Bass guys told him that Ludmilla did not have quite the deal that she originally indicated. They seemed to be saying that the deal was dead and their interest in Ludmilla was at an end. Grajirena found out later, however, that they made at least one more trip to Russia without letting him know. He never found out whether they bought any of Ludmilla's oil. In any event he never got a commission.

But he was not overly concerned. Back from that first trip to Russia in the autumn of 1991, Grajirena spent the rest of the year trying to continue to raise money for the Odessa 200 project. It was slow going. The uncertain economic and political situation in Russia scared off many potential contributors. Besides, it seemed frivolous to many Americans to donate money for a high-tech sailboat to a nation that was having a hard time feeding its people. In addition, the breakup of the Soviet Union had transformed the project from a Russian or Soviet project into a Ukrainian project, and potential donors were not as interested in Ukraine. "Most Americans don't even know where it is," Grajirena groaned after yet another prospective Odessa 200 sponsor backed out.

At the same time, the news was not good from Odessa or Gorky, where the boat was being built. Volga Buran, the company building the boat at the Gorky space center, needed more money. The ruble was losing value, and the cost of materials was skyrocketing. Anatoly Verba went back to the Odessa city officials and other principal sponsors in Ukraine and Russia.

They said they didn't have any more money. The factory said it would soon have to stop construction because it couldn't pay the workers. Verba said he would go to Gorky with his twelve-member crew and finish the boat themselves. The project seemed to be in big trouble. Grajirena asked if he could visit Gorky on his second trip to Russia, in February 1992. Verba said he was closer to getting permission for himself and his crew to enter Gorky, but he still doubted that a visitor's permit to the space center would be granted to an American.

Grajirena, meanwhile, gathered any and all information about setting up an American company that would do business in Russia or with Russians. Lots of information was available from the U.S. Commerce Department and the American Chamber of Commerce. But very little of it seemed pertinent to what Grajirena was trying to do. Moreover, he couldn't get anyone to answer his specific questions. Geoffrey Farrar, the Canadian banker who had been the keynote speaker at the Odessa 200 seminar the previous summer, suggested that Grajirena join the Canadian-Russian Trade Council. Grajirena did, becoming the only American member. It turned out to be a satisfying relationship. He became friends with the officials who ran both the Toronto and Moscow offices of the trade council, and they provided him with considerable information, a number of business leads, and several personal and business favors over the years.

Grajirena made several trips back to Russia in 1992, beginning in February. John Hayhurst, the Missouri orthodontist and old sailing buddy, returned to Russia with Grajirena on the second trip. The lack of modern dental care in Russia had been obvious to Hayhurst and McElwee on their first trip. Most Russians needed only to open their mouths to show that they had bad teeth, with lots of metal. If they were privileged, the metal was gold. If not, the metal was usually stainless steel. The Missouri dentists did some further research and found that the most common form of dental care was tooth extraction. Hayhurst and McElwee decided that Hayhurst would return on that second trip to explore the possibilities of providing dental training and equipment in Russia. They thought perhaps they could start a chain of dental clinic-schools. Anatoly Verba, still beating the drums for the Odessa 200 project, had invited Grajirena and Hayhurst to Odessa for another "seminar," to hear more business pitches from Ukrainians. The Americans also were booked to spend more time with Valery Gadgi, the Mercedes-chauffeured *biznesman* who had tried to persuade them to sell heavy equipment to Syria for him.

On that February trip Lufthansa not only provided cut-rate tickets but also arranged for Grajirena, Hayhurst, and Kuli—who came along as an interpreter—to stay at a discount at the Penta, one of the first Westernized hotels in Moscow. The Moscow office of the Big Six accounting firm that had donated accounting services and management consulting time to the Odessa 200 project invited the two Americans to a dinner at the Kremlin to celebrate a joint venture that the accounting firm had entered with a newly formed Russian management-consulting firm. "Everybody here wants to be a middleman," Grajirena mused, "from giant accounting firms to little old me."

Taking his seat at the banquet and looking over the dignitaries' table at the front of the room, Grajirena saw a familiar face. It was a man who had attended Grajirena's seminar in Tampa the previous summer. He had been a mysterious visitor. He had shown up unannounced, paid his fee, attended all the sessions, and shaken hands with pretty much everyone else there. He had given his name as Kindersohn but offered no business card. He hadn't filled in an address, phone number, or any other contact information on his registration card. He had created a stir by speaking to the Russians in fluent Russian. But no one Grajirena talked to had any idea who the guy was, where he was from, or what he did for a living. "CIA, I bet," someone said. And now here he was, months later, in Moscow, sitting at a place of honor at a banquet in the Kremlin. Who *was* this guy? Grajirena went up to the head table and talked to Kindersohn briefly. He didn't gain any more insight into the man, who said something vague about having various import-export deals going with Russia. Kindersohn did seem interested when Grajirena said that he and the dentists were trying to find business opportunities in Russia, and he promised to call Grajirena next time he was in Florida.

Also at that Kremlin dinner was Valery Leontiev, Russia's chief dental officer and one of the top officials in the Russian equivalent of the American Dental Association. He and Hayhurst quickly got into a deep conversation. Leontiev explained that he was the director of the institute that oversaw the training of all dentists in Russia and set standards for dental equipment and care. Hayhurst explained to Leontiev that he and McElwee wanted to help upgrade dentistry in Russia, and Leontiev seemed extremely interested. It was a good meeting, and the first of many conversations among Leontiev, Grajirena, and the two Missouri dentists about how they might all work together. It was a conversation that would continue off and on, in many per-mutations, throughout the 1990s.

The second trip to Odessa was a rerun of the first, but on a smaller scale: The welcome from city officials was muted, the turnout for the seminar was smaller, and the business proposals presented by Odessans were even more lame. Grajirena resolved that this would be his last trip to Odessa unless the yacht project somehow revived or there was some reasonable expectation of finding a real business opportunity rather than "give me money" pie-in-the-sky schemes. He found no more excitement for the Odessa 200 project in Odessa than in Tampa. Only Anatoly Verba, the would-be skipper, still seemed optimistic, even though the Gorky factory was steadily raising the boat's price tag. From the original million rubles, the factory now wanted nearly 20 million rubles, in large part because of the Russian currency's rapid devaluation. Yet Verba insisted that the boat would be finished by March, the following month. He said he had been granted permission to take his crew to Gorky, and they would finish the work on the boat themselves. Grajirena told him he was worried that the $150,000 contributed to the project by American sponsors—sponsors lined up by himself—was going to be wasted. "People want to see the boat," he said. "I want to see the boat." Verba promised to send Grajirena photographs of the boat as soon as he and his crew arrived in Gorky.

After Odessa, Grajirena, the dentists, and Kuli returned to Moscow, where they hooked up with Valery Gadgi. Gadgi picked them up at the Penta Hotel and put them in a taxi that followed his Mercedes to the station, where they caught an overnight train to his hometown, Ulyanovsk, an old, traditional Soviet city 450 miles to the east on the Volga River, in the valley below the Ural Mountains. Gadgi led the Americans onto the train and into first-class compartments he had reserved for them. Even before the train pulled out of the station, the vodka began to flow. It never stopped for the five days they spent with Gadgi, leading Hayhurst to christen that second trip to Russia the Flatliner Tour. As the train cleared the Moscow city limits and rolled into the countryside, Gadgi called Grajirena over to the shaded window. "Now I show you Mother Russia!" he bellowed, opening the shade. The sky was black and the ground was white, as far as the eye could see, in every direction. It was five o'clock in the afternoon. *What have we gotten ourselves into?* Grajirena wondered.

When the train arrived the next morning in Ulyanovsk, a city of 350,000, the travelers were groggy from the combination of too much vodka and too little sleep. Despite all the turmoil amidst the breakup of the Soviet Union, many of Ulyanovsk's citizens—including Gadgi—remained proud that their town was Lenin's birthplace. Gadgi installed the Americans in the best place in town, a dark, foreboding fortress of a hotel. It was where every Soviet leader from Stalin to Brezhnev had stayed when making the customary pilgrimage to the Lenin museum, built around the modest house where the leader of the 1917 revolution was born in 1870, when the town was still known as Simbirsk. The city was renamed after the 1924 death of Lenin, whose original surname was Ulyanov.

The Americans' arrival at the hotel set off an immediate round of parties, dinners, and meetings where Gadgi introduced them to people he did business with, or wanted to do business with, and with whom the Americans might be able to do business. It was obvious that Gadgi was trying to impress both his Ulyanovsk hometown cronies and the visiting Americans. He was trying to be a middleman for the middlemen, Grajirena thought. Yet it was impossible not to like Gadgi. He had a quick wit and a quicker smile, and he was altogether charming in his roguish way. Grajirena was surprised when Gadgi introduced a thick, heavyset woman, Irine, as his fiancée. What had happened to the beautiful blond wife? Grajirena asked Gadgi in a quiet moment. The Russian's animated face fell, but only for a moment. "Divorce." He shrugged as he poured more vodka. Later he told Grajirena that his new girlfriend—whose prodigious appetite led the Americans to nickname her "Irine, Irine, the Eating Machine" behind Gadgi's back—was well connected. Her family had been high up in the Communist Party, and she had worked as a lawyer for the party.

Of more interest to Gadgi was that Irine's brothers ran a caviar operation. Would Grajirena like to import a large quantity of caviar? Grajirena suspected that Irine, who had a bottomless cavity in her sweet tooth and seemed to be able to eat ice cream day or night, even for breakfast, had replaced the beautiful blonde in Gadgi's affections because she had more hard-currency potential. Gadgi assured Grajirena that the caviar was beluga, the highest quality. He said Grajirena could make $1 million on a shipment of $10 million worth of caviar. Grajirena said he had heard that Russian law strictly limited caviar exports, especially the good stuff. Well, yes, technically that was true, Gadgi said, but Irine's brothers had connections, and there were ways to get the caviar out without paying huge export fees. Grajirena said he would consider it. Later, back in the States, he got in touch with several caviar importers who said they weren't interested. They said it sounded like Gadgi's deal would violate not only Russian law but also U.S. federal import regulations. They urged Grajirena to stay away from caviar, and he did.

Gadgi and his friends came up with many other business offers during that trip to Ulyanovsk. One of Gadgi's pals made cars. Another manufactured airplanes. Another had an air-freight service. A dozen others had a dozen other enterprises that they wanted to peddle to Americans. They were all eager to offer Grajirena exclusive North American rights. Some threw in South America, too. Grajirena collected business cards and brochures and took notes. In nearly every case, when he got back to the States and checked around, he found no market for the Russian product or service. The cars, for example, would have to be rebuilt to conform to U.S. antipollution standards. The same with the airplanes. Some Russian products were too expensive. Most were too cheap—not in terms of price, but in terms of quality.

Gadgi introduced Grajirena and Hayhurst to a big, rough-looking man whom he called Big Boris. Boris what? "Just Boris," the man said in a heavy accent. "All you need know." Boris was six foot four, had a top-heavy, looming torso, and was bald as a cucumber except for a single bushy black eyebrow that slashed all the way across his forehead. All his visible teeth were gold. Big Boris came to Grajirena's hotel room and produced a looseleaf notebook that held photos, descriptions, drawings, and technical specifications for machine guns, automatic rifles, night-vision binoculars, shoulder-held rocket launchers, mortars, flamethrowers, and other light artillery. It was a catalog of destruction. This is like something out of a James Bond movie, Grajirena thought to himself. "Tomorrow," Big Boris promised, "you come my land fifty kilometers outside town. I put on little war for you." Grajirena declined as politely as he could. But he couldn't help wondering if Boris wasn't worried about electronic eavesdropping. Many of the rooms in hotels where Westerners stayed supposedly had been bugged during the Soviet years. What if this room was bugged? What if the remnants of the KGB were listening? Big Boris shrugged dismissively. "I no worry," he said gruffly. "If room bugged, only person listening is my boss."

Gadgi's hospitality continued when he packed up a group of his Russian cronies and took them, along with Grajirena and Hayhurst, up into the Ural Mountains. "We hunt boar tomorrow," he announced. The mountain *dacha* was rustic but well appointed, a classic old Russian hunting lodge with a modern kitchen. Grajirena, a lifelong warm-weather man who was uncomfortable with firearms, begged off the boar hunt. He said he wasn't feeling well, had a lot of reading to do, and would spend the day by the fire. Early the next morning he was awakened by the sounds of the hunting party toasting their hunt with shots of vodka as they trudged off into the snow. It was still dark. He looked at his watch: six A.M. The hunters returned in the late afternoon. They hadn't encountered any boars, but they obviously had encountered several more bottles of vodka. Shouting and reeling, they stomped past Grajirena sitting by the fire, stripped off their clothes, and went straight into a sauna. Twenty minutes later Grajirena was roused from his book by shouting outside. When he looked out the window, he saw the hunters, including Hayhurst, rolling their steaming, pink bodies around in the snow and whacking each other's backs with small branches.

The next evening, down from the mountains, back at the hotel in Ulyanovsk, Gadgi brought along Irine the Eating Machine and one of her girlfriends, an attractive young blonde, for a farewell dinner with the Americans. Grajirena noticed a group of swarthy guys in flashy clothing at a corner table in the hotel restaurant. He had heard about the *mafiya*—gangs, often Georgians, who were operating in the new Russia like old-style Chicago gangsters, but this was the first time he had seen any of them. They lounged conspicuously around a couple of corner tables, drinking and smoking and talking on small mobile phones. Occasionally they would mutter to a small group of young women. The women seemed to drift in and out of the restaurant, lingering near the gangsters' tables but never sitting down with them. Occasionally two or three of the women would take to the small, otherwise deserted wooden dance floor and sway to the sound system's tapes of American soft rock. Gadgi ignored the gangsters until Grajirena asked about them. Gadgi said they were small time, nothing to worry about. He nodded toward his bodyguard—there was only one with him this evening—who gave a tight little smile and patted what appeared to be a gun in a shoulder holster under his jacket.

After dinner, the two Americans and Gadgi's entourage—Irine, her friend, and the bodyguard—decided to have a nightcap up in Grajirena's room. As they got up and walked out of the restaurant, three of the gangsters followed. They pushed their way onto the elevator as Grajirena pushed the button for his floor. The Georgians began speaking harshly to Gadgi in Russian and motioning toward Irine's girlfriend. They thought she was a prostitute who was going upstairs with the Americans, and they didn't like it. They ran the prostitutes at this hotel, and they didn't want anyone doing business on their turf. Gadgi tried to explain, but they said they wanted $200 or someone was going to get hurt. They looked menacingly at the bodyguard, who began studying the floor numbers above the elevator door as they lit up slowly, one after another. Gadgi was still talking to the gangsters, taking sidelong glances at the seemingly oblivious bodyguard, when the elevator stopped at Grajirena's floor. The doors opened and the bodyguard sprang into action. He pushed past the two women, almost knocking them down, so that he was the first one off the elevator. He then ran—he didn't walk fast, he sprinted—down the hall, threw open the door at the end, and clattered off down the stairway.

After a dumbstruck moment of surprise at the bodyguard's escape, Grajirena, Hayhurst, and the two Russian women walked quickly to Grajirena's room. They locked the door behind them. Gadgi stayed in the hallway, talking calmly to the three menacing Georgians. Fifteen minutes later he knocked lightly on Grajirena's door and came in, smiling. The Georgians had disappeared. Gadgi never explained what happened. Maybe he convinced them the blonde was not a prostitute. Maybe he paid them off. He didn't say whether the bodyguard had returned. Grajirena never learned any of the details. It was his first encounter with the *mafiya*. But not his last.

CHAPTER 6

Souvenirs

Back in the States, in the spring of 1992, Grajirena planned another seminar for Americans interested in doing business in Russia. He saw it as a last chance to revive the fundraising momentum for the Odessa 200 project. He still hadn't received any word on how the work on the boat was progressing. The Russians in Gorky, at the space shuttle factory, still refused to work until they were paid more. But Anatoly Verba, the skipper, reported that he and his twelve-member crew were getting ready to go to Gorky and finish the work on the boat themselves. Grajirena, who had supervised the building of yachts himself, had little reason to think the sailors would know what they were doing. But he wasn't quite ready to give up on Odessa 200. Perhaps the second seminar would bring in more contributions. He and the dentists also hoped a second seminar would present more business opportunities for their fledgling company, which they had incorporated under the name First Republic. Kindersohn, the mysterious Russian-speaking American who had been at the head table at the Kremlin banquet, came up with the name.

Kindersohn had telephoned unexpectedly, announced he was in Tampa, and asked Grajirena to play golf the next day. On the front nine, Kindersohn offhandedly suggested the name First Republic. On the back nine, Kindersohn asked for a favor for a friend. The friend, Kindersohn explained, was looking for a North American bank that could facilitate complicated financial transactions between Germany and Saudi Arabia. The first deposit would be $10 million, Kindersohn said, and the account had to be one that could quickly facilitate additional large deposits and could then move them out again quickly. Couldn't any bank do that? Grajirena wondered. Well, yes, Kindersohn said, but his friend was looking for a personal contact. He was an old-fashioned sort of European who liked to deal with a person, someone he could shake hands with and reach on the telephone.

Grajirena took Kindersohn's problem to Geoffrey Farrar, the Canadian banker who had again agreed to be the keynote speaker at the second seminar. Farrar was preparing to retire as president and chairman of the Canadian branch of Barclays Bank. He already had started a consultancy to help North American firms do business in Russia and Eastern Europe. Farrar said he would be happy to talk to Kindersohn's friend and to help him find a personal contact at Barclays for his account and his large wire transfers. Several weeks later, Grajirena asked Farrar what had happened with Kindersohn's friend. Was he using Barclays? No, Farrar said, Kindersohn's friend was definitely not using Barclays. The friend had made contact with the bank and asked for the paperwork to set up the account. Then there was a period of back-and-forth. The paperwork wasn't quite right, the friend didn't fill some forms out correctly, the friend missed a deadline for filing the paperwork, and so on.

Meanwhile, Barclays did some checking on Kindersohn and his "friend"—if there was a friend. The bank suspected it was Kindersohn operating under another name. Kindersohn or his friend was running a scam that had worked on several other banks in the United States and Europe. The back-and-forth over the account would continue for a short time, without the account ever opening. Then there would be silence. Suddenly the bank would receive a notice that the friend had lost a lot of money by not getting the account open in time for a big deal. The lost opportunity cost the friend millions, and it was all the bank's fault. He was going to sue the bank for damages in the millions. In every instance the bank's lawyers said the case was without merit. But it would be expensive to defend and might result in bad publicity for the bank. So the bank would settle— $10,000 or $20,000, usually—and write off the loss in order to get the case to go away. Kindersohn and his friend, Farrar's bank concluded, appeared to be crooks. Kindersohn probabably wasn't even his real name. Grajirena never saw or heard from Kindersohn again.

During his first few trips to Russia, Grajirena spent as much time as he could seeing the sights and looking around. Sometimes, as on that first trip arranged by Ludmilla, he was given tours arranged or personally hosted by the people with whom he was doing business. Sometimes he sought out the landmarks on his own. He often went out walking, just looking, exploring, poking his nose into shops and museums, sometimes simply sitting down in a park and people-watching. Like many other Americans new to Russia, he collected souvenirs. Many Americans suffered Moscow Madness in the form of drinking and debauchery. Grajirena decided his form of Moscow Madness was collecting souvenirs. He found himself buying stuff that he would never have bought anywhere else in the world. Cheap little pins portraying Lenin's head, or the walls of the Kremlin, or the hammer and sickle. Old books published by the Communist Party, awkwardly written in English, that explained and extolled the Soviet system of government. Fur hats—in rabbit for a few dollars, in wolf or reindeer for a few dollars more, in mink for a lot more. Elaborately woven, colorful *babushka* shawls. *Matryoshka* dolls that fit one inside the other, some cheaply made in factories, others hand painted by real artists. Little handmade toys. Hand-painted lacquered boxes.

When he went to the banquet at the Kremlin, Grajirena had noticed at the entrance a seven-foot flagpole topped by a detailed bronze casting of a Russian eagle with the "CCCP" designation for USSR in Cyrillic characters. On the way out of the banquet, he stopped and motioned toward the eagle atop one of the flagpoles. "How much?" he asked two guards standing nearby. They huddled, talking earnestly. One of them drew a four and a zero on the floor with the point of his rifle. Forty dollars, they said. Thirty, Grajirena countered. They looked at each other. "Thirty-five?" Grajirena asked. Big smiles broke out on both soldiers' faces. One of them held out his hand for the money, while the other one tilted the flagpole down, popped the eagle casting off the top of the pole, and handed it over, with the gold twisted rope still attached.

When he went through customs on the way out—a requirement most countries don't have—Grajirena held his breath when the agent motioned for him to open his bag. The agent riffled through the suitcases in a professionally nonchalant manner. When he came to the bronze eagle, he picked it up curiously, hefted it in his hand, and looked at Grajirena with one eyebrow raised. Grajirena, for lack of anything better to do, shrugged and rolled his eyes. The agent tossed it back into the suitcase with the same nonchalance, zipped up the bag, and motioned Grajirena through. That eagle claimed a prized place back in Grajirena's office, along with a handful of other Russian souvenirs.

On free Sunday afternoons in Moscow, Grajirena liked to check out the antiques, arts, crafts, and plain old junk that everyday Russians brought to

Izmailovsky Park, on the northeast side of the city, to sell at an open-air, informal market. He picked up dozens of pins and patches and medals, most of which he gave away back in the States. One thing he did keep for himself was a KGB colonel's full uniform. On the flight back to the States, a stewardess spilled a drink on Grajirena's lap. He had the uniform in his carry-on baggage and went into the plane restroom and changed into it. His family was waiting for him at the airport, and the kids were so upset at the sight of their dad in the uniform that Valerie ordered him to change again before they drove him home. Grajirena didn't object. The heavy wool uniform was scratchy and uncomfortable, and it smelled badly of body odor. Like many other Russians, no matter how important, the colonel apparently did not place a priority on regular bathing. Grajirena had the uniform dry-cleaned three times, but never could get the smell entirely out. Eventually he loaned the uniform to a friend for Halloween. Grajirena never got it back, and never asked for it back.

One Sunday afternoon when he was strolling through the market in the park, a clean-cut young Russian approached Grajirena and asked if he was interested in religious artifacts. Grajirena said he didn't know much about them, but he did know that it was illegal to possess an icon stolen from a church, and that anyone who tried to take one out of the country could end up with a heavy fine or a jail sentence or both. "No, not an icon. No icons," the young Russian said, motioning for Grajirena to follow him behind one of the market's permanent wooden stalls, to an area shielded from view by bushes. Two other young men showed him a Russian Orthodox Bible that appeared to have been handwritten by monks. It was illustrated, with bright gilded flourishes that were probably real gold. "Fourteenth century," one of the young men said reverently. "Six hundred years old." Grajirena gingerly looked at the Bible. He was literally afraid to touch it. Another young man, just as reverently, said, "Five hundred dollars." Grajirena was tempted, but only briefly. It would be marvelous to own something so rare, so historic, so beautiful—if it was the real thing, and he assumed it was. He could donate it to a museum back home.

But no. It wasn't worth the risk, even if the Bible was real. These young guys could be cops running a sting to send a message to rich tourists who were smuggling out icons and other artifacts in their luggage. Or they could be running a con game; they'd sell him the Bible, then steal it back from him or follow him to his hotel and have some buddies, playing cops, "arrest" him but let him go if he gave up the Bible and a bribe. Even if the Bible was legit and the guys were not trying to set him up, customs agents at the airport could catch him trying to smuggle it out. If he got caught with it, he would be in a world of trouble. He didn't need that kind of trouble, and First Republic didn't need that kind of publicity. It wasn't worth the risk. But for years afterward, he thought about that Bible—it would have been an extraordinary souvenir—and whether he could have slipped it out of the country.

On one of his first trips to Russia, Grajirena told Valery Gadgi that Americans loved Russian souvenirs, especially military stuff and folk art. Grajirena mentioned that he was always looking for little things to take home and hand out to people as keepsakes. It was good for business. A few days later Grajirena was about to head to the airport for his flight home when Gadgi and his entourage pulled up in front of the hotel. From the trunk and the back seat of the Mercedes, a beaming Gadgi presented Grajirena with eight boxes—big boxes, a couple of them two feet square—full of souvenirs. Russian army attaché cases. Army pouches worn with a strap across the chest. About a hundred brass belt buckles emblazoned with the red star and the hammer and sickle. Epaulets from the shoulders of dress uniforms. All sorts of artwork—paintings, carvings, statues, ceramics. One ceramic painting of the skyline of St. Petersburg was dated 1890. Gadgi had a stack of fifty of them. Two cases of Russian champagne. And much more. "Souvenirs!" Gadgi exulted as he presented them to Grajirena. On the way out of Russia, the customs agents watching passengers leave Sheremetevo barely gave Grajirena and all his boxes a glance. They just presented him a written bill for about $400. He shrugged and paid.

It was a different story when the plane landed in Miami and Grajirena came through customs pushing and pulling two heavily laden luggage carts. The customs agent raised his eyebrows and asked what was inside. Grajirena recited the list, as much as he could remember. He told the agent the stuff had been given to him, that he wouldn't sell it or even keep it, and would give it away to help promote the Odessa 200 project—all toward the greater good of peace on earth, good will toward man. "Well, okay," the agent said. "Let's open one of them up." The first box produced a case of Russian champagne. The agent made a note and looked dubious when Grajirena tried to explain that Russian champagne is not like French champagne. "You can buy it for a dollar a bottle in restaurants, fifty cents a bottle in a grocery store," Grajirena said. Next the customs agent encountered some old Soviet army belts. "What are they worth?" the agent asked. "I have absolutely no idea," Grajirena said. "And it doesn't matter to me because I'm going to give them all away." The customs agent told Grajirena to sit down and wait. The agent went and consulted with a supervisor. He and the supervisor eventually returned. "Okay," the supervisor said. "Let's open it all up. We've got to go through it all." An hour later, with souvenirs strewn across three big tables and onto the floor, the customs agents had a two-page list. They huddled over it, talked about it, punched figures into a calculator, and presented Grajirena with a bill for $400—the same as he had paid to get the souvenirs out of Russia. "No," Grajirena told the U.S. customs inspectors. "I won't pay it. Keep the stuff. Good-bye." He started walking away. "Hey, wait, you can't just leave this stuff here!" the agents called, running after him. "How about $300?" they asked him. "How about zip?" Grajirena countered. They suggested $250. Eventually they came to a compromise: Grajirena would pay $150 in duties, and the customs agents would help him repack everything. Years later Grajirena would sometimes see similar souvenirs in catalogs of old Soviet knickknacks, selling for anywhere from $10 to $35. "And I handed out hundreds of them to people like I was giving away candy," he said with mock chagrin.

Grajirena handed out many of those souvenirs to people who, in March 1992, attended the second seminar in Tampa on doing business in Russia. It was not as big a deal as the first seminar the previous July. The publicity was good, but the second seminar didn't create quite the same splash. More than a hundred people attended, down slightly from the first seminar. Hardly anyone was interested in making a donation, either corporate or individual, to the Odessa 200 project. But several people seemed interested in getting involved with First Republic. They seemed impressed that Grajirena, Hayhurst, and McElwee had made so many contacts in their first two trips to Russia, even if they hadn't made any deals. There were lots of possibilities over there, Grajirena said. It was just a matter of finding the right ones.

One of the people who attended the seminar was Mark Mroczkowski (pronounced Maris-KOW-ski), a Tampa accountant who was interested not only in investing in the company but possibly in working for First Republic full time. Meanwhile, John Hayhurst and Dale McElwee, the Missouri dentists, decided they wanted out of First Republic. They were still interested in Russia, but they wanted to establish a nonprofit corporation to set up a series of dental clinics there. Their idea was to bring Russian dentists to their offices in Camdenton, on the banks of the Lake of the Ozarks, for training. The Russian dentists could then go home and work in teaching clinics, which the Missouri dentists would set up with the latest American dental technology.

The Russian dentists would treat patients while teaching more Russian dentists, who could then work in other teaching clinics. Hayhurst and McElwee didn't want to be in the Russian import-export business. They weren't looking for Russia to make them any richer than they already were. What they wanted to do was reform the dental care system in Russia.

Grajirena got in touch with Peter Harken, who built the 470-class sailboats that Grajirena had sailed to so many victories two decades before. Harken had done well in those years. His yacht-equipment company, based in Pewaukee, Wisconsin, with operations in California, Italy, France, and elsewhere, was renowned throughout the sailing world for its yacht hardware and fittings. Harken had a longtime interest in Russia and Russians. Since 1978 he had been providing training and tooling for the Russian Olympic sailing teams. Grajirena thought Harken could not only get components from Russia but sell finished products to Russia. They agreed that First Republic could serve as a possible conduit for various business deals for Harken Inc. Harken and Mark Mroczkowski, the Tampa accountant, were both interested in putting money into First Republic. It felt right to Grajirena, too. Harken was a seasoned international businessman and trusted friend. He would be a great addition to the board of directors and could advise Grajirena. Mroczkowski could compensate for Grajirena's own lack of financial expertise. Once the company got going, Grajirena would be the president and CEO, the main marketing man, and the chief deal-maker. Mroczkowski would be the CFO and would crunch the numbers. All the company needed now was a deal—or preferably lots of different deals. In April 1992, Grajirena flew back to Russia with Harken and Mroczkowski.

The goals of this trip were more focused. Valery Gadgi had again invited Grajirena to Ulyanovsk, this time to meet with a smaller, more select group of Russians, nearly all of them in charge of manufacturing operations. Some of them could conceivably be suppliers for Harken yacht equipment. "Okay," Grajirena told Gadgi. "We'll come again. But this time no boar hunting. And no *mafiya*." Before returning to Ulyanovsk, however, Grajirena wanted to see the Odessa 200 boat, or else. Anatoly Verba, the would-be skipper, was waiting for Grajirena in Moscow. He and his crew had indeed been working on the boat, and he had a stack of photographs to show Grajirena. He handed them over without comment. Grajirena began thumbing through the photos with great anticipation—maybe these snapshots would bring the project back on track. His heart fell, however, as he went through them. The boat was a disaster. There was still a tremendous amount of work to be done. Moreover, the work done thus far was unacceptable. It looked as if the Russians building the boat had ignored completely the computerized designs that the Odessa 200 sponsors in America had financed. This boat might float someday, but it would never be a high-tech racing yacht capable of winning the Whitbread round-the-world race.

Grajirena put the pictures down and looked at Verba. Verba had hoped this boat and this race would make him a yachting hero and a wealthy man. He was still determined not to give up the project. He and his crew would finish the boat, he said. They would put in the engine, electronics, and fittings provided by sponsors. They would get the boat into the water and sail it to Southampton for the start of the Whitbread race the following year. The entry fee already had been paid with money raised in Tampa. The Russian crew would sail *Odessa 200* around the world. Verba said he would honor all the American sponsorship deals that Grajirena had arranged. He wouldn't erase a company's name just because it had come through with only part of its pledge. He asked Grajirena to stick with him and keep trying to raise more money.

Grajirena said he was sorry, but he couldn't support the project any longer. As far as he was concerned, the fundraising effort in Florida was dead. Verba said he understood and thanked Grajirena for all the help. The two men shook hands and parted. Grajirena went to Ulyanovsk to meet people who he hoped would make deals with First Republic. Verba went to Gorky to rejoin his men, sleeping in a railroad car on a factory siding, working eighteen hours a day. After dreaming of what the yacht might be, now they were breaking their backs just to get it into the water.

The Russian crew eventually did finish the boat, and it was christened *Odessa 200*. Because of early construction flaws, it did not meet the technical standards of a Whitbread yacht. The race's organizers realized the Ukrainian entry was more a threat to sink than to win the race. But they were eager to enhance the international aspects of the Whitbread and to encourage entries from nontraditional world-yachting countries such as Ukraine. The race organizers allowed *Odessa 200* to enter the Whitbread despite its shortcomings. A wealthy Ukrainian family in Odessa led an effort to come up with enough financial support to finish the boat. In return, the family would get the boat after the race—if *Odessa 200* made it all the way around the world. Verba, his crew, and the *Odessa 200* did sail in the race and did make it around the world, though they finished far behind the other competitors. The boat was returned to Odessa, where the rich Ukrainian family used it in the Black Sea. Grajirena heard that during a stop at a port in Turkey, the family's oldest son was killed when he was struck by a car driven by a drunk driver. That was the last he ever heard of *Odessa 200*.

Chapter 7

Spring 1992

In that April 1992 trip, Gadgi, his bodyguard, and Irine, Gadgi's girl-friend with the caviar connections, met Grajirena, Harken, and Mroczkow-ski in Moscow. The three Russians and three Americans took a train to Ulyanovsk and were to return by plane a couple of days later. But when they arrived at the Ulyanovsk airport for the scheduled seven A.M. Aeroflot flight back to Moscow, there was a problem: The flight was canceled. There was another at eight A.M., but it was full. "No problem," Gadgi said. "I have friends at Aeroflot." Irine did most of the talking to the Aeroflot staffers at the gate, and they seemed happy to help. But Gadgi's group had to have new tickets for the eight A.M. flight. The ticket desk didn't open till nine A.M. So the group sat in the airport and waited till the desk opened. Meanwhile, the scheduled eight A.M. flight, fully loaded with passengers, sat outside on the tarmac. When the desk opened at a few minutes after nine, Gadgi bought new tickets. Two uniformed Aeroflot gate staff went out onto the tarmac, boarded the plane, and a few minutes later led off several very unhappy passengers. Gadgi, his bodyguard, Irine, and the three Americans boarded the plane, took the newly vacated seats, and tried to ignore the stares of fellow passengers as the plane took off for Ulyanovsk.

On the way to their seats, Mroczkowski, an accomplished amateur small-plane pilot, stuck his head into the open door of the cockpit of the airliner. He handed the startled pilot and copilot several copies of American aviation-hobbyist magazines and told the Russians that he was a pilot back in the States. After takeoff, just as the plane was leveling off, the copilot suddenly appeared in the aisle next to the Americans. He motioned for

Mroczkowski to swap seats with him. In the cockpit the pilot gave Mroczkowski the controls. Grajirena leaned out into the aisle and snapped a picture of Mroczkowski, who never had flown a jet, much less a commercial
airliner. The plane briefly shuddered and dipped while Mroczkowski got
used to the controls. After a few minutes of smooth and otherwise unevent-
ful flying, the copilot again swapped seats with the beaming Mroczkowski.

To Grajirena, meetings with potential business partners in Moscow and
Odessa felt much more promising on this trip. Several of the deals involved
supplying parts in titanium, an extremely light but strong—and expensive—metal that first came into common use in the aircraft industry and
was just starting to be adapted for sports equipment. The Ulyanovsk area
had titanium, as well as factories that could process it relatively cheaply.
Three of the would-be deals encountered by Grajirena, Harken, and
Mroczkowski on that trip were typical. An Ulyanovsk factory that did a lot
with titanium said it could make the blocks for a new sailboat that Harken
was designing. Another Ulyanovsk factory that worked with titanium
seemed like a potential supplier of handlebars for a U.S. company that made
mountain bikes. And a Moscow factory that made the big rockets for the
Soviet space program said it could make anything.

Here's what subsequently happened to those three potential deals over
the ensuing months. From the first titanium factory, Harken ordered samples of the sailboat blocks. The initial sample delivered to his workshop in
Wisconsin was crudely made and totally unsatisfactory. Subsequent samples
were better, and it looked as if the quality was improving as the Russians got
the hang of the specifications for Harken's complicated mold. Guiding the
Russians toward what he needed was a painstaking process. It was as if
Harken had to teach them remedial design, engineering, and production
techniques. But he told Grajirena it could be worth the effort. Not because it
was saving him a lot of money—with the shipping, communications, and
extra time involved, the savings were marginal. It could be worth it, he said,
to get First Republic up and running, and to help the Russian economy take
one small step toward free-market capitalism.

Harken was about to place a big order when, without warning, the
Russian factory stopped communicating with him. He tried to fax and
phone the factory, but there was no answer. With his own production deadline approaching, Harken reluctantly gave up and ordered the sailboat
blocks from one of his old reliable American suppliers. The Russian factory

finally got in touch a few days later. "Our electricity was cut off for three weeks," the manager said. He admitted it was because he was unable to pay the bill. The manager was stunned to learn that his factory had lost the Harken contract. Things like that—the electricity being cut off—happened all the time in Russia. It wasn't his fault. Why couldn't they still do the deal? Harken's explanation that reliability is needed in business, and that Harken Inc. had to meet its own deadlines, was lost on the manager.

At the second factory the deal for the titanium handlebars for mountain bikes also seemed promising at first. First Republic would be the middleman, taking a small commission from each handlebar sold by the Russians to the Americans. The Americans asked to see twenty-five samples. Most of the samples were fine. They were light, strong, and well formed. And the price was right. But several of the samples were inferior. Either they were poorly shaped, or there were flaws in the metal, or both. The American bicycle company said no thanks, we can't take a chance on this kind of inconsistency. It produced an expensive, high-tech bicycle, and if it ordered twenty-five handlebars, it needed to know that all twenty-five would be usable. Again, the Russian factory couldn't understand why it hadn't received the contract. Its managers, in all their years of making products for the state, had never received any complaints or sanctions or penalties for making a few substandard products or parts. It was expected—nobody was perfect. To the Russians, the Americans were being unreasonable. They told Grajirena at one point that they thought they had lost the contract not because there was anything wrong with their work, but because Americans had a bias against Russians from the Cold War and were looking for an excuse not to do business with them. If that was true, Grajirena retorted, the Americans would never have considered the deal in the first place.

The Moscow rocket factory had several possibilities for deals. First the factory director, knowing of Harken's and Grajirena's sailing backgrounds, thought he could make sailboats for them to outfit and sell in the States. Without telling the Americans, he began construction on two 80-foot yachts, one a racer and the other a cruiser. "We have been told that these maxi-yachts sell for millions in the West," the factory director said when they visited, and he unveiled the two partly finished hulls. He reckoned that he could sell the boats to First Republic for $750,000 each. First Republic could outfit them, then sell them for $1.5 million or more apiece. Grajirena and Harken glanced at each other. Sure, every once in a while some billionaire might commission the construction of a big yacht like this. But the big boats commissioned by ROs were typically custom-made, not off-the-rack. And they certainly weren't made in Russia. "The design is a mess," Grajirena said. He and Harken told the factory director that his two hulls, once finished, might be worth $200,000 apiece, not $750,000. And they said they weren't interested in fitting out and selling maxi-yachts at any price. It just wasn't part of their business. The factory director seemed disappointed but remained convinced that the hulls were worth millions. Grajirena later was told that the hulls eventually were sold to purchasers in Europe, but for even less money than he and Harken had estimated.

At one point Grajirena brought the Moscow factory director a proposal. An American manufacturer needed a small, uncomplicated component. How much would the Moscow factory charge to make the piece? Grajirena asked. The factory director huddled with his managers and came back with a price: $23. That was ridiculous, Grajirena said. The company was getting the part made in the States for $6. "What price would we need to charge to get the contract?" the factory director asked. Grajirena said $3.50. "Done," the factory manager said. The exchange didn't inspire much confidence in Grajirena, however, and he let the deal die.

The proposition that seemed most promising was for the rocket factory to make impellers—large parts that push air into turbine engines. First Republic arranged for the rocket factory to make the impellers for a large U.S. heavy-equipment company, and samples were ordered. With the promise of hundreds of thousands of dollars in commissions, First Republic put the factory director on its payroll as a consultant for $1,000 a month, several times his regular earnings as director of the rocket program. First Republic got the specifications for the impellers from the U.S. heavy-equipment company and sent them to the director. Grajirena didn't hear anything for several weeks, then was dumbfounded when the director said the specifications from the States were in inches, and he needed them to be in metric. He wanted Grajirena to send the plans back to the American company to be converted to millimeters and centimeters. Grajirena couldn't believe it. "Why couldn't you just do the conversions yourself when you got the specs?" he demanded. "I mean, this is the Russian space program. How did you guys copy all those American space vehicles and all our atomic submarines for all those years without being able to convert inches to metric? You guys really do rocket science, and this kind of simple conversion isn't rocket science." The director insisted, for a variety of reasons that Grajirena didn't understand, that the American plans must be in metric, and that the plans would go wrong if he did the conversions in Russia. It took another month to get the plans back from the American company with the metric conversions, and three more months to actually produce a sample. First Republic paid the factory director $1,000 a month through those five extra months. During those five months he came back to Grajirena several times asking for small amounts of money for colleagues. The factory chief of design needed $200 a month. The production supervisor needed $150 a month. A couple of other people needed $100 a month each. Grajirena seethed at the nickel-and-dime pleas but paid them without protest.

The sample impeller finally was produced, and it was a disaster. "It looks like a Neanderthal banged it out of a rock," Grajirena said. He urged the Russians to try again, but they said they were satisfied. They wanted Grajirena to show it to the American company. So he did. The American company took one look at the prototype and called off the deal. Grajirena sat down with the factory director and fired him. "It has become clear that you cannot do what we need to have done," Grajirena said. "Our relationship with your factory is over." The factory director was stunned. He had never been fired. He had assumed that the $1,000 was for life, and that he had years and years ahead to build up the list of cronies receiving monthly stipends from First Republic. He was angry, and he showed it. His English was good, and he spoke harshly to Grajirena before stomping away. Years later Grajirena learned that the rocket factory, still managed by the same director, had developed a successful relationship with a Western company, making titanium heads for golf clubs. The director had apparently learned something from his experience with First Republic.

Grajirena felt that he had learned something, too. "No more dealing with older Russians—they're almost all a waste of time," he told his First Republic partners. "Almost every Russian over age thirty-five has been ruined by working in the old Communist system." Under the Communists, every enterprise was owned by the government, and therefore every manager was a government employee. The manager's only job was to meet his or her production quotas for the year. The manager was not interested in—and did not need to know anything about—marketing, distribution, management, or finances. That was the government's job. The manager did not need to care about quality, keeping customers happy, meeting investors' expectations, or making a profit. The manager was not concerned about the impact of his or her enterprise on the environment. Again, that was the government's job. Example: A shoe factory got an annual production goal for shoes. It had to produce that many shoes. It didn't matter whether the size or color or quality matched what people wanted to wear. If the factory pumped out the right number of shoes, the manager got a medal. That was one of the reasons so many Soviet citizens wore ill-fitting, ugly shoes. Things did not necessarily get better after the collapse of the Soviet Union. When a Russian car company came out with a new model compact, the average car had ninety-two defects.

"The director of the rocket factory was typical," Grajirena told his investors back home. "A guy in his fifties, a really smart guy. But the only thing he's ever known is a state economy and central planning. He was always told what to make, and then who to sell it to. The buyers were told to buy from him. Old Russians used to say, 'We pretend to work, and they pretend to pay us.' To them, the whole idea of work is creating delays so they don't have to do it, or better yet finding a way for someone else to do it. Another month that the rocket guy didn't work was another month he got paid. Meanwhile, everybody involved needs more money. And they think we Americans have no limit on how much we can spend. They don't understand supply and demand. Their state economy never made money an issue. Their bosses in the government always had the money. They think we're like that, too. And if we tell them we don't have a bottomless money pit, they don't believe us. They think we're lying." The First Republic partners talked a lot about who they should be doing business with, and how they should be doing business in Russia. They realized the significance of what they were trying to do. "We're the pioneers, showing everybody who will follow us all the things that can go wrong," Grajirena said.

———————

One small incident, toward the end of that April 1992 trip to Russia, took on great significance. On the flight from Ulyanovsk back to Moscow, the same one where Mroczkowski briefly took over the controls, Grajirena ended up sitting next to an overweight Russian, who kept overflowing into Grajirena's space. As the plane bounced to a landing, this man, along with all the Russians on the plane, cheered and applauded, as they often did. While they were taxiing toward the gate to deplane, the Russian next to Grajirena bent down, pulled a battered leather briefcase off the floor, and opened it. He extracted a dented can of Milwaukee's Best beer, popped it open, and quaffed it like fine champagne to celebrate the successful landing.

The odd little scene stayed with Grajirena. "That can of plain old cheap American beer was like a treat for this guy, like a delicacy. It wasn't even cold," he told Harken in the taxi on the ride from the airport into central Moscow. They needed to find something that the Russian public would embrace the same way that fat guy on the plane grabbed the can of Milwaukee's Best. "We may have to keep looking for a while, but I'm sure we're going to find some opportunities in this country," Grajirena told Harken. Coincidentally, a few weeks later, an American in Moscow approached Grajirena. He wanted to import several containers of American beer to

Moscow, the American said. Could Grajirena help? Grajirena said he didn't have any immediate contacts but would look into it. But it wasn't a high priority for Grajirena, largely because it was a one-time deal. First Republic was interested in continuing relationships.

So Grajirena was reluctant to do much research on importing beer. But he remembered the fat Russian celebrating with his old can of warm Milwaukee Best. And he remembered his first trip to Moscow, when he had moved from Ludmilla's hotel to the Metropol. Walking into the Metropol's bar and ordering a cold beer—albeit a Danish beer, rather than American— was a relief, a delight, a return to civilization. Maybe Grajirena and his partners shouldn't be looking for a product like beer to import. Maybe they should be looking to import beer.

Peter Harken liked the idea. He said he knew a vice president at Miller Brewing who happened to be a yachtie. Harken's friend set up an appointment for Grajirena with the head of the brewing company's international operations. Grajirena flew to Milwaukee. The Miller executive was cordial and encouraging. Yes, Miller was interested in doing business in Russia. The company had received many inquiries about a distributorship there but had not made a deal. No one had proposed a legitimate, reasoned, researched plan. Yes, if Grajirena could come up with some marketing studies and a business plan, Miller might consider doing business with First Republic. No, there would be no problem with an exclusive for Russia if the numbers were right. The executive said it would be a good idea to focus the business plan on Moscow, since that would likely be the first market and the platform for expanding into other parts of Russia.

Grajirena flew back to Moscow in June 1992, intent on putting together a marketing study that would be the foundation of a business plan for First Republic to import and distribute Miller beer in Russia.

CHAPTER 8

A Plan

Telephone books, as Americans know them, did not exist in Moscow in 1992. There were no Yellow Pages. There was directory assistance, but more in theory than in practice. If a caller could get an operator at all, it probably wouldn't be one who spoke or understood English—or American-accented Russian—well enough to help. Even if the operator seemed to understand what the caller wanted, that particular operator might not have access to phone numbers. If the caller could manage to get transferred to an operator with a directory, the odds were that the number wasn't in it. At that time there weren't even very many accurate city maps of Moscow. For decades, the Communists controlled information in order to control the population. Their own revolution, back in 1917, had been fueled by word of mouth, in small meetings, by secretive writings passed from one person to another. The Communists did not forget that information is power, and they built their system on propaganda. All information was to come from the state. Unauthorized, unofficial information that was passed from person to person was dangerous. The party knew that if people could not find each other, they could not pass unauthorized information to each other. Consequently, only the party's elite had access to phone numbers and maps. The public also had no access to information on consumption or consumer preferences—studies, reports, surveys. Besides, what was the point of finding out what kind of toothpaste people liked if there was only one kind of toothpaste?

It was a marketing man's nightmare, in other words. And it was what faced Rick Grajirena in the summer of 1992, when he returned to Moscow to put together a business plan supporting First Republic's bid to become the exclusive Moscow distributor for Miller beer. The heart of any business plan, of course, is a market study. Grajirena needed to show Miller Brewing's international executives that Moscow bars, restaurants, and grocery stores would buy Miller beer from First Republic. No matter what the business plan said about First Republic's ability to pay for the beer and get it into Moscow, there would be no deal unless First Republic could convince Miller that it could get beer—the Russian word is *piva*—to people who would buy it. In Moscow Grajirena quickly learned that Russia is not one of the great beer-drinking nations. In 1992, Russians drank 18.8 liters of beer per person—far down the list, in forty-second place, among industrialized nations. In contrast, Czechs and Germans drank more than 140 liters of beer per person in 1992, nearly eight times as much as the Russians. The United States consumed 86.2 liters of beer per capita, in fourteenth place.

From the beginning of history in other countries in Eastern and Central Europe, people both rich and poor drank beer daily. But beer was never a staple in Russia. Beer did become popular for a time in the late eighteenth century among Russian nobility and aristocrats, largely because Catherine the Great loved it. A woman of prodigious appetites, historians tell us that Catherine "looked her best" in masculine clothing, had twenty-one known lovers, and died a sudden death. (Hence all those grade-school rumors that she met her demise in a failed bedroom experiment involving a horse and a large sling.) Catherine's preferred tastes included beer from England—the darker and stronger the better. English brewers created a style to export to her court, Russian Imperial Stout, that has enjoyed a comeback among American microbrewers.

By the time Rick Grajirena came to Russia, all that was ancient history. Russia still had a tradition of small breweries, many of which brewed "village beer" in small batches for local consumption. In the United States, the big beer companies had become big through mass marketing and national advertising. In the old Soviet Union, there was no mass marketing, no national advertising, no television commercials, no billboards, no ads in magazines—hard to imagine for Westerners, who grew up amid advertising seemingly everywhere. Along with little advertising, the old Soviet Union had relatively little beer. Many small store windows had temporary signs, hand-lettered on paper: *Piva nyet*. No beer. Some of the signs looked as if they had originally been put up for a day or two but had been in the windows for years. Some Russians said they gave up drinking beer during the Brezhnev era, when they suspected that any beer for sale in Moscow had been watered down with horse urine. Really. But most Russians didn't seem to mind the scarcity of beer. Russians ordinarily didn't relax after work over a beer, or go meet friends for a beer, or have a beer after mowing the lawn or playing golf. (Of course, few Russian had lawns or played golf, either. For many years, the only golf course in Russia was the one that Nikita Khrushchev built in Siberia in the 1950s before a visit from Dwight Eisenhower.)

Many Russians did not regard beer as an alcoholic beverage. It was a soft drink, a cousin to *kvass*, the unfermented "liquid bread" that was sold primarily as a children's drink for a few kopecks out of tanks wheeled around on the streets. Historically, Russians have drunk to get drunk, and that means vodka. While Americans—and people from other industrialized nations—drink much more beer than Russians, the gap is considerably narrower for consumption of all alcohol. Studies show that Russians rank just behind Americans in consumption of pure alcohol. If wine and beer are disregarded, Russians are the world's leading consumers of spirits—principally vodka. The Russian tradition was—and is—that once a bottle of vodka is opened, the cap has to be thrown away. The bottle must be finished at that sitting. As in many northern climates, alcoholism rates are high. Correspondingly, so are the rates for domestic violence and divorce. Serious drinkers regard beer as little more than a chaser, or at best a hangover cure the next morning. "Beer without vodka is money to the wind" is an old Russian saying. Grajirena's daunting task was to prove to Russia that beer wasn't just for breakfast.

Grajirena couldn't do market research. He couldn't round up groups of beer drinkers and have them do sample tastings; he could not report back to Miller, for instance, that 37 percent of Russians in the top three demographic groups would switch to Miller beer if it was for sale in their local pubs. There weren't any defined demographic groups. There weren't competing brands from which they could switch. And there were almost no pubs or bars as Westerners knew them—very few places where ordinary people gathered after work to relax and talk over drinks. The few places that served alcoholic beverages—vodka, a short list of mostly sweet wines, and maybe a bottle or two of local beer of questionable age and quality—were hard to find. Most of them had no advertising outside, not even a sign that let passersby know this was a place to get something to eat or drink. Americans have described their atmosphere, at best, as similar to a high school cafeteria, but a cut below due to hygiene issues. A place that had a keg of beer would typically have a thirty-minute queue to get in. Many thirsty drinkers brought their own mugs or pitchers from home because few establishments had glassware or were willing to hand glasses out to customers, who might walk away with them. A beer lover would stand in line for half an hour, get his mug filled, head straight back to the end of the line, and try to make the beer last—almost always unsuccessfully—until he got back to the head of the line. Some would fill up a big pitcher and carry it home.

Many restaurants were family-run neighborhood places, and the neighborhood residents knew where they were. They didn't need a sign. But since the late 1980s a handful of new restaurants, some actually with signs, had popped up in Moscow, as one of the baby steps toward free enterprise under *perestroika*. Several of those restaurants were still around when Grajirena came to town to do his market study in the summer of 1992. He made them his first target. Would they like to buy Miller beer from America? The response was unanimous: Yes, they would. Most of the restaurants carried some type of Western beer when they could get it, often canned beer from the Netherlands or Scandinavia. They looked forward to the prospect of having a regular supply of American beer, especially in bottles. A bottle looked better on a table than a can. Bottles were classier. Bottles were how beer was served in good restaurants in Western Europe and the United States. Some restaurants said they wanted to pay by credit card. Was that all right? They did as much of their business as they could on credit cards backed by American or European banks. Diners were advised in advance not to bring cash or checks—credit cards only were accepted. Dollar credit cards. This was because the restaurants wanted to keep as little cash as possible on the premises. The less cash on hand, they reasoned, the less interest they would draw from the *mafiya*, and the less they would lose if the *mafiya* robbed the place.

———

Payment by credit card was okay with Grajirena. He was happy that the restaurants were eager for Miller beer, no matter how they paid for it. But he could not go back to Miller with responses from only a handful of restaurateurs. He needed more. A public relations man in Tampa who had done some work to help publicize the Odessa 200 project gave Grajirena the name of a Russian professor as a possible contact. The Tampa PR man had met the professor, Alexander Borisov, at an international public relations conference and been impressed. Borisov taught public relations and marketing courses at Moscow State University, one of Russia's best universities. The Tampa PR man told Grajirena that the professor spoke good English, seemed to understand American marketing, and was eager to help American firms in Russia.

When Grajirena called him, Borisov said he would be happy to get together. He suggested Sunday brunch at one of the Western-style hotels, and he promised to bring some ideas on how to go about doing market research and then marketing American beer in Moscow. Grajirena had never been to Sunday brunch at one of the Westernized hotels in Moscow. He was more of a bacon-and-eggs-at-seven-A.M. sort of guy. It was a remarkable scene. The hotel set up dozens of extra tables, flowing out from the restaurant into the lobby. A quartet played classical music. A queue of people in the hallway waited behind velvet ropes to pay $36 apiece—at a time when the average Russian was happy to be making $50 a month—to get a crack at the long buffet table laden with all manner of eggs, sausages, ham, pancakes, French toast, omelets, rolls, croissants, buns, fruit, yogurt, cereals, and more. The crowd was almost entirely foreigners—American, European, and Japanese business travelers and a mix of expatriate businesspeople, journalists, and diplomats living in Moscow. For Borisov and any other Russian who wanted to make foreign business contacts, it was the place to see and be seen.

The professor fit right in. He was of average height and trim, and he wore a nice-fitting European suit: not flashy, not expensive, but understated and serious. He had a good haircut, not long and swept back like old Communists, not greased up like the gangsters. He nodded and smiled at people. He was in his element, Grajirena thought—or rather, what he wanted his element to be.

Over this and several other meetings, frequently at hotel restaurants, Borisov put forth a grandiose plan for marketing Miller beer in Moscow. He sketched out prospective advertising campaigns that included television commercials, radio spots, and print ads. He said he could get things started for a quarter-million dollars. He suggested a contract. But Grajirena realized that despite his apparent sophistication regarding Western advertising, marketing, and public relations, Borisov had little practical business sense. Like so many other Russians whom Grajirena met, Borisov thought that he and First Republic had deep pockets. He didn't realize that First Republic was a near-penniless startup, consisting of little more than three guys spending their own time and money. "We just don't have that kind of money," Grajirena told him. "Maybe we will someday, but not for a long time." Grajirena tried to explain it several times. After a time Borisov stopped talking about TV spots, but Grajirena was never confident that the professor really believed First Republic didn't have a lot of money.

Nonetheless, Borisov was eager to assist. He told Grajirena that even if he couldn't oversee a multimillion-dollar advertising campaign, he wanted to help First Republic get started. Grajirena said First Republic really didn't need TV commercials featuring Swedish bikini teams. What it needed was solid information about the market: where and how Miller beer could be distributed and sold in Moscow. Grajirena had his short list of hotel bars and new Western-style restaurants that wanted to pay by credit card. But he needed many more prospective customers than that. He needed to be able to show Miller that he could sell beer in Moscow neighborhood restaurants and grocery stores and kiosks, the little hutlike streetcorner shacks that had become tiny beacons of free enterprise in Russia. He needed to get in touch with as many of those potential Miller customers as he could. Could Borisov help gather that marketing information?

Yes. Yes, he could, the professor said. He had an idea. He had never heard of anyone trying it in Russia, but it might work. He came up with an old KGB map of Moscow—distinctive because it was complete and accurate, with all the streets and all their correct names. Borisov recruited about fifty of his best marketing students from Moscow State University and gave them copies of a questionnaire Grajirena had made out for potential customers. What is your name? Address? Phone number? What kind of business do you do: Restaurant? Grocery? Kiosk? Who are your customers? Do you sell beer now? What kind? How much do you sell? Would you be interested in carrying American beer? Miller beer? In cans or bottles? How much would you sell if you could get a steady supply of as much Miller beer as you ordered? How much would you pay per case? How much would you charge for the beer? Grajirena agreed to pay the students two dollars a day—the most they had ever earned, more than they could earn in any other part-time job, and probably more than they could have earned at any full-time job. Armed with their photocopied maps and questionnaires, the students plunged out into Moscow. They were assigned neighborhoods, and they walked up and down all the main streets and many of the side streets, looking literally door to door for restaurants and groceries, and stopping local residents to ask them about more places. Many times a local citizen would say yes, there's a restaurant right there, across the street, downstairs in that apartment building, but the family that runs it opens only on Saturday nights. The student would come back on Saturday night and get the questionnaire filled out.

As far as anyone at First Republic knew, it was the first legitimate market research of its kind ever done in Russia. Within six weeks, at a total cost of less than $2,000, Grajirena had a stack of several dozen completed questionnaires. The response was extremely positive. Eighty-eight potential accounts —restaurants, grocery stores, kiosks, a handful of new nightclubs—indicated that they would order Miller beer and sell as much of it as they could. Some of the more enterprising students gathered comments from their respondents, and one of the most common was: They could not believe there would be a steady supply of beer.

Borisov never received any payment from First Republic—not beyond a couple hundred dollars' worth of Sunday brunches, anyway. But he did ask permission to use First Republic and Rick Grajirena as a reference for the public-relations and marketing agency he was establishing to supplement his university teaching. Grajirena said that would be fine. He thanked Borisov and promised to get in touch if First Republic ever did need a big advertising campaign. The professor did set up his agency, and he did use his work for First Republic to open doors for work for other Western firms setting up in Moscow.

Back in the States, Grajirena began putting together the business plan, writing it and creating charts and graphics himself on his home computer. He and Harken and Mroczkowski agreed that First Republic's top priority was raising money. With a Miller deal on the horizon, this was the time to raise it. So they put together a prospectus to raise $325,000. It sold out quickly, mostly to friends of Grajirena in Florida and to friends of Harken in Wisconsin. Part of the cash was used to buy out the two-thirds of the company owned by McElwee and Hayhurst. Grajirena became president and CEO of the reconstituted First Republic. Mroczkowski became chief financial officer. Their starting salaries were about $40,000 each. Harken joined them on the board of directors, along with Tom Fotopulos, a Tampa area lawyer who helped with the legal formalities of setting up the company, and his brother George Fotopulos, who recently had retired as an executive with a Coca-Cola distributor and who would act as a consultant in setting up the distribution operation in Moscow. The Fotopulos brothers each took a small percentage of the company in exchange for their respective expertise in law and the beverage distribution business. First Republic also purchased a small Tampa duty-free operation that sold liquor, cigarettes, and small luxury items such as perfume to cruise ships. The duty-free operation had an office in a bonded warehouse, which became First Republic's headquarters. The duty-free company's office and warehouse staff became First Republic's office and warehouse staff. Rick Grajirena was pleased. First Republic was taking shape.

And so was the distribution proposal for Miller. Decorated with color photographs of Moscow restaurants, nightclubs, and groceries scanned in by Grajirena himself, the business plan was not a slick, highly professional document. It looked more like the work of earnest amateurs who had done their homework. The proposal gave a brief—what else could it have been?—

history of First Republic, and thumbnail sketches of Grajirena, Harken, Mroczkowski, and the brothers Fotopulos. There were also profiles of Alexander Borisov, touted as "public relations, marketing and advertising support," and of a young Russian woman, Larissa Moskalenko, who was listed as First Republic's first—and to that point, only—sales representative. She came to Grajirena and Harken through Russian sailing contacts, who had urged them to give her a job. A world-class sailor, she had won a bronze medal in yachting for the Soviet Union in the 1988 Olympics and just missed a medal in 1992 in Barcelona. She had many contacts within the Russian sports hierarchy and spoke good English—and it didn't hurt that she was gorgeous. "When she walks toward you, all you can think of are two zeppelins in a dead heat," someone told Grajirena and Harken. They hired her. She didn't last long after a trip to Wisconsin to meet with Miller executives and to talk to potential First Republic investors. She impressed the potential investors so much that one of them developed a severe crush on her. The potential investor's wife knew something was up when her middle-aged, overweight, out-of-shape husband began getting up two hours earlier than normal to go jogging with Moskalenko. The wife objected strenuously and said First Republic was relying on Moskalenko's charms to seduce money out of potential investors. Her husband kept his money rather than put it into First Republic. Moskalenko decided First Republic wasn't for her. Grajirena and Harken tried to smooth things over with her, but she took a marketing job with a European sporting-goods company instead.

In September 1992, Grajirena and Harken presented their marketing plan to several top Miller executives in Milwaukee. The meeting was held in a conference room at the brewing company's headquarters. As Grajirena walked the Miller executives through the proposal, his principal message was that First Republic had a big advantage over other would-be distributors, largely because Grajirena had spent a lot of time on the ground in Russia meeting a lot of people and gathering a lot of information. The Miller executives smiled when Grajirena described hiring the Moscow State University students to fan out through the city and conduct the first grassroots market research ever in Moscow—all for Miller beer. They liked the image. They nodded knowingly when the business plan's overview of First Republic summed up Grajirena's general economic view of the region. "Russian and Ukrainian market economies are developing through personal initiative, and many successful business leaders are emerging," the plan said. "These businessmen, having recently entered the free market, are actively seeking to establish lasting ties with responsible Western companies that can assist in the profitability and growth of their enterprises." Without government statistics or any market research beyond what his Moscow State University students had turned up, the "Marketing in Moscow" section of Grajirena's business plan was largely seat-of-the-pants guesstimates. This, in its entirety, was his plan's "Beer Market Overview":

> Consumption per capita, while not measurable, is judged to be very high. Beer is consumed as a thirst quencher, a food companion, at business and social functions, as a stress reliever, and on the street at all hours of the day. Consumption of beer occurs in the same manner and ease as the consumption of soft drinks in the U.S. The downside of this phenomenon is that it indulges young people below the age of eighteen. (There appears to be an absence of any effort to address this problem due to higher priorities.)
>
> The total market volume of all brands is not known. There is no data collection system in existence. It is a multi-brand market, with brands too numerous to list. Except for the few upscale retail outlets, there is poor consistency of brand availability. This is due to a "good only while supplies last" wholesale and retail system. German brands seem to dominate the mid-price beer market, while locally brewed beer dominates the low-price mass market.
>
> The winter months of November, December, January, February, and March have historically affected beer sales considerably, but aggressive marketing and continued development of retail outlets should boost wintertime sales.

The report went on to assess retail outlets in Russia in similarly vague terms. The number of bars was "unknown," and the bar market was "very underdeveloped." Taverns were "unlisted and under-developed." Liquor stores were "unlisted and definitely under-developed." Thirteen casinos were identified and regarded as "good prospects for premium beer," and so were the three Pizza Huts. "Pizza Huts serve German beer at $4.00 a bottle, and a locally brewed private label at $3.00 per bottle. Pizza Hut estimates 40 percent of their customers are Americans. The three Pizza Huts average a total of 1,000 cans of beer per day. This account should be a top priority for Miller and First Republic." The report said First Republic had identified 180 well-established restaurants, plus many others "too small to be counted." The report identified twenty-six "Western-style" supermarkets and predicted,

"This is the future." Cans of Miller would sell for a dollar or more apiece, six dollars for a six-pack (twice the price, roughly, of what Americans typically paid for Miller beer). The report said, "First Republic representatives discussed the possibility of stocking a prestigious American beer with numerous retail supermarkets, and received very favorable reactions without exception."

Finally, the report said small neighborhood food stores, located every six blocks or so, were "unlisted and too numerous to research. They supply mostly staples and are always short of inventory. Not good premium beer marketing prospects presently, and time will tell whether they will survive. If they do, a low-price imported beer might be effectively marketed through this channel." Kiosks, the marketing report concluded, "exist in the thousands," ranging in size from eight by ten feet "to a space equal to that of a TV tray." Grajirena's report predicted that the kiosks would disappear as the Russian economy stabilized and improved, and that their demise would provide a boost to neighborhood grocery stores. "Kiosks will be a route delivery system's worst nightmare: low price only, low inventory, no way to park and deliver, and high delivery frequency. Should kiosks survive and should the price-point become reasonable, a 'cash and carry' operation might work. One concept is to park a beer truck near a cluster of kiosks and let them buy directly from the truck. The truck becomes a mobile warehouse."

The report's brief assessment of the distribution system noted that there was no Western-style beer distributor in Moscow. Anybody who could get his hands on some beer could bring it into the city and sell it to a middleman, who might sell it to another middleman, before it finally ended up with a retailer. City officials issued permits to sell beer, but "other organizations" had considerable control over where beer could be sold—Grajirena's euphemistic nod toward the *mafiya* and the old-line Communist Party operatives who still controlled distribution of some products in some areas of the city. The report concluded that the development of free and open markets could mean an end to such "facilitators," but for now the facilitators "must be recognized and managed." If someone from Miller had asked Grajirena point-blank what he meant, he would have explained that First Republic might at times find it difficult to do business without paying a bribe or conducting its business according to the strict letter of the law. But nobody from Miller asked what he meant.

CHAPTER 9

Groundwork

The Miller executives loved First Republic's amateurish little business plan. They wanted to do business in Russia, and no one else had shown as much interest or initiative as Rick Grajirena. In the month after he presented the plan, the two companies held a series of uncomplicated negotiations over their proposed distribution agreement. Then Grajirena and Harken flew to London and made their presentation to Miller executives at the company's European headquarters. Grajirena's sales projections, which the business plan conceded were based on "educated guesses," predicted that First Republic would sell 236,505 cases of Miller beer in Moscow in 1993. Each Pizza Hut would sell five cases a day. Each of the nearly two hundred restaurants would sell an average of one six-pack a day. Each of the twenty-six supermarkets would sell fifteen cases a day. If that happened, Miller Brewing would gross more than $1 million by doing business with First Republic. It was promising.

But Miller executives knew that the sales forecasts were simply Grajirena's guesses. First Republic's research convinced the Miller executives that this was the company to go with—but not that it would necessarily be successful. They were willing to give First Republic a chance, and some support—minor support. They would not put up any money or even any beer. First Republic had to pay cash in advance for its beer. Perhaps if things went well and there were reasonable assurances of rapid growth, the company eventually might offer some terms that would allow First Republic to pay for the beer sixty or ninety days after delivery. But that was down the road.

Grajirena would have liked better payment terms, but he was convinced that cash flow would not be a problem. Miller beer was going to fly off the shelves in Moscow. First Republic would use the revenue to buy more Miller beer, then just keep plowing profits back into the company to promote growth. First Republic agreed to pay Miller cash in advance for all beer shipments to Russia. Miller offered First Republic a one-year exclusive distributorship in Moscow. The contract was drawn up, and Grajirena flew to Milwaukee and signed it at a simple boardroom ceremony with Miller executives in October 1992.

Meanwhile, working out of the offices in the duty-free warehouse in Tampa, Grajirena hired an office manager and began laying the foundation for the Moscow operation. As president and CEO, he considered moving to Moscow himself, but quickly rejected the idea. His wife, Valerie, and their sons, soon to be teenagers, were settled in Florida. They didn't want to live anywhere else, and neither did he—especially in a place as far away, as foreign, and as difficult as Moscow. He and Val discussed it briefly but never seriously. They figured that he would probably spend a week or ten days each month in Moscow. Other people, yet to be hired, would be based in Moscow for First Republic. The retired Coke distributor, George Fotopulos, swung into active consulting mode and began traveling to Russia with Grajirena. Through the Canadian-Russian Trade Council, they found a Canadian lawyer who helped them file all the necessary legal documents. The lawyer also helped them find office space and rent delivery trucks. Looking for an office manager, either an American already living in Moscow or a Russian who was well versed in American business culture, Grajirena and Fotopulos made contact with an employment agency in Moscow that specialized in finding Russians to work for American firms. They were impressed with the American expatriate named Carolyn who handled their account at the employment agency. She quickly recruited several smooth young Russians to work in the office and in sales. Grajirena and Fotopulos were pleased when she herself applied for the job of office manager, and they hired her immediately.

Grajirena and Fotopulos placed advertisements in the *New York Times* and the *Chicago Tribune* for a general manager. They were looking for an American who knew both the beer business and Russia. Dozens of applicants knew the beer business, and dozens more knew something about Russia. But none knew both.

Grajirena and Harken huddled. Which was more important: knowing the beer business or knowing Russia? Russia, they ultimately decided. The American beer distribution business could be learned. But someone who knew it would never work out if he wasn't comfortable living and working in Moscow. Two candidates stood out. One of them had four young children, the other was single. Grajirena and Harken, for a variety of reasons, focused on the single guy. Stanley was of medium height, a dark complexion, and a stocky build. He was in his mid-twenties, but he seemed older. Smooth and polished, he seemed a person of culture and substance, the type of man who could get a job done. His parents had emigrated from Russia to Cleveland when he was small, and he spoke fluent Russian. He had visited relatives in Moscow many times and had a business degree from a Big Ten university. He said he was eager to do everything he could to learn the beer distribution business. George Fotopulos had a friend who had a beer distributorship, and he lined up a crash-course internship for Stanley. Stanley worked there for several weeks and did well. He moved to Moscow as First Republic's general manager for Russia in the late autumn of 1992.

The first offices were in the same building as the offices of First Republic's lawyer, Jack Robinson, a tall, slender, balding Canadian who had been working in Moscow for several years. Robinson's chief assignment was to set up a corporate structure for First Republic that would allow the company to get its profits out of Russia—something that could be difficult for Western firms at the time. Robinson set up an offshore shell corporation in Cyprus, one of the few countries that had a foreign-exchange agreement with Russia that would allow companies incorporated there easier movement of money in and out of rubles. Cyprus also offered a favorable tax rate: profits repatriated from Russia by a Cyprus-registered company were taxed at Cyprus's rate of 4.25 percent, as opposed to the typical 35 percent Russian tax on repatriated funds.

Like most Western lawyers helping Western companies, Robinson offered lots of other advice and made lots of other connections. For example, when Grajirena said he needed office and warehouse space, Robinson introduced him to Robinson's own landlord, Arkady An, a *biznesman* of Korean descent who had a thriving business in real estate development and the automobile trade. An once showed Grajirena one of his warehouses, full of imported Mercedes, BMWs, and other expensive imported cars, dozens of them. Robinson said An was also trying to corner the market in Lada cars, the Russian-made automobiles that passed for midquality in Russia but were regarded as cheap and poorly made in the West. (One Russian joke was that the new model Lada had a rear-window defroster—so the owner could keep his hands warm while pushing it. Another joke: How do you double the value of a brand-new Lada? Fill it with gas.) Arkady An moved around Moscow swiftly, often in a convoy of Mercedes limousines, with assistants and bodyguards ever present. While he himself was a smooth-looking, well-dressed, polished sort of man, he always had his brother with him, and his brother looked much rougher. Grajirena thought the brother looked like *mafiya*, but there was no evidence that either Arkady An or his scary brother was a gangster. They were obviously rich, and in the early days of post-Soviet Russia, pretty much anyone making money was generally suspected of doing something—or lots of things—that were at least technically or party illegal. Most Russians believed that the only way to make money—unless you were a Westerner, and sometimes not even then—was illegally.

An was happy to rent office space to First Republic on a temporary basis, along with the first of several warehouses he was building in a new development on the outskirts of Moscow. The warehouse would be completed by the time the first shipment of Miller beer arrived in December, he promised, and in the spring First Republic could move into new offices that were being built adjacent to the warehouse. Grajirena toured the warehouse-office site. The nearly completed warehouse looked good. It was huge— 20,000 square feet, much bigger than First Republic needed at the time— but the price seemed reasonable, and there was plenty of room to grow. Grajirena envisioned using all of that warehouse within a couple of years and perhaps taking over one of the others that An planned to erect nearby. The roof was just above ground level, while most of the side and back walls were belowground. The entrance was a big driveway carved into the earth, sloping down from ground level to the level of the warehouse floor. The sides of the driveway were massive concrete walls built into the earth. There was an automatic sliding door big enough for a semi-trailer truck, and a normal office door next to it for people to walk through without opening the big door. Grajirena liked the fact that the warehouse was built into the ground. It would attract less attention, and the earth-backed walls would provide natural refrigeration for the beer. He thought the design was a good one. He would find out how wrong he was.

The First Republic office in central Moscow, in the same An-owned building where Robinson had his law offices, needed to be furnished and outfitted. Some American companies imported American office furniture, but Grajirena wasn't that picky. Desks and chairs, made either in Russia or elsewhere in Eastern Europe, were fine with him. But computers, software, and other electronic equipment—phones, fax, copier—had to be brought in from the States. If it was available in Russia at all, the equipment typically cost twice as much. Grajirena became an expert at getting electronic equipment through customs. He probably should have filled out form after form in triplicate, he probably needed some special permits, and he probably should have paid some sort of special taxes on the equipment. Instead, he and other First Republic employees and investors brought everything in as regular luggage. The first time he tried it, Grajirena was nervous. What if the customs people took away the desktop computer he had lugged onboard as his hand baggage?

But the customs officials waved him through without even looking into the bulky box, which was clearly marked as a computer, complete with a picture of the machine. Other Westerners in Moscow told Grajirena that while a lot of the equipment they brought into Russia may have come in illegally—no one seemed sure of the rules—the unofficial policy for customs officials was to look the other way. The country needed computers, the reasoning went, no matter who was bringing them in. And the more Western businesses operated in Russia, the more Russians would get better-paying jobs. Occasionally a customs officer would stop Grajirena and inspect the equipment. As one inspector lingered over the machine, Grajirena was sure he was waiting for a bribe. He decided to take a chance. "What are you doing?" he boomed, waving his arms. "Don't you realize this machine is the future of your country? You can't keep out computers. You can't stop progress. I need this for my business, and my business will hire Russians for good salaries. How can you do this?" The startled Russian customs officer, who wasn't used to people speaking to him at all, much less shouting at him in a language he didn't understand, packed up the computer equipment and waved Grajirena through. The next time it looked as if a customs officer was going to slow him down with an inspection, Grajirena went into his act of aggressive indignation right away. Every time he was waved through immediately. There was a bigger problem with the computers once they were safely in the office. It turned out to be not so safe, in a country wired for 220 volts, to run equipment that was built to run in a country that had 110-volt wiring. In their excitement at the new equipment, the staff would plug in the computer or printer, and it would blow. "You gotta stop frying these machines," Grajirena grumbled after the second or third time. The expense was an issue, but his real complaint was the prospect of another twelve hours on a plane with a box of electronic gear on his lap.

The initial Moscow staff consisted of Stanley, the general manager; Carolyn, the office manager; and three salesmen. Arkady An rented First Republic some trucks to use for deliveries, and he provided the drivers, too. All First Republic needed was some beer to sell. Grajirena ordered five containers of beer, each containing 1,240 cases of Miller Genuine Draft in bottles. He sent Miller a check for $60,000—about $10 per case. Arkady An, who suddenly seemed interested in expanding his empire beyond vehicles and real estate, said he would buy the entire shipment, all five containers, for $80,000—about $13 per case. The margin was less than Grajirena anticipated. He had expected to sell the beer for about $14 or $15 per case. But this deal had the advantage of being a quick, big-volume first sale that would provide immediate cash flow. The beer would be delivered directly to Arkady An's warehouse. First Republic wouldn't even have to handle it. And An said he would pay cash on delivery—provided delivery came in the first week of December. The holiday season in Russia usually began not on December 25 but on New Year's Eve, a night of feasting and drinking, and continued through January 7, the Russian Orthodox Christmas. During the decades of official state atheism in the Soviet era, Christmas had been a nonholiday. But many people had celebrated behind the closed doors of their homes, and Father Frost often brought gifts for the children. With the Communists and the Soviet Union seemingly consigned to the scrap heap of history, the New Year's-to-Christmas holiday season to welcome 1993 promised to be the most festive since czarist times three-quarters of a century earlier. It was the perfect time to create a stir with plentiful supplies of a premium American beer that was new to the market. All that First Republic had to do was take delivery of the beer, hand it over to Arkady An, and let him distribute it and start building a buzz for Miller Genuine Draft. They would use the cash flow from that first delivery to get even more beer delivered by January, to meet the expected demand. "We're off to a flying start," Grajirena exulted to his board of directors.

First Republic's shipment of beer left the United States on schedule in November. But during the Atlantic crossing the ship threw a prop, and ended up in Rotterdam for repairs. The beer didn't arrive in time for Christmas. A great opportunity was lost. But Grajirena wasn't worried—it was just bad luck. Instead of getting started in December, First Republic would unveil Miller beer in January. One month wouldn't make that much difference. Grajirena decided to focus on a Super Bowl party instead.

CHAPTER 10

1993

The first shipment of Miller Genuine Draft, delayed in Rotterdam, finally made it to Moscow in early January 1993. Arkady An, who had wanted to buy the entire five containers if the beer arrived in early December, wanted none of it. Grajirena was not discouraged. He was spending a lot of time in Moscow, and so was George Fotopulos, the retired Coca-Cola distributor working as a consultant to First Republic in exchange for a small piece of the company. They had been working with the office staff and the salespeople, and they were convinced that Miller beer was going to be a big product in Moscow, and that First Republic was going to be a raging success. After all, there had never been a Western-style beer distributor in the Russian capital. Moreover, First Republic was selling service as well as beer. A restaurant or bar owner, a supermarket or a kiosk could order beer delivered the next day, and it would be delivered the next day—the exact number of cases ordered, at the price that was agreed upon.

Each establishment was assigned a First Republic salesperson who personally looked after the account. The salesperson not only checked in every two or three days—more often if necessary—to see if beer was needed, but also did much more. The salesperson brought in point-of-sale material, such as posters and table cards, and helped arrange special promotions for bars and restaurants. In groceries and supermarkets the First Republic salespeople became informal consultants on retailing. They not only showed managers how to display and sell Miller beer, they often advised them on making their entire operations more effective. Mark some popular item on sale each week. Put signs in the windows. Have big floor displays. Install displays of small items near the checkout counters. Pipe in some soothing music. Make sure the store is clean and well lighted. Make sure the bottles, boxes, and cans on shelves face out. Train staff to be courteous, pleasant, and most of all, helpful.

These most basic concepts of Western retailing were all but unknown in Russia, which had never had a free-market service economy. "What we are selling is not just beer," Grajirena kept telling his staff. "We are selling service." The First Republic salespeople, often with Grajirena or Fotopulos, walked into shops unannounced, asked to see the manager, and made their pitch. They had no trouble selling the idea of Miller beer. Virtually every account wanted it—if they could get it, and if they could keep getting it when they needed it. That wasn't the way the Russian economy had worked for decades. In the old days stores, shops, and restaurants had placed orders for certain products, but what was delivered to them often had little resemblance to what they had ordered. They sold what the state delivered. A restaurant might have beer and chicken on the menu, but if all the state supplier sent them was sweet wine and black sausage, that was all they sold. "If you sell our beer, we will deliver it to you within a day or two of when you order it," Grajirena and his salespeople told the bar, restaurant, and store owners. Many of the Russians buying Miller beer were skeptical, but they had nothing to lose. If First Republic did not keep its promises and deliver the beer, their establishments would be no worse off than they were before.

First Republic introduced another foreign concept to Moscow retailing: consignment. The salespeople took orders with the promise of payment within a couple of weeks. They would often arrive at the Moscow establishment with the beer, help unload it, and help store it, emphasizing the importance of keeping bottles of beer in dark, cool places to keep them from "skunking." Many Russian managers never gave any thought to preserving and protecting their products to keep them fresh. Their customers came to them over and over, no matter what, because there was nowhere else to go. "Now, with capitalism, there will be competition," Grajirena warned the managers. "You can't just take your products and shove them out on the floor or on the shelves. You've got to give people a reason to buy from you rather than from the new place around the corner. Make sure your beer is fresh and displayed well." It was, he reflected, like giving hands-on lessons in free-market retailing.

Grajirena wanted to have a Super Bowl party to kick off Miller's entry into the Moscow market in January 1993. One of his salespeople told him that an American journalist was putting on a party at one of the Westernized hotels, and that much of the expatriate American community planned to attend—even though, because of the eight-hour time difference, the kickoff wasn't until 2:18 A.M. Moscow time. No matter—the party would start long before the game and would go on well toward dawn. Thousands of Americans had moved to Moscow since the fall of the Soviet Union, and this would be a rare chance to celebrate America's unique, albeit unofficial, holiday. Grajirena got in touch with the American journalist, who had arranged for a special closed-circuit showing of the game to be channeled into the hotel. It would be the first time the Super Bowl was shown live in Russia. Grajirena paid the journalist $5,000 for the right to sell Miller beer exclusively at the party, and to be listed as a sponsor in all advertising and promotions. Miller banners and posters decorated the party, and First Republic staffers sold beer from seven P.M. to seven A.M. First Republic made a tidy profit, but even more important, the party heralded Miller's arrival in Moscow.

There was a big turnout, and it barely mattered that the football game wasn't a particularly good one: Dallas Cowboys 52, Buffalo Bills 17. "I can't believe I can watch the game here. I'm so sports starved, it's scary," said one young American who had just moved to Moscow to work in a food import business. "If I couldn't watch the game, I'd be calling my mom and dad every five minutes," said one Marine from Texas who showed up in his ten-gallon cowboy hat. Besides the expat community, a number of Russian movers and shakers, the "new Russians" embracing capitalism, turned out in force for the Super Bowl party. For many, it was the social event of the year. And Miller beer was the cool new beverage of choice for the beautiful people. One of the Americans at the party who had been in Moscow the longest was Jeffrey Zeiger, who had moved to Russia four years earlier to set up Tren-Mos, the city's first American-run restaurant. "For several hundred Western people to sit and watch the Super Bowl in an American establishment is proof that this city has come a long way. It doesn't matter who wins the game. Moscow wins today," he told the *Los Angeles Times*. The newspaper noted that the Budweiser commercials seen by American viewers were not aired in Moscow. Instead, the Bud commercials were blacked out, and the partygoers at the Moscow hotel saw Miller commercials.

In the days and weeks after the Super Bowl, Miller sales took off in Moscow. Anheuser-Busch was also entering the market with Budweiser, but its distribution system was not nearly as developed as First Republic's. Jeff Zeiger had been carrying Budweiser in his restaurant, which was the unofficial social headquarters for the American expat community in Moscow. He dropped Budweiser and switched to Miller. Grajirena, flying back and forth, dividing his time between Tampa and Moscow, suggested that his salespeople set up "tastings" in groceries and supermarkets. He asked Chris Mitchell, one of the young Americans working as a salesman for First Republic, to set up and oversee the Moscow Cold Patrol. "Here's the idea," Grajirena told Mitchell. "We'll get together a bunch of good-looking young Russian women. We'll put them in those little costumes that Miller uses for Cold Patrol girls in the States. They can do tastings in groceries and supermarkets and out on the street near kiosks. We'll have them making appearances at bars and restaurants and nightclubs that agree to do special Miller promotions. They have to look good, but the personality is just as important. They've got to be outgoing. They've got to be fun to be around. They've got to get people to try the beer."

Mitchell took to his new assignment eagerly. "I'm your man," he told Grajirena. He posted flyers in windows and on lampposts near Moscow State University, announcing interviews that promised high-profile, good-paying, part-time promotional work with a Western company. He put classified ads in two Russian newspapers that were similarly vague. He didn't know any Russian words to describe the work, probably because this kind of work was unknown in Russia. "It sounds like you are looking for prostitutes," a Russian in the office told Mitchell. "Hey, why don't you just go out and hire some beautiful prostitutes? They know how to work with the public." Mitchell considered it briefly but decided that First Republic needed young women with a wholesome, innocent look. Literally hundreds of young women applied for the dozen spots as Cold Patrol members and the right to hand out samples of beer in tight short-shorts or a cowgirl microskirt. Grajirena at one point arrived at the First Republic office and was barely able to make it through the hallway, which was crowded with gorgeous young women waiting for a few minutes of Mitchell's time. "I've got to see every one of them," he told Grajirena. "It's my responsibility." Each young woman filled out a detailed application form and brought in a photo that Mitchell stapled to the form so that he could remember her. Several prostitutes, misled by the vague wording of Mitchell's ads, did show up. But they quickly lost interest when they found out that First Republic was not in the market for their particular commercial talents, and that the job paid only a dollar an hour.

After Mitchell pared down the applicants to a couple of dozen, Jeff Zeiger offered the use of his restaurant, Tren-Mos, for the "finals." The competition was held like an informal beauty-and-talent contest, with Zeiger, Mitchell, and the other First Republic salesmen acting as "judges." Mitchell hired ten young women, nearly all of them college students. They began making appearances, six or eight at a time, depending on their class schedules and other commitments. If a store agreed to order a certain amount of beer, First Republic would—with considerable advertising and promotion—bring in the Cold Patrol. The pretty girls, smiling at the women and flirting with the men, passed out samples of Miller beer to shoppers. The Cold Patrol was the first "tasting" promotion group in Moscow, though many other companies selling consumer products quickly copied the idea. At first many shoppers refused the Cold Patrol's proffered samples, and not because the samples were in urine specimen cups—the closest thing to tasting glasses that Grajirena could find in Moscow. Many Russian shoppers, who never had been offered a free sample of anything, thought they had to pay for the samples. Or that taking a sip would mean they had to buy a six-pack of Miller Genuine Draft. It didn't take long, however, for the Cold Patrol and their free samples to catch on. Once they were assured that taking a small plastic cup of beer from a pretty girl in a belly shirt didn't mean they had to buy a six-pack, customers typically took a sip, then maybe another, and then more often than not bought a six-pack. Business boomed, particularly for sales of Miller beer, whenever the Cold Patrol showed up. Bars and nightclubs were jammed when they made appearances. These girls were not ice maidens. Some of them drank as much beer as they handed out, and they all chatted, flirted, and danced with customers. They became celebrities in Moscow in their own right, much like the Dallas Cowboys cheerleaders were in the United States at the time. Nightclubs and bars began buying more beer just to get the Cold Patrol to make an appearance. "Every place they have appeared has become a good customer of ours," Mitchell reported to Grajirena. First Republic, recognizing the value of the Cold Patrol, gave the women a raise to two dollars an hour after a few months, and then three dollars an hour a few months after that. It was widely regarded as probably the best part-time job a coed could get in Moscow.

There were, however, some early problems with the Cold Patrol. Out of the first group, Mitchell let two or three go within a few weeks. "They're really good at standing around and looking cute, but they're too shy to talk to people they don't know," Mitchell explained to Grajirena. Replacements were easy to find. Mitchell dipped into his stack of applications, or occasionally hired the daughter or sister or cousin of a First Republic customer, or someone who worked in the office. Every few weeks he had to make a replacement. A couple of the girls liked to drink too much. At first Grajirena didn't mind them drinking on the job or even getting a little tipsy, but when they started ignoring customers, he told Mitchell to get rid of them. Similarly, nobody seemed to mind the Cold Patrol flirting with customers, but later one of the young women was fired amid suspicions that she was arranging after-work assignations—for pay. Cold Patrol girls often danced with each other, especially early in the evening to get the party started. But two Cold Patrol girls were dismissed after they danced only with each other all night, and ended up soul-kissing and groping each other in a not-dark-enough corner of the bar. Grajirena set down a code of conduct for Cold Patrol girls—no drinking on the job, no dancing with other First Republic employees—and issued a memo to all First Republic employees telling them not to drink other beers or wear the logos of other beer companies in public.

American beer was all the rage in Moscow in 1993. Exports of beer from the United States to Russia nearly quadrupled. And Miller beer was the trendiest of the trendy. Within weeks of the Super Bowl party, Miller beer was in virtually every popular nightspot, particularly any establishment that aspired to Western levels of service or ambiance. By the spring of 1993, First Republic's Moscow operation was sending money back to Tampa and was on the verge of operating in the black. First Republic and Miller did many more promotions in Moscow, including sponsorship of the city's first softball tournament. Miller beer seemed to be everywhere. Chris Mitchell attended a meeting of American businesspeople at the U.S. Embassy, and when he introduced himself as a salesperson for First Republic, "the exclusive importer of Miller beer," the crowd burst into applause. A top Russian rock band called Time Machine made a point of drinking the beer during a much-anticipated and highly publicized live interview and performance on Russian television. Miller was so hot that other advertisers began placing Miller bottles in their own ads and commercials to show how hip they were.

Things were going well for Rick Grajirena. For the first time in more than two years, since he left his last sailmaking business and started helping Russians raise money for round-the-world yachting, he felt that he had some time for himself. He missed sailing. So he traded a share of First Republic stock, worth $21,000 on paper, for the *J. Maxie,* a two-person sailboat in the popular Star class, for which there were many races in the waters off Florida. He renamed the boat *Valhalla*—he had to get his wife Valerie's name on there somehow—and recruited one of his former oceangoing crew members to crew on the smaller boat. They raced the boat on weekends in and around Tampa and sometimes in other parts of Florida. Despite little time for training or practicing, they dominated their races during the spring and summer of 1993, winning half a dozen and finishing near the top in several others. Grajirena felt as if he was on top of the world, and that things would only get better.

As First Republic was getting off to its strong start in Moscow, Miller executives took notice. It looked like their Moscow distributor was going to be a winner. A Miller executive called Grajirena and said that the Miller distributor in Switzerland was flying in an American country-western band, Tom Grant and the Nashville Ambassadors, to play at promotional appearances in Swiss bars and restaurants for a week in late June. If Grajirena would pay for part of the airfare and arrange a place for the band to stay in Moscow, First Republic could have the band there for the week of the Fourth of July.

Grajirena jumped at the offer. This could be even bigger for First Republic than the Super Bowl party, he told himself. He booked the band into some of First Republic's best accounts—the Moscow bars and restaurants that were selling the most Miller beer. For the week that the band was in town, Grajirena took Valerie along to Moscow for the first time. Several months earlier, First Republic had rented a small two-bedroom apartment in central Moscow, a typically drab place with a furniture-cramped living room, a bathroom-sized kitchen, and a closet-sized bathroom. All the furnishings and floors were worn, the faucets leaked, the windows rattled, the phone line was bad, the cracks in the walls were partly covered by dark hanging rugs, and there was a vaguely sour smell that no amount of spraying or scrubbing could remove. It was an apartment that probably cost the previous Russian tenants the equivalent of $30 or $40 a month in rent. First Republic was lucky to get it for $800 a month. The four band members—singer-guitarist-leader Tom Grant, a drummer, a bass player, and a guitarist—stayed in the apartment. Rick and Val Grajirena stayed in a hotel for the week. While her husband was working, Valerie spent her days hanging out with the band, mostly sightseeing with a First Republic office worker as a guide-translator. In the evenings Val would meet Grajirena and the rest of the First Republic crowd at the bar or restaurant where the band was playing. Onstage was the only place the band seemed at ease. "We're just a bunch of good ol' boys who ain't never been anywhere," one of them said. "We always thought Russia was a scary place. Bad things can happen to Americans here."

But the Nashville Ambassadors caused more damage than they suffered, beginning at their first gig, when the drummer leaped from behind the band and set off running and drumming through the room, smashing some glasses with his drumsticks and knocking others over when he leaped onto tables. The crowd went wild, and Grajirena happily paid the ninety-dollar bill for broken glassware, which the bar owner presented even before the band finished its set. Word of mouth spread about this crazy country band that also did lots of rock 'n' roll and had a wild drummer. For the rest of their stay, Tom Grant and the Nashville Ambassadors became the hot ticket in Moscow. Every night the show would start quietly, then the drummer would seemingly go berserk, and so would the crowd. "He's pushing the Russians over the edge," Mitchell told Grajirena. "They see one guy on stage getting out of hand, and they think, hey, I can do that, too." There were turn-away crowds, culminating in a July Fourth outdoor barbecue at the flagship restaurant in Jeffrey Zeiger's Tren-Mos chain, which had grown to include three restaurants in central Moscow. Homesick Americans queued up for burgers just off the grill and promised lifelong devotion to Miller beer in gratitude. Russians ate corn on the cob for the first time and congratulated themselves for embracing an American lifestyle they previously had seen only on TV. In Moscow, First Republic had become synonymous with Miller beer, Miller beer had become synonymous with America, and America was what was selling in Moscow.

CHAPTER 11

Mitchell

When Chris Mitchell got the assignment to put together First Republic's Cold Patrol in the spring of 1993, he was twenty-two years old. He had grown up in a small town in Pennsylvania, where he was an adequate student and captain of his high school wrestling team. By the time he graduated from high school and was accepted at Bucknell College, he hadn't particularly distinguished himself academically, and he had shown no more interest in foreign affairs or international events than any typical American teenager in the 1980s. Then he was late turning in his form to register for classes. He had to take a language, and the only one left was Russian. He was the worst student in his Russian class. "You deserve an F, or maybe a D if I'm generous," his professor, a native Russian, told Mitchell. "But I'll make you a deal. I'll give you a C if you promise never to take Russian again." Mitchell turned him down. For some reason he loved the idea of speaking Russian and learning about Russian culture. He changed his major from political science to international studies, and he signed up in the autumn of his senior year for a semester-abroad program to study at Kiev State University, in the historic capital city of Ukraine. It was the autumn of 1991, right after the coup attempt that led to the fall of the Soviet Union—exactly the same time that Rick Grajirena was making his first trip to Russia. While living and studying in Ukraine, and making occasional trips into Russia, Mitchell quickly picked up the language. What had been extremely difficult for him to learn out of a book, he picked up easily and naturally in conversation with native Russian speakers. In a short time he was using slang, laughing at jokes, and sometimes even thinking in Russian. "I've found my destiny," he told his surprised parents when he went home. "It's in Russia."

After graduating from Bucknell in the spring of 1992, Mitchell packed his bags and moved to Moscow. He had no job, but he was confident that his near-fluent Russian would open many doors for him. For several months, however, all he could find was poor-paying work as an English instructor for private language firms. He had expected life to be like it was in Kiev, when prices and the ruble-dollar exchange rate were controlled by the government and someone with a few dollars could live very well. A few months later, when he arrived in Moscow, the Soviet government no longer existed, and the price restraints and exchange controls were gone. Mitchell earned several thousand rubles a month as an English teacher, which in Kiev a few months earlier would have been a princely sum. A bottle of vodka had cost only three rubles then. But a year later, in Moscow, with the government's artificial support of the ruble a thing of the past, Mitchell's several thousand rubles a month were worth barely $20. Calling home twice a month ate up his entire salary. He had to use his savings to pay the rent.

Mitchell called the American Chamber of Commerce in Moscow and asked if any new American companies in town needed help. The Chamber gave him the number of First Republic, and he called Stanley, the general manager of the Moscow office. Stanley liked the fact that Mitchell was an American who spoke fluent Russian. Mitchell had no sales experience, but he had worked one summer in a beer distibutorship as a "handtruck slave." That was more beer experience than most First Republic employees had, so Stanley hired him on the spot. Mitchell never even asked how much money he would get. He figured it must be better than teaching English. His first week's pay was $60, and he was ecstatic. He could barely believe his good fortune when he learned that he would get a commission on top of that: a dime on every case of beer he sold.

He joined two other First Republic salesmen. Cary Scardina, another recent American college graduate, had moved to Moscow for fun and fortune. Misha, a thirtyish Russian, spoke excellent English and had some experience working with an American import-export firm that had an office in Moscow. Misha was the head salesman, and he taught the two young Americans how to sell in Russia. The main thing to remember, Mitchell learned, is that Russians hate to say no to someone face to face. They would say, "I want to think about it," or "Your beer is too expensive for me right now," but they would rarely say no. Mitchell was persistent, showing up at potential accounts over and over. He would explain why it made sense for them to buy Miller beer, and he urged them again and again, "Just take one case, see how it sells. What have you got to lose?" He promised that he would come around a lot, help arrange promotions, give them advice on their business. "I'm your friend. I'll be keeping an eye on your business with you. You can count on me," he said more than once.

In many ways it was easier for an American to be a salesman in Moscow than for a Russian. Russian shop and restaurant managers were often too busy to meet with a Russian salesman who showed up unannounced, but they usually had time for Mitchell—if only out of curiosity, at least at first. Foreigners were still an oddity. They were fascinating to Russians, most of whom had not seen many foreigners, much less sat down and talked to one. Americans were particularly interesting, since they had been the hated and feared—and envied—enemy through all the years of the Cold War. "These Russian guys love the idea of having an American salesman coming to see them," Mitchell told Grajirena. For many of his accounts, it was as if he was their pet American. They could tell other businessmen, their friends, their relatives, that they were doing business with an American. "A lot of these guys like the idea of an American kissing their butts, trying to get their business," Mitchell said. He developed a large Russian vocabulary—a salesman's vocabulary. His grammar was still weak at times, "like a country Georgian," Mitchell said, so nobody would mistake him for a native Russian. But many Russians were pleased and flattered that he could speak their language at all.

In the early days of First Republic, not even the Americans who lived there drove themselves around Moscow. Driving in Moscow was regarded as too dangerous because of bad Russian drivers; too inefficient because it was so easy to get lost amid the road layouts and signs; and too troublesome because of the many obscure Russian traffic regulations. Moscow traffic policemen, the GAI (pronounced guy-EE), frequently stopped cars, especially those carrying what appeared to be foreign businesspeople, and assessed the drivers "fines," to be paid on the spot, for violations real or imaginary. The driver that First Republic assigned to Mitchell was a big man nicknamed Cartoon, because he bore a slight resemblance to a monster in a popular Russian Saturday-morning animated children's program. Mitchell and Cartoon became close friends, spending six to seven hours a day driving the streets of Moscow, the Batman and Robin of the Moscow beer business. "Cartoon can smell out new places," Mitchell told Grajirena.

Cartoon's salary, $50 a month, was a bargain. He would hear about a place that was supposed to be a bar or restaurant or nightclub, and he would drive Mitchell there to knock on the door, cold. Or they would get together in the morning with no plan, look at one of the city maps Grajirena got from Borisov for the marketing study, and then head for a neighborhood where they had never been. They trolled the streets for bars and restaurants. Cartoon screeched to the curb whenever he saw a place that looked like a potential customer and knocked on the door. It was usually opened by a large, scowling security guard. Cartoon would explain who Chris Mitchell was, emphasizing that he was an American, and they would be shown in and ushered past the manager right into the rear office of the owner.

About one in five of these cold calls resulted in a sale that developed into a good, continuing account for Chris Mitchell. About one in five refused to see him. "Get this boy out of here," one nightclub owner snarled at a bodyguard who had brought Mitchell in without checking first to make sure the boss wanted to talk to an American. Three in five would see Mitchell that first time and place a small order, or not place an order but leave the door open for a possible future sale. "I think some of these guys ordered from me just to get me to come back and see them regularly," Mitchell said. "They loved to talk about their business, to explain it to an outsider. They wanted to know what I thought of their places. Some of them had lots of questions, especially about how things were done in the restaurant or nightclub business in America. A lot of them were curious about how I ended up in Moscow. I became friends with some of them." Many of the Russian restaurateurs encouraged Mitchell to come back to their places in the evening, and to bring Western friends along. Foreigners were trendy, and if foreigners were hanging out at a Russian place, it must be trendy. The *mafiya* and other high-spending new Russians were sure to follow.

The typical nightspot was a restaurant that had a small stage or dance floor at one end of the room, flanked by waiter stations, with the tables fanning out toward the opposite wall. Diners often spent the entire evening in the restaurant, smoking and drinking and eating food that was ordered not all at once but a dish or two at a time. If Mitchell dropped in any time after noon, many of his regular customers expected him to sit down to eat—and drink—with them: champagne, appetizers, mixed drinks, food, beer, more food, wine, dessert, cognac. Mitchell and Cartoon learned to pack their sales calls into the mornings. They ultimately stopped scheduling anything after three o'clock in the afternoon because they were likely either to blow it off or show up in no shape to do business.

Mitchell's social life revolved around his work. His best friend in Moscow was Cary Scardina, the other young American salesman, and they spent a lot of their free time together. They traveled through much of Russia, the former Soviet Union, and Eastern and Central Europe together, often on spur-of-the-moment weekend trips. "We'd just pick a city on the map, anywhere we could get to in eight hours, and jump on a train for the weekend," Mitchell said. He met many of the employees at his accounts and became friendly with some of them. His first girlfriend in Moscow was the Russian accountant at a hotel where he sold Miller beer. He went out almost every night with colleagues from First Republic, customers, or people he met selling beer. Usually he frequented places where First Republic delivered Miller beer, where he was known by owners and staff who expected him to drink a lot of beer. He did. When Grajirena or other First Republic staff came into town, he was often their guide to the nightspots of Moscow. Potential investors were the most difficult duty for Mitchell because they were often first-time Moscow visitors who seemed intent on getting drunk.

Moscow Madness was the term for it, and every American expatriate in Moscow knew what it meant, many of them from experiencing it themselves. As *Sky*, Delta's inflight magazine, reported, American businesspeople came to Russia for two main reasons: to get rich, and to have fun. Not necessarily in that order. Many Americans came to Russia and acted totally out of character, usually with excessive drinking. There were a variety of reasons, often in combination. For so many years Russia had been the dreaded enemy. No matter how much Russia changed, it would always be the enemy to Americans who had grown up to fear the old Iron Curtain. For those people, finding themselves actually in Russia—still forbidding and intimidating—could be unnerving. Sitting down with someone over a drink was reassuring. Tying one on was a way to feel better, more comfortable—at least until the next morning.

The experience was all the more meaningful, perhaps, if one or more of the drinking buddies were real Russians. After a couple of drinks, they didn't seem so dangerous. "We're not so different," untold legions of American visiting Russia were heard to slur. "You Russians are just like we are. People are people." Chris Mitchell saw it dozens of times. "You'd go to whatever was the latest trendy spot," he said, "and see these American bankers or lawyers in town on business, drunk out of their minds, dancing on the bar, tearing their shirts off, then blowing chunks on the floor. They would never in a million years act like that back home. It took them less than twenty-four hours in Moscow." When an American disgraced himself, it was often with a Russian's encouragement, Mitchell believed. A Russian who was used to drinking a lot, especially a lot of vodka, might get an American visitor into a man-to-man toasting contest with shots of vodka. The American would inevitably lose, thereby giving the Russian a feeling of superiority over this foreigner who had a much better life, by every standard of the capitalist world, right down to his $200 shoes, but who at the moment was passed out with vomit on those $200 shoes.

Potential investors in First Republic were among the worst sufferers of Moscow Madness, Mitchell believed. Rick Grajirena would bring them or send them to Moscow. "Chris, show these guys around," he would say. Mitchell would squire them around—the First Republic offices, the warehouse, and then to the most Westernized of his accounts. Grajirena might join them for dinner and then, as he almost always did, turn in. "Show them a good time, Chris," he would urge. Time after time, in the wee hours, Mitchell would deliver a staggering would-be investor back to the hotel. It was his job to clean up after them, if necessary, and keep them out of trouble if they got into an argument with a prostitute or said the wrong thing to a *mafiya* gangster. Too often, Mitchell found himself staggering, too. Sometimes the potential investor shared a hotel room with Grajirena. The next day, Mitchell would smile through his own throbbing headache as Grajirena complained about being awakened by a bumbling, incoherent roommate. Once Grajirena awoke to find a potential investor standing at their hotel window urinating—onto the closed window—and muttering, "Piss on 'em. Piss on 'em all." That potential investor did not put any money into First Republic, nor did many of the others who came over to Moscow "to look around." Few of them were really interested in investing, Mitchell felt. Most were simply looking for an excuse to come to this political and economic frontier now that it was relatively "safe" and they had connections, through Grajirena, to take care of details such as visas and hotel rooms. They paid all or most of their own way, but First Republic nonetheless put forth considerable effort and expense on their behalf, showing them around and entertaining them. They were historical tourists, getting a close-up, personal look—largely thanks to First Republic—at the the biggest political, social, and economic upheaveal of the late twentieth century.

In those heady days in the early 1990s, the gathering spots for Chris Mitchell and many other Americans in Moscow were Jeff Zeiger's restaurant, Tren-Mos, and his nearby brasserie-bar, the Tren-Mos Bistro. The thirty-five-seat bar at the Tren-Mos Bistro was typically busy from early afternoon until well after midnight, with American tourists, visiting businesspeople, expatriates working in Moscow, diplomats, and news crews. Zeiger was First Republic's first customer for Miller beer, and he also had one of the first TV hookups in Moscow for CNN. His restaurants and bar, which also drew many well-known and influential Russians, were the places to see and be seen in Moscow. The bar was the place to find out what was going on, and Zeiger became the highest-profile American in Moscow. But in 1994 he left Moscow abruptly. Mitchell and other Americans there were never sure why Zeiger left. Some noted that his Russian partner was killed, presumably by the *mafiya,* and that he may have been afraid he would be next. Other Americans remembered that Zeiger had been embroiled in tax problems with Russian authorities, and said perhaps he was afraid he would be arrested. Whatever the reason, no one at First Republic, not even Mitchell and others who considered themselves good friends of Zeiger's, knew what had happened to him. Several later said they had tried to track him down over the years, to no avail. To them, it seemed like the man who was "Mr. American" in Moscow in the first years of the new Russia had simply dropped off the face of the earth.

CHAPTER 12

Zeiger

Jeff Zeiger's father's family emigrated to the United States from Eastern Europe after World War II. Zeiger's father, Shelley, built up a successful liquor distribution business, and young Jeff grew up in a happy upper-middle class home in Trenton, New Jersey. Shelley Zeiger spoke seven languages and did business all over the world. He began going to the Soviet Union in 1973, when it was rare for American private businessmen. He first hoped to make a deal to import Russian vodka. The liquor market was leveling off in the United States for traditional American favorites such as whiskey and gin, and Shelley Zeiger thought that a new product, such as genuine Russian vodka, might have growth potential. He made arrangements to meet with the Russian authorities who controlled chemical exports—alcohol was considered a chemical—but was told that the government recently had made a deal with Pepsi-Cola to swap Stolichnaya vodka for Pepsi. The authorities suggested that Zeiger might be interested in another alcohol-based chemical product: perfume. So Shelley Zeiger began importing Russian perfume to the States. He took care of the importing, and his wife ran the American distribution side of the business.

Over the years, the Zeigers added more products to their import and distribution business, including arts and crafts, such as carvings and paintings and *matryoshka* nesting dolls. In the mid-1980s, Shelley Zeiger, seeing still more opportunities, led a trade delegation from Trenton to Moscow. He and Trenton city officials proposed to Russian authorities that Trenton and Moscow become "sister cities." But officials in Moscow, a city of nearly 10 million, thought it would be beneath the Russian capital to become sisters with the New Jersey capital, a city with a population of barely 100,000. Instead, they suggested that Trenton become sisters with one of Moscow's districts. Happily, they offered the Lenin district, in the very heart of the city, home to the Kremlin, Red Square, the Pushkin museum, and the Bolshoi ballet. In 1986, when the Kirov ballet decided to perform in the United States, it could have picked virtually any major American city. It chose Trenton. Thus began a remarkable, long-running exchange of arts, culture, and business between Trenton and Moscow.

In 1988, when President Ronald Reagan had his historic meeting with Soviet leader Mikhail Gorbachev in Moscow, the American contingent brought along a pizza wagon—a self-contained trailer truck with a kitchen that produced pizza and passed it out the window to gleeful Russians who had only heard of the wonders of American pizza. People queued up on the streets for hours to get a warm slice. "Hmmm," said Shelley Zeiger, who had made perhaps thirty trips to the Soviet Union over the previous fifteen years and was still looking for his first good restaurant meal. He knew of an Italian restaurant, of sorts, in Moscow, and a French restaurant, of sorts. But neither was very authentic or very good. Both had trouble getting ingredients, keeping everything on their menus, and training staff to provide proper service. This was the period of *glasnost* and *perestroika*, however, and the Russian government was gingerly, cautiously allowing people to form small private businesses. Many of those new businesses were neighborhood restaurants. To Shelley Zeiger, the time seemed right. He asked his friends in the Moscow city government about the possibility of opening an American restaurant in the Lenin district. They offered him a choice of two government-run canteens—dirty, grubby, infested places that offered a scant list of mostly greasy, sometimes stale food to people who had nowhere else to go out to eat.

Jeff Zeiger by then was twenty-three years old and on the executive fast track with Hyatt hotels, managing the chain's hotel restaurant in Princeton. When his dad called and suggested they have dinner to talk over a business proposal, Jeff had no idea what was on his mind. Jeff had never been to Russia. He hadn't studied Russian history or language or literature. He knew very little about Russia. He had little or no interest in it. The business had always been his dad's, not his. So the proposition put forth by his dad was surprising but also fascinating. "I want to open the first American restaurant in Russia," Shelley said. His son smiled at him, relishing the parent-son role reversal. "Well, good, Pop. I want a beautiful blonde and a million bucks. But you're the one who always told me we don't always get what we want." Jeff didn't think his dad was serious. But as dinner progressed, it became clear that Shelley Zeiger had never been more serious. He really did intend to open the first American restaurant in Russia, and he really did want his son to be his partner and go to Moscow and run the place. The Zeigers, father and son, would be partners in a joint venture. Their additional partner would be a branch of the Moscow city government. The Russians would put up the building; the Zeigers would put up the money, the equipment, and the know-how. Jeff Zeiger would be the owner-manager.

Jeff was intrigued. He wasn't married. He had no reason not to take the job, except that he might lose his budding career at Hyatt. But he discussed the opportunity with his boss, and the boss told Jeff he couldn't pass up a once-in-a-lifetime chance like that. He also promised that Jeff could always come back to the Hyatt chain, probably in a much higher position. The experience would be invaluable in an international chain such as Hyatt. Jeff told his father yes. They went to Moscow and picked what they thought was the better of the two restaurant locations offered. After being issued the license for Russian Joint Venture No. 444, they renovated the place from top to bottom, much of it with equipment, furnishings and facilities they brought in from the States. They decided to name the restaurant Tren-Mos—Trenton and Moscow—and opened it in November 1989, the same month as the fall of the Berlin Wall and a year before the first McDonald's opened in Russia. From then on, whenever Shelley Zeiger encountered American businessmen boasting about how much they had invested in Russia, he would dismiss them by saying, "Hey, that's nothing. I contributed my firstborn son."

Jeff Zeiger came to Russia in 1989 not speaking a word of the language. He had no idea how to set up an American-style restaurant there or manage it American style—to make money, in other words. But nobody knew how to do those things in Russia because nobody have ever done them. The first McDonald's would not open for six months, the first Pizza Hut a year after that. The problems were immense: getting equipment and money into the country, having renovation work done, hiring and training staff, finding reliable sources of food and drink. Zeiger thought he had found a Russian meat supplier, but he had to look elsewhere when the supplier wanted to deliver the entire first year's supply of meat—five tons—before the restaurant even opened. "In some ways it was harder because we had to figure out for ourselves how to get everything done," Zeiger reflected a decade later. "Nobody had ever done it before. But it some ways it was easier than it is today. Back then you didn't have to pull out a hundred-dollar bill every time you needed something. People in Russia welcomed us. They wanted us to succeed. And business was more personal then. The vegetable market guy, for instance. I drank with him, I told jokes with him, we talked about our families, we talked about our problems and the world's problems. We did all the toasts. We became friends, business friends. And I got good fresh vegetables when a lot of other people wanted them but didn't get them. When I needed something special, he got it for me. All business back then was based on personal relationships."

Within a year Zeiger spoke fluent but coarse Russian, the kind spoken by taxi drivers and delivery men and cooks and bartenders. Tren-Mos was a raging success, what Zeiger described as a Moscow version of Rick's American Cafe in the classic film *Casablanca*. It was the hangout, the place to go, not only for American tourists and expatriate diplomats, journalists, and businesspeople, but for many European and Asian visitors as well. It also became the place for new Russians, the entrepreneurs, to see and be seen. Politicians came in, their wives came in, sports figures, poets, pop singers, cosmonauts. Bob Hope. Edmund Muskie. Paul Laxalt. Buzz Aldrin. Many of the Russian politicians who moved in and out of Boris Yeltsin's cabinet. Not Yeltsin, but his wife came in with friends. Zeiger became friendly with one of the old Soviet Union's foremost heroes, one of the first cosmonauts, one of the first men ever in space. "You know," he told Zeiger late one night as they sat drinking, "I went all the way to outer space and came all the way back. Of all the places on Earth I could have landed, I had the bad luck to land right back in the Soviet Union."

Ordinary Russians also came into Tren-Mos to celebrate weddings and anniversaries. Tren-Mos was the most expensive restaurant in Moscow, but unlike other expensive places—including those owned by Russians—it encouraged Russians off the street to come in and eat. Some of the new "private" or "capitalist" restaurants run by Russian entrepreneurs made it all but impossible for regular Russian citizens to be their customers. One of the most frequent practices to discourage ordinary Russians was to refuse to accept cash. The "credit cards only" rule kept cash off the premises, thereby reducing the chances of a *mafiya* robbery. But it also kept most Russians off the premises, since no ordinary Russian had an American or European credit card, or any way to get one. The banks simply did not do that sort of retail business in Russia. It was a country where nobody made much money, and the money they did make could not be sent out of the country. Even if money was spirited out, it wasn't worth what the Russian government said it was worth. American and European banks wanted nothing to do with credit card customers from Russia.

A handful of new "private" restaurants in Moscow did accept rubles and did allow ordinary Russian customers. But those restaurants usually had a separate dining room for the Russians, keeping them apart from the Western customers. The Western dining room was plusher, nicer, better appointed. The waiters were smoother, spoke some English, and provided a measure of service. The menu in the Russian dining room was different, not only because it was written in Russian, but because the selection of dishes was more limited, simpler, and cheaper. Jeff Zeiger changed all that at Tren-Mos. There would be only one dining room, he decreed, and one menu, focusing on typical American fare such as steaks and chops, french fries, and salad. Each menu item listed the price in both rubles and dollars. Zeiger's only special treatment for Westerners was to ask them to pay with dollars or dollar credit cards. That was his profit. The rubles paid by his Russian customers—on a typical night the clientele would be half Russian, half Western—would stay in Russia and be used for his overhead, salaries, operating costs, ingredients, and other expenses. After the initial costs of setting up the restaurant, when he changed a considerable amount of dollars into rubles, Zeiger did relatively little currency exchange. Rubles paid his bills, dollars were his profit.

Business boomed, and Zeiger helped it along with his natural flair for networking and personal marketing. Back in the early 1990s, many Americans traveled to Moscow on Pan Am. So did Zeiger. On one flight he overheard a couple of flight attendants bemoaning their regular layover in Moscow. They were talking about how their per diem was paid in rubles and, as one of them said, "There's no place to spend them on anything you'd want to buy. You can't even go out and get a burger." The two flight attendants compared notes on the food stuffed in their flight bags in order to survive their two days in Moscow: cheese, cans of tuna fish, crackers, fruit. They were going to eat in their hotel rooms. Zeiger struck up a conversation with the flight attendants, invited them to Tren-Mos, and ended up making a standing offer for all flight crews for Pan Am and any other American airline flying to Moscow. Tren-Mos would accept payment from them in rubles, allowing the flight crews to spend their per diems for decent food. In turn, if a passenger asked the flight attendants where they ate in Moscow, they would tell the truth—"We all eat at Tren-Mos"—and hand the passenger Zeiger's business card. During his five years in Moscow, flight attendants gave out more than five thousand of Zeiger's business cards—and he estimated that more than half of those people came to the restaurant at least once. Many of them became regulars.

Tren-Mos was the American hangout, the place to get a good meal, the place to rub shoulders with the famous and would-be famous. Finally, it didn't hurt that Tren-Mos was the place where young flight attendants let their hair down in Moscow. "I want to meet this Jeff Zeiger," one American executive announced upon entering Tren-Mos. When Zeiger appeared, the executive shook his hand. "I don't know what you've got going for you, young fella," he told Zeiger. "But on the flight over here three different stewardesses gave me your card and told me to come here to eat." Like many other Americans doing business in Russia, that man became a regular when his company sent him to Moscow to live. When friends and families visited from the States, he took them to Tren-Mos. When associates came in on business, he took them to Tren-Mos. When the company's CEO visited Moscow, he took him to Tren-Mos. The state-run restaurant formerly on site had grossed the equivalent of a few thousand dollars a year, probably not enough to cover its payroll of twenty or thirty employees without a state subsidy. Tren-Mos quickly grew to gross revenues of $2 million a year and 150 employees, all Russian except for Zeiger and his French-born executive chef. Moving about Moscow, Zeiger was often stopped by people who recognized him and wanted to shake his hand and tell him thank you. Thanks, Americans said, for bringing a decent restaurant to Moscow. Thanks, Russians said, for bringing a nice restaurant to Moscow that is not just for foreigners, where we regular Russians are welcome, too.

Advertising was not a prominent feature of the Moscow airport. Indeed, Zeiger saw no commercial signs or posters on its walls when he first arrived in Moscow. He found out who to talk to, who to ask, who to pay, and put one of the first advertising signs on the walls of the airport: a prominent sign for Tren-Mos, right above the baggage claim area for passengers arriving on international flights. Rick Grajirena noticed that sign on one of his first trips to Moscow. When First Republic was doing its marketing studies for Miller Brewing, Tren-Mos was one of Grajirena's first stops. "I'll be your first customer," Zeiger promised, "and probably your best." He was. As Miller grew to become *the* American beer in Moscow, when Zeiger replaced his sign at the airport—he made it much bigger—he included a picture of a Miller truck. His bar became the first in Moscow to have draft Miller, the first to have popcorn machines, the first to have CNN, the first to undertake charity work through well-publicized donations of food and money to orphanages. The decor of the restaurant was simple, in the beginning. The only obvious American touch was the tablecloths, which were striped red, white, and blue. Not long after Tren-Mos opened, the governor of New Jersey came to visit on a trade mission. He brought along a New Jersey state flag, which Zeiger hung on the wall. A few days later some customers from

Ohio said, "Hey, why a flag from New Jersey but not Ohio? We'll fix that." Next time they came in, they brought an Ohio flag. Within a few months, Tren-Mos was decorated with the flags of all fifty states, all contributed by customers. Regulars from other countries began bringing in their flags, too.

———————

Tren-Mos was so successful that the Zeigers soon opened two more spots, the Tren-Mos Bistro, which featured quick dishes such as pizza and pasta, and, next door, the Tren-Mos Bar. The bar, with only nine stools at the bar itself and a couple dozen chairs around tables, was a small place, but it assumed a large role in Moscow's expatriate social scene. It was where journalists and diplomats and businesspeople met to swap information and rumors and speculation that often made its way into print, into broadcasts, into State Department briefings, and into memos back to the home office. The *mafiya* was never a large presence at any of the Tren-Mos establishments, unlike many of the other new "private" restaurants and night spots in Moscow. Zeiger refused to cater specially to them. He also refused to pay them off—or, rather, he would have refused if he had been asked. "I know it happened to a lot of other places, but the *mafiya* never approached me," he said. "I don't know why. Maybe they all assumed I was already spoken for, that some other gang was already protecting me. Or maybe it was a political thing. Maybe my profile was too high because I had the first American restaurant, or I was too well known for all the charity work. Because of the kind of people who came to the restaurants, maybe they figured that coming after me would have caused them more problems than it was worth. Maybe I was just tougher to shake down than the other guys."

That's not to say there were no problems for Zeiger, even after his three spots were up and running and making money and he was the toast of Moscow. Shipments from the States, or from suppliers in Western Europe, were stolen. Customs regulations seemed to change at whim. Workers needed to be retrained or replaced. The first—and at the time only—bank doing dollar transfers when Tren-Mos opened went bankrupt overnight. Zeiger lost $220,000 that credit card companies had paid him for charges at his restaurant but that the bank had not yet processed. At one point Moscow was awash in rumors that the government was going to begin charging the new "private" restaurants a value-added tax (VAT)—in effect, a sales tax. Zeiger and other restaurateurs protested, especially when there was speculation that the government might charge the VAT retroactively and demand that the restaurants pay the tax on sales made in the previous month.

"That's not fair," Zeiger told a top tax official who often ate at Tren-Mos. "At least give us a chance to charge our customers and pass on the tax to them. It's not right to charge us for business we've done in the past." The tax official agreed with Zeiger and told him not to worry. A few days later, in January 1993, the VAT went into effect, retroactive to January 1992. The government issued a demand to Tren-Mos. News reports at the time said the figure was $400,000, but Zeiger would confirm only that it was "well into six figures." He hired American and Russian lawyers, wrote letters, had meetings, filed appeals, and lobbied anyone and everyone who might help get the new VAT requirements reversed, or at least have the retroactive requirement reversed. "You guys don't understand what heavy taxation does," Zeiger told government officials and politicians. "It kills business. It discourages people from starting more businesses. You're killing the goose that's laying the golden egg." None of it did any good. He paid the full six-figure demand, $400,000 or whatever it was, retroactive a year. Looking back, Zeiger said it was a testament to the strength of his business—including the nearly 80 percent profit margin that he achieved most months—that he was able to survive hits such as the bank closing and the VAT demand.

In February 1993, Tren-Mos achieved another first, a historic footnote in the new Russia's march toward a free-market, capitalist economy. The branch of the Moscow city government that had been the Zeigers' partner in the Tren-Mos joint venture sold its share of the partnership to a private individual. It was the first Russian-American joint venture to be privatized. The buyer was Sergei Goryachev, the Russian who had been in charge of the Russian side of the venture. Goryachev was an old friend of Shelley and Jeffrey Zeiger. Years before, he had been the mayor of the Lenin district of Moscow. He helped Shelley Zeiger get his foothold in Moscow and did much to further the "sister city" relationship with Trenton. Zeiger never was sure where Goryachev came up with the money to buy out the government's half of the joint venture. Maybe profits that were supposed to be turned over to the government had been skimmed. Maybe Goryachev had backers—presumably *mafiya*—who put up the capital. Maybe it came from some other shady business in which Goryachev was rumored to be involved—black-market currency exchanges, or money laundering. Jeff Zeiger didn't know and didn't care. None of Goryachev's other businesses were related to Tren-Mos. As far as Zeiger was concerned, Goryachev was a friend, a mentor, a hard-working, competent partner.

For Zeiger, things didn't change at all after the Russian replaced the government as his partner. Five months later, however, Goryachev was murdered on the street, shot three times in the head and neck at close range. The killer was never found, but it was widely assumed that a *mafiya* gang was behind the murder. To Zeiger, that was entirely possible. But he was also convinced that the killing had nothing to do with Tren-Mos. He was sure it involved Goryachev's other, shadier dealings. *Pravda* wrote a number of stories about the murder, using it as a hook for an exploration of the growing *mafiya* influence. *Pravda* interviewed Zeiger, seeking to link the murder to Tren-Mos and other successful private businesses as one of the costs of capitalist growth. Nonsense, Zeiger said. He denied ever having any dealings with any gangsters, and he told *Pravda* that the day the *mafiya* came in and told him he had to pay protection money was the day he handed the gangsters the keys and walked out. Zeiger's legend grew in Moscow. He had been the hardworking entrepreneur, the schmoozing host, the astute manager, the compassionate philanthropist. Now he was also the defiant tough guy, spitting in the eyes of the bully. Everyone who heard or read about Zeiger wanted to meet him, and business got even better.

One of Zeiger's regular customers was the director of the Bolshoi ballet. One day the director brought in Natasha Lushin, a ballerina, and introduced her to Zeiger. They began going out and were married in mid-1994. By then Zeiger began to sense a change in Moscow. From a handful of Americans when he had arrived five years before, the number of expatriates now numbered in the tens of thousands. Tens of thousands more were visiting on business. Americans were setting up their own social circles, dining and entertaining in each other's homes. Many of the recent expatriates had families and didn't go out every night after work. A dozen other American restaurants had sprung up in the wake of Tren-Mos, with talk of more new ones every day. There were new French and Italian and Chinese restaurants. McDonald's was building new outlets, and so was Pizza Hut. When his wife got pregnant in late 1994, she and Zeiger decided they wanted the baby to be born in America and raised as an American. A Russian customer had been asking Zeiger for a couple of years, repeatedly, how much he wanted for his restaurants and bar. It had become a joke between them. But when the customer asked again, Zeiger surprised him by naming a price.

Three days later the full amount was on deposit in Zeiger's bank back in New Jersey. Not long after that, he and his pregnant wife got on a plane and left Moscow. They opened a restaurant in Trenton, and when that failed, Zeiger took a job as a food and beverage manager for the Marriott hotel chain. "How did you find me?" he asked when contacted for this book. He scoffed at the rumors, still widely circulated and believed in Moscow, that he had been run out of town by the *mafiya* or the tax inspectors or both. He pointed out that he stayed in Moscow for a year and a half after his Russian partner was murdered, and that he had resolved all his tax difficulties before he left by biting the bullet and paying all the tax demands in full. "Business was actually better after the murder," he said. But he insisted that when he left Moscow four years earlier, he closed that chapter of his life. He didn't keep in touch with anyone he knew or worked with in Moscow. He hadn't been back and had no plans to go back. But he would not say he had closed the door forever. "My wife is from Moscow, but her parents are here in the States with us now," he said. "We have two daughters, and maybe we'll want to take them back at some point. But would I live there again? No. Would I work there? Maybe."

CHAPTER 13

Moscow Madness

Rick Grajirena had his own brushes with Moscow Madness, but he had a built-in immunity: He was physically incapable of staying up late. "I didn't always go to bed sober in Moscow," he said, "but I was almost always in bed by eleven o'clock, usually closer to ten. That kept me out of a lot of the trouble these other guys got into when they went out to the bars and clubs till three or four in the morning. Or five or six in the morning, judging by some of the times they would come roaring in and wake me up." In those early days in 1993, he felt good about the way things were going for First Republic. But like any small startup business, it still encountered problems. There were many telecommunications problems due to the poor service in Russia. It was difficult to get a clear line to make a telephone call to Tampa. Even if repeated efforts, over and over, got a clear line to the States, it often abruptly disconnected. It was all but impossible to send a long fax in one attempt, especially during the day. Grajirena ultimately worked out a way for the fax machine in the First Republic office in Tampa to automatically call the Moscow fax machine in the middle of the night, when the phone lines were clearer, and pull in waiting faxes.

Other typical problems for small startups—problems with money and people—were not as easy to resolve. There were cash-flow problems, but surprisingly, the usual reason for such problems—customers failing to pay their bills on time—wasn't the main issue for First Republic. The Moscow accounts, despite wanting their beer delivered on consignment, were reasonably good about paying within thirty or sixty days, depending on the terms arranged with their First Republic salesmen. A bigger problem was the money deposited in First Republic's Russian banks. Grajirena arranged for bigger customers—the Westernized hotels, for example—to wire their payments directly to First Republic's bank in Tampa. For money collected in Moscow, First Republic set up accounts with several banks. New banks were popping up all over Russia and competing to do business with Western firms, and Grajirena figured that having accounts with different banks would spread the risk in the event of a bank failure. Those accounts were all special Western-business accounts that allowed for the movement of foreign currency into Russia and rubles out of the country for conversion into some other currency. Most of First Republic's revenues were collected in Moscow and deposited in those Russian banks. In theory, First Republic's structure allowed for easy withdrawal and movement of money out of Russia through Cyprus—thanks to the offshore corporate structure and the Cyprus-Russia treaty on currency exchange—and then on to the United States. The theory did not always work that way in practice, however. A wire transfer could take three to four weeks. First Republic staffers had to fill out several forms for a wire transfer, and then literally stood in line at the bank to turn in the forms. The wait merely to turn in the forms could be two hours. Once the forms were turned in, it took the bank several days to review them and act on them. If there was anything wrong with the forms— any blank not filled in, anything at all the clerks could find wrong—the forms were kicked back to First Republic. They had to be filled in again, and a staffer had to go stand in line again. It was just like the old Russian bureaucracy. As a result, money that First Republic wanted to use to buy more beer was sitting in banking limbo, somewhere between Moscow and Nicosia and Tampa.

The problem was made worse by the fluctuations in the value of the ruble. "Fluctuation" is the word the newspapers used. Grajirena didn't see any fluctuation. To him, fluctuation meant up and down. The ruble was only going down. When First Republic was first contemplating doing business in Russia, the official exchange rate was one dollar for one ruble. The real exchange rate, on the street, was more like thirty rubles to the dollar. Then, after the collapse of the Soviet Union, the new Russian government cut the ruble loose in order to attract new investment from other countries. It was part of a "shock therapy" economic strategy that had more or less worked, despite some wrenching readjustments, particularly in the form of unemployment, in other Eastern European countries such as Poland, Hungary, and the Czech Republic. On the face of it, the reformers in charge of Russian economic policy at the time thought the shock therapy would work equally well for Russia. After all, Russia was a highly industrialized nation with abundant natural resources and a population of 150 million. The reformers aimed to privatize as much state property as possible, lift as many subsidies as possible, open as many markets as possible to free competition, and institute sound fiscal policies. The laws of supply and demand would work, and within no time Russia would be humming along in a free-market democracy.

Things didn't work out that way. Poland, Hungary, and the Czech Republic all had more experience in dealing with the West and in doing business Western style. The reformers seemed to forget that it took centuries, not months, for the West's business culture to develop. And the fact that those other Eastern European countries were smaller made them more nimble in retooling their economies. Russia's shock therapy did attract foreign investment. But if it was supposed to be a mild jolt, it wasn't. It was closer to an electrocution. Without subsidies, factories closed and production plummeted. Inflation was rampant, and so was unemployment. People who had never seen prices rise or who lost their jobs were indeed shocked. Millions of miners and soldiers got their paychecks late or not at all. The government owed billions in back pay. People were angry. Was this the supposed freedom they had heard so much about—the freedom to be poor? The social dissension gave rise to right-wing nationalist movements and a Communist revival. The political turmoil climaxed in early October 1993, when Yeltsin dissolved Parliament and Russian troops besieged a group of his political opponents in the Russian White House, the Parliament building. Martial law was declared, there were firefights as soldiers besieged the building, and dozens of people were killed. Jack Robinson, First Republic's Canadian lawyer in Moscow, was hurrying into a client's building near Parliament when gunfire broke out, and a woman was killed by a stray bullet as he walked past her. The siege ended, order was restored, and Yeltsin remained in power. But the economic upheaval, particularly in terms of currency exchange, continued for First Republic and other American companies that had moved quickly into the new Russia.

At the old, artificial one-to-one exchange rate, no foreign company doing business in Russia could get its money out of the country. In the new Russia companies could bring hard currency in and take it out—with severe restrictions. Foreign companies such as First Republic always knew the value of the dollars they were bringing into Russia to invest. They knew they would be earning money in rubles—or at least they hoped they would. But they could never be sure of the value of the rubles they would earn, and how much the rubles would be worth when they wanted to repatriate their profits. Inflation in Russia during 1992 and 1993 was 1,600 percent. During some *months* inflation was 25 to 30 percent. Grajirena watched, in pain, as the ruble dropped from 30 to the dollar to 1,000, then 2,000, then 3,000, then 4,000 to the dollar. At one point the ruble lost 30 percent of its value literally overnight. Grajirena came into the office to learn that $20,000 worth of rubles on deposit in First Republic's banks in Moscow was now worth $14,000. That made the quick movement of money out the country critical.

First Republic would change its prices to reflect the latest exchange rate. But between the time an account placed its order and the time the money was collected and wired out of Russia, the real value in dollars was much less. Even if things went smoothly, the inevitable downward march of the ruble meant that First Republic received 10 to 20 percent less. It was no wonder that for years after the end of the Soviet Union, the U.S. dollar was the unofficial currency of Russia and other former Soviet republics. The U.S. hundred-dollar bill came into common business use and was widely counterfeited, which is one of the reasons that in 1998 the U.S. Treasury introduced a new harder-to-copy design for the hundred-dollar bill. People and businesses, both Russians and foreigners, hoarded dollars and did business with one another in dollars. For a time First Republic tried to collect from all its accounts in dollars, but the Russian government outlawed business payments in dollars. Many other companies continued to do all or most of their business in dollars, and some staffers urged Grajirena to let them do business in dollars. He refused. "We may have to get around some of these crazy laws in Russia, when and where we can," he said. "But we don't want to be blatant by breaking the law and shoving it in the government's face. If we openly do business in dollars, everybody is going to know it and we're going to get caught. It's not worth the risk."

The exchange rate also affected the staff in the early days of First Republic. Under Russian law at the time—it was later changed—First Republic's payroll taxes were more than its payroll. So the goal was to show as little payroll as possible. First Republic paid all its staff the minimum wage in rubles, then supplemented their salaries in dollars paid on the side. The staffers didn't have to declare the dollar payments for their personal income taxes, and First Republic didn't have to declare the dollar payments for the payroll tax. It was skirting the law, but Grajirena reasoned that (a) there was little risk of getting caught since the employees would not inform on themselves, (b) it was a widely accepted practice among Russian companies, and

(c) First Republic might not be able to stay in business otherwise. Even with this dodge, however, the staff often clamored for more money. The constant devaluation of the ruble also meant rampant inflation, and it was getting more expensive to live in Moscow every month. Chris Mitchell, who had originally been thrilled to be hired as a First Republic salesman at $60 a week, became increasingly disgruntled. He and the other young American salesman, Cary Scardina, at one point went "on strike" for several days before Grajirena agreed to raise their salaries to $200 a week. It was meager by American standards, but even with inflation the cost of living was still low enough in Moscow that it was a good living wage. During the first year of business, a number of other staffers, both American and Russian, had to be similarly placated with raises.

Some of First Republic's early missteps were such obvious mistakes that Grajirena found them hard to believe. He was surprised, for example, when Chris Mitchell told him that he and the other two salesmen had no territories within Moscow but instead roamed the entire city. Two salesmen might have separate accounts near each other on one side of town, and two more separate accounts near each other on the other side of town. "And it takes two hours to drive from one side of Moscow to the other," Mitchell said. He suggested that the salesmen swap around their accounts so that they had geographic territories. They would spend less time driving around and more time selling beer. Grajirena quickly gave his approval. It had seemed obvious to him. It had also seemed obvious to him that the salesmen would be paid their commissions after they had collected from their accounts. But in the early days First Republic was paying salesmen their commissions based upon their sales orders rather than on collections. At a time when First Republic was trying to build cash flow, this was a drain. Grajirena quickly ordered a change. "From now on, you get your commission when your accounts pay their bills," he told the salesmen.

Another mistake was buying a big truck. The thinking was that the small trucks rented from Arkady An could handle many of the smaller deliveries to diverse neighborhoods, but it would be much more efficient and productive for a big truck to make the big deliveries to the big customers, mostly Westernized hotels, clustered in the center of Moscow. But the first time the truck ventured into central Moscow, fully loaded with beer, a traffic policeman pulled it over. He not only wrote a ticket that required the driver to pay a fine on the spot, he also ordered the truck to turn around. Moscow had a city ordinance prohibiting big trucks in the center of town. Nobody had told First Republic. Nobody at First Republic had checked it out first. The big truck was redeployed to make deliveries in the suburbs and outlying areas of Moscow, and Grajirena had to rent more small trucks from Arkady An, and hire more drivers. "Making all those small deliveries instead of a few large ones is costing us money," Grajirena told several First Republic investors, "but there isn't anything we can do about it. We've talked to all sorts of city officials explaining our problem and trying to get an exemption, but they say there's no way." The city ordinance finally was changed when bigger Western companies came in and threw their weight around. "When Coca-Cola said it couldn't bring in Coke unless the rules were changed, the rules were changed," Grajirena said.

Meanwhile, business was growing and First Republic was adding staff, both in the warehouse and in the office, both American and Russian. The turnover was high among the Russians, especially the blue-collar guys hired to work in the warehouse or as drivers making deliveries. While they were all pleased to get decent-paying jobs with an American company, many of them were shocked to learn that they were actually expected to work hard. All day. Every day. Like the currency rules, Russia's employment laws were holdovers from the Soviet era, and it was almost impossible to fire a Russian worker, even for cause. And many of the first Russians hired by First Republic certainly provided the cause. Absenteeism was rampant, as it had been under Communism. In the Soviet economy nobody had expected anybody else to really take any initiative and work hard, to really care about doing a good job. Back then, people hadn't even been required to show up on time or every day. Why now? They literally had no understanding of what it meant to work hard at a job. For all their working lives, it had been no big deal to miss work, or to show up drunk. It hadn't mattered to their old Communist bosses. Why did it matter so much now to these capitalist bosses? First Republic, rather than take on the red tape associated with the near-impossible challenge of firing someone, sometimes paid off workers to quit. Eventually many workers were hired informally, unofficially, off the books. They wouldn't have to be fired if they had never had a job.

First Republic had its share of Moscow Madness. A young Canadian hired to oversee the office's computerized inventory and billing system became a serious drunk. He would go on binges and miss work for days at a time, to the point that the office accounts were so hopelessly behind that no one knew exactly how much inventory there was, let alone how much in accounts receivable. Carolyn, the American office manager, began taking long lunches and sometimes wouldn't come back in the afternoon. Grajirena spoke to her about it several times and warned her that she wasn't getting her work done. Once she went to Finland for the weekend, then called to say she had made a mistake in her visa and couldn't get back into Russia. It took another whole week for her to get back to work. Grajirena was going to tell her to shape up or ship out, but Carolyn beat him to the punch. She said the job wasn't what had been promised her and that she was going back to the States to law school.

On top of the currency-exchange drain on the cash flow, First Republic seemed to be bleeding money. To Grajirena, it seemed as if expenses were too high, but he couldn't figure out where the money was going. Mark Mroczkowski, the chief financial officer, had a suggestion. When he joined First Republic, he had brought along Ellen, a young woman who had been working at his accounting firm. She had joined First Republic's Tampa office with the title of controller. She seemed smart, and Grajirena and Mroczkowski both trusted her. Mroczkowski suggested that they send her to Russia to go over the books in the Moscow office, and Grajirena readily agreed. It was the first of several trips to Moscow as she took a larger and larger role in the company. During that first trip she reported back to Grajirena that someone may have been stealing, but she wasn't sure where or how. Perhaps she could find more evidence on future trips. She was sure that the Canadian computer guy wasn't stealing, but his drinking made his work hopelessly sloppy and lazy. She said he should be fired. Grajirena fired him over the phone, and he never bothered to come in and pick up his last check.

Ellen then said that Stanley, the general manager, had a lot of expenses. Grajirena had been concerned about this from the moment Stanley arrived in Moscow. First Stanley had wanted a European car. He thought it wouldn't do for the company, and it would be bad for his own image, to be seen being driven around Moscow in a plain old Russian car. Grajirena argued that First Republic wanted to be seen as a regular Russian company rather than as a rich Western company. But he relented and approved a European car. Stanley also insisted that he needed a cellular phone, which had become a trendy symbol of significance for *mafiya* and other new Russians. The Moscow phone lines were terrible, Stanley said, and he needed to be in constant touch with the office. Grajirena approved that expense too, but smoldered every time he got a monthly bill for $1,000 or $1,200 for Stanley's cell phone. He fumed even more whenever he spent a little time with Stanley and saw the phone glued to his ear at night in Moscow bars and nightclubs—when the office wasn't even open. At one point Grajirena hired an old friend from Tampa to come to Moscow and do marketing for First Republic, to be sort of a supersalesman and offer Stanley some guidance. The friend was an old sailing and drinking buddy who wore open shirts and liked gold chains and other jewelry. The friend spent a lot of time in Moscow, staying in the company apartment and going around with Stanley both during the day and at night. Grajirena found out that his old friend's nickname, around the First Republic office and in Moscow expat bar circles, was "Vegas." He decided his friend had to go. He flew to Moscow, called the friend, took him out to dinner, and fired him. The personnel problems at First Republic were becoming a constant headache. To Grajirena, handling the dozen or so people on the staff in Moscow was much more cumbersome than overseeing the thirty or more who had worked for his sailmaking company in Florida.

CHAPTER 14

Underground Work

Rick Grajirena was weary as the plane landed in Moscow on the last Tuesday in April 1993. First Republic was off to a small but promising start, heading into its first summer of selling beer in Moscow. But it was hard work. The long flights back and forth from the States were starting to wear on him. At this rate, he calculated, he was going to spend one-quarter to one-third of the year in Moscow—far too much time away from his family and the head office in Tampa. "Besides, I'm getting too old for this," he grumbled to himself. Adding to the stress, on this particular trip he had an entourage, which always slowed him down. He was glad that one of the three men traveling with him was Peter Harken, his old sailing buddy from Wisconsin who had become a principal partner in First Republic. Harken was not averse to having a good time in Russia, but he was also keenly interested in the business and would not get in Grajirena's way. The other two men were among the fledgling company's thirty-three other investors: Ron Finger, a plastic surgeon from Georgia, and his cousin, Jerry Finger, the chairman of a small bank in Texas. "We just want to come and look around, check on our investment," they told Grajirena. They'd never been to Russia before, and their investments in First Republic were the most daring they had ever made. To them, both their investments and this trip to Russia represented adventure—a personal and financial fling, a small reward for their middle-aged success. They wanted to see the sights, have a good time, and be treated like visiting dignitaries. Grajirena knew he was expected to shepherd them around, organize their schedule, and make sure they were kept happy—even though that almost surely meant he wouldn't be able to get as much done.

But Grajirena was hoping he wouldn't have all that much work on this trip anyway. It would be a short visit, for just a few days over the upcoming May Day weekend—Russia's biggest holiday, dating back to the old Communist days, when the party leaders would stand on Red Square and salute their missiles and tanks rolling past. While the party faithful saluted, millions of other Russians seized on the holiday as an opportunity to get drunk. The fall of Communism meant no more parades and salutes. But the May Day holiday was still an excuse to get drunk, and First Republic's Moscow office was set for its first really big sales push. The entire warehouse inventory—14,000 cases of Miller Genuine Draft—was presold and merely had to be delivered, beginning the next day, Wednesday. Collecting his bags at the airport, Grajirena was tired but relaxed, and looking forward to simply being part of a big holiday weekend and a big payday. First Republic had paid about $15.50 a case for the beer, including customs and shipping, and was wholesaling it in Moscow for about $22.50 a case. For this one weekend Grajirena was counting on a gross profit of nearly $100,000.

The four men cleared customs and immigration, and the cab ride into town went smoothly. They checked into their rooms, then met at the hotel bar for a quiet nightcap. Grajirena had a beer and then turned in, as usual, shortly after ten o'clock. The other three Americans ordered the second of what was to be several more rounds. When the phone in his room rang at six A.M., Grajirena was glad he had abandoned the party. It was Stanley, the manager of First Republic's Moscow office. For some time Grajirena had been uneasy at the way Stanley sometimes presented himself, appearing at meetings with his cell phone always at his ear, like a cheap *mafiya* gang member. Grajirena thought most of Stanley's cell phone calls were going to his women friends or his many Russian cousins. At the time First Republic hired him, Stanley, whose parents had moved to Cleveland from Russia when he was a child, had seemed completely Americanized. But what Stanley told Grajirena on the phone that morning made him realize that the Americanized Russian had become Russianized again in a very short time. It was another example of Moscow Madness, but a daylight example. Stanley's job performance was not being hindered by adultery or promiscuity or alcohol and drug abuse. Stanley's Moscow Madness was that he had become more Russian than the Russians. A *nyet* attitude had replaced the "can do" optimism that distinguished Americans in Moscow.

There was a big problem, Stanley told Grajirena over the phone. A huge problem. An insurmountable problem. The entrance to the underground warehouse—which had seemed like such a good deal when First Republic rented it from Arkady An, the Korean-Russian auto importer and real estate mogul—had collapsed. The entire inventory of 14,000 cases of beer was buried inside. There was no way, Stanley assured Grajirena, to get the beer out and deliver it to restaurants, bars, hotels, and shops in time for the holiday weekend. Grajirena tried to focus Stanley and get the details over the phone. Stanley blamed the disaster on poor Russian construction techniques and the spring thaw.

The warehouse, in effect, was a hole in the ground lined with big concrete slabs, four by ten feet, with walls a foot thick. Similar slabs formed the roof. These slabs also lined the walls of the ramp down to the warehouse's below-ground doors: one a normal-sized doorway and the other a truck entrance big enough to allow a semitrailer to pull in with full containers. The slabs lining the driveway had been installed the previous November, when the ground was firm. Now, in May, the ground had softened and turned to mud, and the slabs on the right-hand side had crashed down onto the ramp, sealing both doors shut under tons of concrete and mud. Grajirena later learned that the construction would have been stronger, and probably wouldn't have collapsed, if the warehouse walls had been built with small concrete blocks rather than huge concrete slabs. But blocks were not available, he was told. The concrete had come from an old Soviet factory that had a quota to produce a certain amount of concrete. The quota did not cover quality or style, so the factory managers had met their quota in the cheapest, quickest way: by producing relatively few huge slabs instead of more time-consuming—and higher quality, more useful—concrete building blocks.

It was yet another example of why the old Soviet Union had failed. That gave Grajirena no joy at the moment, however. He wanted to get the beer out. But that was proving difficult. Stanley had "fully explored" getting the beer out, but nothing could be done, he told Grajirena. This was Wednesday, the May Day holiday was approaching, and all of Russia was winding down to take off the long weekend. Muscovites would want to buy a lot of Miller beer. But they wouldn't be able to buy any if it was all buried in this rubble landslide. Over the phone Stanley told Grajirena there was no way to line up the workmen and heavy equipment to dig out the warehouse until after the weekend. Stanley promised to get right on it at the beginning of the next week, after the holiday. "I don't accept that," Grajirena told him. "You've got to get that beer out and get it delivered. Our whole company could go down the tubes if we don't deliver that beer. Find a way. We're not Russians, we're Americans. We will find an answer. Don't say it can't be done. Work on a plan, and get back to me this afternoon to let me know how you're going to get the beer out. Good-bye." Grajirena roused Peter Harken, and the two Americans, both jet-lagged, grabbed a taxi out to the warehouse, an hour outside central Moscow. It was a mess, and they had to admit that maybe Stanley was right. Maybe it *was* impossible to get the beer out. But they weren't ready to give up, and they weren't happy about having a manager who was so willing to give up. Sliding around in the mud, looking at the collapsed concrete from all angles, Grajirena and Harken finally agreed that if nothing else worked, they might bring in jackhammers to drill through the concrete roof and hoist the beer out to delivery trucks. But that would be terribly expensive and time-consuming, not counting the time and expense of making repairs to the warehouse roof later.

Grajirena went into the office in central Moscow and waited for Stanley, who didn't show up until after lunch. Stanley said he was sorry, but he had done everything he could, and the beer could not be rescued. First Republic and Grajirena would simply have to write off the weekend, he said. Stanley told Grajirena he already had canceled the rental trucks and drivers who were supposed to pick up and deliver the beer. Moreover, he said, since nothing could be done, he was taking the weekend off as planned. He said he would spend the holiday with his Russian cousins, and he'd report back to Grajirena sometime the following week. Grajirena was astonished, but not too astonished to react quickly. "You're fired," he told the surprised Stanley. "I'm too busy to talk to you anymore right now. We'll negotiate a severance package for you next week, after we've gotten the beer out of the warehouse and delivered. Now please leave." Grajirena turned to Misha, First Republic's head salesman and Stanley's unofficial number two in the Moscow operation. Grajirena did not particularly like Misha's cocky manner, and he had an uneasy feeling about whether to trust the young Muscovite. But he had little choice at the moment. "Misha, you're the manager now," Grajirena told him. "You've got twenty-four hours to get that beer out, or you're history, too." Misha nodded and rushed out of the office, heading toward the warehouse. Grajirena stayed behind in the office, working the phone to line up another warehouse and arrange trucks to move the beer there, if and when it was excavated. By the time Grajirena and Harken got back out to the warehouse, Misha was negotiating with a Latvian construction crew that was building four other warehouses nearby. With Grajirena's wholehearted approval, Misha gave the Latvians $100 and promised them as much beer as they could drink that evening if they would haul their big tractor-crane over to the collapsed First Republic warehouse and pull away the slabs blocking the ramp doors.

The Latvians drove the tractor-crane into position, on the intact left-hand side of the driveway, opposite the side that had collapsed. They began hooking thick steel wires to the iron rings that were still in the fallen concrete slabs below. "The original construction crew left those big rings in the slabs. Shabby work, but it's a good break for us. It will make it even easier to yank those babies out of there, and then we just have to dig through the mud to clear the doors. We're gonna be able to drive our trucks into the warehouse in a couple of hours," Grajirena told a smiling Peter Harken. They were so confident, and they thought Misha had things under such complete control, that they took their cab back into Moscow to the First Republic office. When Grajirena walked into the office, however, Misha was on the phone, waiting to talk to him. The weight of the crane had collapsed the left side of the driveway, the side that had been standing. Now there was twice as much concrete and mud blocking the doors, and the big tractor-crane was stuck in the mud on top. "Do whatever you have to do," Grajirena told Misha. "Don't give up. Get that beer out. I'm on my way back out."

He returned to the warehouse, where Misha had upped the ante for the Latvians—another $100, and all the beer they could drink all weekend. The construction crew brought in more trucks. Keeping the trucks away from the sides of the driveway, which could further collapse at any moment, they ran steel lines to their bogged-down tractor-crane and gradually pulled it out of the mud. Then they hooked their lines onto the concrete slabs and slowly began pulling them out of the morass of mud that now clogged the driveway. By nightfall, the slabs were all off the ramp and out of the way. But a hundred yards of mud, up to a man's waist, still blocked the warehouse doors. "Get men, and get shovels, and have them here at daybreak," Grajirena told Misha. "I'll have a big truck here to move all the beer."

Grajirena had a quick dinner with the Finger cousins, the investors from Georgia and Texas, and apologized about being unable to party with them for at least another day or two. He spent a fitful night, tossing and turning and waking up every hour or so despite being bone-tired. By sunup Thursday he was back at the warehouse, where he was met with the welcome sight of Misha leading thirty Red Army soldiers across the muddy field to the warehouse. Each soldier was carrying a shovel. "Ten bucks and a case of beer per man," Misha told Grajirena. Grajirena knew there was probably something illegal about bribing on-duty Russian soldiers, but at that point he had no objections. With the Russian government finding it so difficult to pay its soldiers, who was going to object to them moonlighting a little? The soldiers dug a path through the mud to the point that the smaller, normal-sized door could be opened. Then they formed a human chain, like an old-fashioned fire brigade, and steadily moved the beer out of the warehouse and onto a twenty-foot delivery truck that Grajirena had hired. The truck held 1,200 cases—essentially a full container. It took the soldiers two hours of handing out beer, case by case, to fill the truck. But things were looking good, Grajirena thought to himself. A number of First Republic staffers, trying to help out during the emergency, showed up and joined the human chain, passing beer from the warehouse to the truck. The only break came when several links in the chain had to rescue Chris Mitchell, the salesman. Mitchell was walking across the muddy area when a workman blocked the way. The workman told Mitchell to go around because it was dangerous. Mitchell thought the workman simply was being officious in the typical Russian style, giving orders for the sake of giving orders, so he wouldn't have to do any of the work himself. Mitchell responded with an offhanded curse he had learned from a taxi driver and strode straight across the muddy area that the workman was blocking. Suddenly he was up to his armpits in mud, and sinking. He shouted and flailed about, and the workman and several people from the beer-case fire brigade rushed to help. They threw him ropes and held out long boards to him. Mitchell grabbed one of the boards and eventually was pulled to safety. He never did get one of his shoes back. "I thought the guy was just being a typical Russian asshole, trying to tell me what to do," he spluttered. No, someone said; Mitchell was just being a typical American, not believing what a Russian told him just because the person was a Russian.

When the truck was loaded with beer, the driver jumped in the cab, fired it up, popped it into gear, and took off for the new warehouse Grajirena had just rented. The truck went ten feet and then stopped, stuck in muck up to its axles. It wouldn't budge. Trying to move it forward or backward just spun the wheels and sent it deeper into the mud. Grajirena couldn't believe it. "Go get the Latvians again," he instructed Misha. The Latvians, eager for more cash and more beer, were happy to bring back one of their trucks to pull out the beer-laden delivery truck. They ran a steel line to the hook on the truck's front bumper (most Soviet-made trucks had such hooks, for easy and all-too-common towing) and began to pull. The pulling truck gunned its engine, the stuck truck's wheels began spinning, the mud made sucking sounds, and the bolts holding the respective truck bumpers groaned with the strain. Grajirena instinctively moved away, watching from a distance. The Russian soldiers, who had been lounging around, waiting to load another truck if the stuck one ever got out of the way, cheered the effort. Suddenly the inch-thick braided-steel towline snapped like a string. The line whip-curled across the mud-clogged ramp like a powerful and angry snake, snapping just short of some soldiers, who no doubt would have been badly injured or killed if it had struck them. They shouted curses at the Latvians. The Latvians shouted back, then gathered in a small circle, scratching their heads and talking among themselves. They did this for twenty minutes. They returned to their construction site and came back with a huge steel cable, four inches in diameter. It took six of the Latvians to lift the cable into place and hook it onto the stuck truck's front bumper. They powered up the trucks again and began to pull. The soldiers moved back to where Grajirena was standing, well beyond the reach of the cable. It didn't break this time. This time the whole front bumper of the stuck truck came flying off.

After more hollering and arguing, the Latvians decided to try the stuck truck's back bumper. They hooked the steel hawser to the back bumper, then pulled that off, too. By then some of the Red Army soldiers were laughing so hard, they were rolling in the mud. But they weren't laughing for long. Grajirena put them to work offloading the beer from the stuck truck, and then had them pass it hand to hand, case by case, fifty yards across the muddy field to the nearest street. Meanwhile, Grajirena went off and rented two bigger trucks, a pair of forty-foot Mercedes rigs. The drivers parked them on the street, and the soldiers slowly filled up the big trailers with beer. When the stuck truck was emptied of its 1,200 cases, the Latvians' truck could pull it out of the mud. It was moved over to the street and parked alongside the two Mercedes trucks. By nightfall Thursday the three trucks had each made five runs and delivered all 14,000 cases of beer to the new warehouse Grajirena had rented sight unseen over the phone. That warehouse was owned by another American and, perhaps more important, was aboveground. The deliveries began to go out to retailers the next day, Friday—two days late, but better than never. First Republic delivered 6,000 cases of Miller Genuine Draft for the May Day weekend—not quite half what should have been delivered, but enough to keep the company and its reputation afloat for the moment.

To Grajirena, Misha was the hero of May Day. He had found the Latvians, whose eagerness ultimately made up for their equipment failures. He had also found the soldiers; if the entire Red Army always worked as hard as those soldiers did, Grajirena thought, Russia never would have lost Afghanistan. "Misha saved us," Grajirena reported back to the office in Tampa. "We would have lost a lot more money if we hadn't delivered at least some of the beer, but the bigger loss would have been in our credibility with our customers. That would have been more serious. As it was, they heard what happened to us, they knew what we had to go through to get the beer delivered, and they were impressed with us. It helped our credibility for them to know just how far we would go to honor our commitments to deliver beer and fill their orders."

CHAPTER 15

Old Beer

A week after moving into the new Moscow warehouse and office, chosen primarily because of its sturdiness and security features, First Republic's office was burglarized. Someone broke in, ransacked the place, and stole virtually every electronic device: computers, printers, photocopier, calculators, fax machines, even the phones and the answering machine. Grajirena had to bring all that gear in from the States all over again. He never found out who stole the equipment. The police came, took a report dutifully, made a list of missing items efficiently, saluted crisply, and disappeared, never to be heard from again. Grajirena suspected the American warehouse owner's staff, perhaps the night watchmen, of pulling off an inside job. But he never had any proof, only vague suspicions.

Despite all the problems, Grajirena remained confident about First Republic's future in the beer business in Moscow. The ruble would stabilize eventually. The staff problems would never totally disappear but would diminish with the weeding out of unsuitable staffers—Russians who couldn't function for an American company, and Americans who couldn't function in Russia. Grajirena believed in the strength of his product, and in the support he expected to get from Miller Brewing. By the summer of 1993, when Tom Grant and the Nashville Ambassadors cut a noisy swath through Moscow, Miller Genuine Draft had become the dominant American beer in Moscow. Grajirena believed that the only thing that could hurt First Republic's beer-distribution business in the long run would be problems with Miller. So far things had gone reasonably well, though there were a few difficult patches.

In the early days Miller had insisted on sending First Republic beer in cans, even though Grajirena's market research showed that Moscow customers preferred bottles. More significantly, Grajirena wished the big brewing company were more forthcoming with favorable credit terms and promotional support. First Republic still had to pay cash in advance for beer, instead of the ninety-day credit terms that Grajirena wanted. He would also have appreciated more free or reduced-price promotional materials from Miller—menus, posters, cardboard table tents, beer openers, hats, T-shirts, and the like. Young Russians were intensely interested in American products and clothing and were eager to wear anything bearing an American logo, especially a logo of the American beer that had become so trendy on the Moscow social scene. Grajirena thought Miller could have helped its young little distributorship—and Miller sales—by providing more brand-name gear for free.

The promotional gear, especially the hats and clothing, was also a touchy subject with Grajirena because he suspected Miller's European operation of dumping stuff on First Republic that it couldn't unload anywhere else. It seemed that whenever Miller had a lot of a certain style of Miller-logo sweatshirts or hats that no one else wanted, First Republic would end up with them at full price. Part of the problem, Grajirena knew, was that his staff in Moscow loved all the gear, and they were easily talked into anything that the Miller European office proposed. Grajirena was thinking that perhaps he needed to institute some closer controls on what was purchased. He also suspected that much of the gear that was coming into First Republic in Moscow was not finding its way to customers. He was afraid staff members were keeping it for themselves or, even worse, selling it on the side and keeping the money for themselves.

And then there were the beer shipments. Like many breweries, Miller had a "best-by" dated stamped on each case. It was a matter of quality control for breweries, which did not want distributors or retailers to sell their beer when it was old. Best-by expiration dates force retailers to rotate their stock. Typically, for beer sold in the United States, the date is about three months after the beer is bottled. In truth, there is no magic date by which a batch of beer will go bad. For most brewing styles, fresh beer usually tastes better than old beer. Beer will "oxidize" with age and become stale, marked by a cardboardlike taste. But it is a long, slow process, especially if the beer is kept in a cool, dark place. Beer that has been properly stored for a year tastes better than month-old beer kept in a warm room. Light, and particularly sunlight, kills beer, giving it a "skunky" taste. Miller was sending First Republic cases of beer from the same batches it sent to distributors in the United States—with the same best-by dates stamped on the cases. This was no problem for American distributors, who typically received the beer within a few days and sold it within a few weeks. But for foreign distributors, the three-month dating was a problem. It could take a couple of months just for the beer to get to them, especially in remote Moscow. That was why most big brewers, including Miller, typically carried one-year expiration dates stamped on cases shipped overseas. But many Miller shipments to Moscow had domestic dating, with a three-month expiration date. It wasn't an issue during First Republic's first few months of operation, when First Republic customers didn't know or care about the dating. They were just happy to be getting regular, reliable deliveries of beer. Then the Budweiser distributorship in Moscow, playing catch-up, began pointing out Miller's expiration dates. Even if First Republic delivered the beer to its Moscow accounts before the expiration date stamped on the cases, retailers could not always sell the beer before then. "They're selling you old beer," the Bud salesmen told First Republic's accounts.

In truth, the beer was the same. The only difference was that Budweiser's best-by date on its cases was a year, not three months, after production. First Republic's salesmen tried to explain this to their accounts, but it took a lot of time and trouble. Many of the accounts understood and remained loyal to Miller and First Republic. But some never bought the First Republic explanation. It sounded too much like the kind of tap dancing that had been so common in the Soviet era—a far-fetched explanation for why something went wrong or, more likely, why someone was trying to cheat you. For a time First Republic's salesmen tried pasting labels with one-year expiration dates on top of the factory's three-month stamps. This backfired when Budweiser salesmen came around later and peeled the labels off in front of the retailers. It got to the point that some retailers wanted to inspect First Republic deliveries before allowing them to be unloaded. If the best-by date stamped on the cases wasn't at least a month away, some retailers refused to accept the delivery. Grajirena made many complaints to anyone and everyone at Miller who would listen to him, from the regional office in Lausanne, Switzerland, to the European headquarters in London, to the headquarters in Milwaukee. "You're treating us like we're some distributor just down the road from you in the States," Grajirena said. "I know that you do one-year dating for your distributors in the U.K., in Switzerland, and other places in Europe. Why can't you do one-year dating for us? Or are you just shipping us beer that was brewed and stamped for the domestic market, but that you can't sell in the States? Why are you treating us like a dumping ground?" Miller finally agreed to have one-year dating stamped on cases going to Moscow. But by then the damage had been done. Some customers never believed the explanations. They switched to Budweiser and never came back to Miller. In any event, First Republic's heretofore sterling reputation with its customers was tarnished. Grajirena was troubled not so much by the original dating problems as by Miller's slow response. This was supposed to be a big international company, but Miller had reacted, he thought, in a provincial, narrow-minded, and largely unresponsive manner to an international problem that could have been solved easily and quickly.

Grajirena was wrestling with his first doubts about Miller Brewing when he got a call in Tampa one morning during the summer of 1993. It was from the First Republic office in Moscow—a clear phone line for once. But the message was one Grajirena did not want to hear: Moscow was suddenly awash in Miller beer, and it wasn't beer that First Republic was distributing. First Republic's accounts were turning away its salesman and not refilling their orders because they were getting Miller beer more cheaply from some other source. It wasn't the same twelve-ounce Miller Genuine Draft bottles that First Republic sold. Instead, these were ten-ounce cans of Miller, an odd size that was not sold in the United States. But it was Miller beer, and it was being sold cheap in Moscow. First Republic's sales had come to a screeching halt. Where had this beer come from? Who was selling it? What had happened to First Republic's exclusive distribution rights in Moscow?

Grajirena, agitated, hung up and immediately called Miller. No one seemed to know anything about ten-ounce cans of Miller beer in Moscow. They promised to find out and call back. The call came shortly. The explanation was a bit sheepish, perhaps mildly apologetic, but it offered nothing that Grajirena wanted to hear. A huge shipment of beer—fifty containers— apparently had been brewed to order for Miller's distributor in Puerto Rico, and then the distributor didn't want it. As usual in such cases, Miller offered the beer on the open market. One buyer, a so-called "wildcatter," took it all. Miller executives said that they never would have sold the beer to anyone knowing that it was going to be dumped in Moscow, or in any other territory where Miller had granted exclusive distribution rights to one of its distributors. They had thought this particular shipment of beer would go to one of the smaller former Soviet republics where no one was selling Miller beer at the time. But the truth was, the Miller executives admitted, that they didn't always know the beer they sold was going to be distributed. We're sorry the wildcatter lied to us, and we're sorry about all the beer being dumped on the Moscow market and hurting First Republic's business, the Miller executives said. They also said there was nothing Miller could do. It was simply bad luck for First Republic. There was no offer of compensation, monetary or otherwise.

Another snafu came shortly after the expiration-date problem was straightened out. Miller's regional headquarters sent First Republic a shipment of beer from Saudi Arabia. No one could explain how or why the beer had come to be shipped to Saudi Arabia in the first place, or why it was sent subsequently to First Republic. But Miller was offering a very good price, about half what First Republic paid for beer. The Moscow office of First Republic called Grajirena. Suspicious, he asked the staff to check the best-by dates stamped on the cases. The expiration date was almost up. Angry, Grajirena called Miller's regional headquarters in Lausanne. Who ordered that beer delivered to Moscow? Miller insisted that someone at First Republic in Moscow had approved the shipment but couldn't say who. Grajirena asked for paperwork to show who had ordered the beer, but Miller could not come up with the documents. Grajirena refused to accept the beer and issued an edict to the Moscow office: No beer was to be accepted from Miller without written notification to him in the Tampa office. "You know," Grajirena told Miller executives, "we have investors who are always calling me and asking how First Republic is doing in Moscow. One of their big questions is always, 'How is Miller treating us?' In the past I've always been able to say that Miller is treating us pretty well. I don't think I can say that anymore. Not right now."

———————

Another problem with beer in the summer of 1993 came up after First Republic began importing kegs of Miller beer. But this time it wasn't Miller's fault. Instead, it was one of the many uniquely Russian problems that came with trying to run a Western-style business in Moscow. First Republic wanted to sell draft Miller beer in Moscow, but few Moscow bars had draft systems at that time. Most of First Republic's accounts had never offered beer on tap and had never even thought about it. They sold beer in bottles or cans, and people bought it. Why change? First Republic's salesmen had to explain. Beer on tap is popular in bars around the world. Many drinkers think it tastes better. It is usually a little less expensive than bottled or canned beer, but there is a much higher profit margin for the retailer.

There are many other overhead costs, of course, but the actual beer out of a keg and served in a glass—6 ounces, 10 ounces, 12 ounces, a pint—costs literally pennies. But it can be sold for a dollar or more for a small glass, and up to $3 or $4 for a big glass, depending on the bar.

First Republic's more sophisticated accounts grasped the concept quickly. They wanted draft beer, and First Republic wanted to sell it to them. But distributing kegs presented a whole new set of logistical challenges. First, the tap systems, with their own built-in refrigeration units, had to be installed in the Moscow accounts. Bartenders had to be trained to use the draft systems, and to clean the draft lines weekly. Otherwise the beer would taste bad—like old beer. Kegs were more cumbersome and required more people to warehouse and deliver, especially in the small trucks that carried only a few kegs each. Once the kegs were empty, First Republic had to pick them up and arrange for them to be shipped back to the States to be cleaned and refilled. A new mountain of paperwork presented itself for shipping kegs out of Russia. Russian bureaucrats did not have forms for something like kegs, which were shipped in full and then shipped back out empty. They wanted to make sure that the kegs were not manufactured in Russia, that shipping them out was not somehow hurting Russian employment or the Russian economy, and that there was no smuggling. In order to accommodate both full kegs coming in and empty kegs waiting for their paperwork to be shipped out, First Republic needed to rework its entire warehouse operation. Grajirena asked Miller if First Republic, like some major distributors in the States, could get beer in giant barrels of beer shipped in, and then clean and refill kegs for its accounts right there in Moscow. It would save a lot of time and trouble and sell more beer. Miller said no, not yet, maybe later. It was a quality-control issue.

Few Moscow bars had existing draft systems where they could just plug in Miller beer. Even fewer were willing to pay hundreds of dollars to install one. So First Republic bought twenty draft systems from Miller—again, Miller required cash in advance—and installed them in bars where the managers promised to push Miller Genuine Draft on tap. Grajirena consoled himself over the expense of the draft lines with the fact that First Republic would "own" the draft systems. If a Moscow bar manager tried to serve anything except Miller Genuine Draft through First Republic's draft lines, then First Republic would pull out the draft system and install it in some other bar. In the first few months First Republic did go into several bars and pull out the draft systems when the bars did not sell as much Miller on draft as they promised.

Miller helped out by sending a couple of men over from its European headquarters in London to help install the systems and show the managers and bartenders how to use and maintain the lines. Throughout the rest of the world, wherever Miller installed draft lines, the vast majority of bars cleaned them weekly. There were occasional exceptions here and there, one bar or another, but most bars knew it was good business to keep the beer tasting fresh. Grajirena had not anticipated that Russian bartenders would refuse to clean their draft lines. Good maintenance had never been a prominent feature of the Soviet era. Everything, in theory, belonged to the people, so why should one person take it upon himself to fix something if someone else was just going to break it again? Within a short time First Republic was deluged with complaints about bad beer. "The beer is fine," the salesmen tried to tell their accounts. "You've just got to clean your lines." Many accounts, for whatever reason, were unable to accomplish that. The quality of Miller on draft became an issue, with the Budweiser salesmen again circling like vultures. Regular Miller drinkers stopped ordering Miller in their favorite bars because it didn't taste right. The less beer they ordered, the longer the keg sat open, the more the draft lines clogged with gunk, and the worse the beer tasted. Grajirena finally ordered First Republic to hire two men whose sole job was to travel around Moscow cleaning draft lines for bar managers who would not or could not do it themselves. It was a large and unnecessary expense, at least by American standards. But it was necessary in Russia.

CHAPTER 16

Winter 1993–94

First Republic needed money, as any growing young company does. But First Republic's needs were particularly acute given the losses due to changing currency-exchange rates, problems with Miller, and management mistakes on both sides of the Atlantic. It simply cost more to do business in Russia than Grajirena and his partners had imagined. The unforeseen expenses—currency exchange, customs foul-ups, the collapsed warehouse, the ban on big trucks, keeping the draft lines clean—all piled up, on and on. In addition, the travel costs were more than anticipated. Grajirena had not expected to spend as much on airfare, hotels, meals, and other expenses for himself and two other First Republic staffers: Ellen, the controller, and Karen, the corporate attorney. Karen, another young woman brought on board by Mroczkowski, joined First Republic after Tom Fotopulos, the lawyer who had done much of the early legal work, bowed out once the company was on its feet. The two women made several trips to Moscow, both to familiarize themselves with First Republic's office in Russia and to coordinate the two operations.

The Moscow staff naturally resented the two women coming in to try to find and plug financial leaks—especially when no one seemed to be watching the women's own expenses. Moscow staffers grumbled that it was costing First Republic $1,000 a day, counting airfare, hotels, meals, and other expenses, to send the two women to Moscow. The Moscow staffers felt as if the women had come to catch them cheating and stealing—but never did. To them, the women's trips to Moscow were doubly destructive, both an insult to the staff and a waste of company money. Grajirena heard some of the grumbling but ignored it. He was not, as he called it, a "financial guy." Instead he concentrated on pursuing growth opportunities. If First Republic made more money, expenses wouldn't be such a big issue. Grajirena had been courting other companies in order to diversify so that First Republic was not totally dependent on its one big supplier, Miller Brewing. Other companies were impressed with First Republic's distribution network for Miller. Grajirena made tentative deals for exclusive distribution rights in Moscow with a number of other companies, including Seagram and Hiram Walker, both of which were eager to plug some of their liquor products into First Republic's distribution network.

The expansion plans were a prominent part of the second prospectus put out by First Republic in the autumn of 1993. Through its first offering and subsequent individual investments, First Republic to that point had gathered just over $1 million in investments for common stock. The second offering aimed to raise $525,000 in the form of 25 shares, each valued at $21,000. Each share was listed as an equity interest worth 0.8 percent of the company, which meant the $525,000 offering constituted—on paper—20 percent of a company worth $2.6 million. The financial statements included in the prospectus showed assets of $879,289, along with an operating loss of $323,591 in 1992 and $312,432 in the first half of 1993. The company had $157,085 in sales to that point, but it had also paid more than $200,000 in salaries and spent nearly $160,000 for travel. The prospectus mentioned other business possibilities for First Republic. All were tenuous, including the various titanium-manufacturing opportunities and a deal to broker plywood that never happened. One section of the prospectus recounted the Super Bowl party in Moscow. "This innovative marketing led to some of the most prestigious liquor firms in the world approaching First Republic with requests to distribute their products." The prospectus not only mentioned Seagram and Hiram Walker, but also suggested that First Republic was "currently negotiating" with Gallo in the United States and other wineries in France, Italy, and Chile.

Interest in First Republic's second offering was not as keen. The process dragged through the winter, but investors eventually did take up the entire $525,000, probably on the strength of First Republic's continuing strong sales performance. From a mere $14,744 in sales in January 1993, monthly sales climbed past $100,000 in December 1993. In January and February, traditionally slow months in the beer business, sales marched on, to more than $120,000 and $150,000, respectively. The distribution network was working. Behind the scenes, however, there were more management problems. Misha, who had been the hero of May Day when he replaced Stanley as Moscow general manager and got the beer out of the collapsed warehouse, turned out to be not so heroic as an everyday general manager. The staff in Moscow seemed to worship him, but to Grajirena it seemed like he ran a loose ship. Mark Mroczkowski, the CFO, agreed. To help sort out the personnel and financial problems in the Moscow office, Mroczkowski volunteered to spend more time in Moscow—as much as three weeks per month. Grajirena welcomed the help. He wasn't eager to spend more time in Moscow himself, but it was becoming apparent that First Republic needed a stronger management hand on the ground. Mroczkowski took over the company apartment.

But Grajirena and Mroczkowski quickly developed a CEO-CFO rivalry. The basic problem in those early days was that First Republic could not keep up with the demand for Miller beer. It could have sold much more beer, but it couldn't sell beer it didn't have. Miller still refused to grant longer-term credit, so First Republic couldn't order beer until it could pay for beer. The cash-flow problems were stunting the business. Grajirena told Mroczkowski, the CFO, that he needed to keep a tighter rein on expenses so that the company could make more profit and buy more beer. Mroczkowski told Grajirena, the marketing expert, that he should be bringing in more business and investment so the company could buy more beer. They had a loud, heated argument one afternoon in front of the office staff in Tampa, and things were never again the same between them. In the autumn of 1993, when First Republic played a major role in hosting a Wisconsin trade delegation to Moscow led by governor Tommy Thompson, Mroczkowski played host in Moscow and Grajirena stayed in Tampa. Grajirena suspected Mroczkowski of suffering from his own form of Moscow Madness, evidenced in part by Mroczkowski's desire to become the first American to get a private pilot's license in Russia. Grajirena resented the time that Mroczkowski devoted to taking flying lessons. When Mroczkowski was featured in a Fortune story about Americans doing business in Moscow—complete with a photo of him in front of a plane—Grajirena seethed. The article never even mentioned First Republic. At a ceremony where First Republic received an award as the Tampa Bay area's 1993 "International Business of the Year," a photo was taken of the two of them, Grajirena and Mroczkowski, the CEO and CFO, standing shoulder to shoulder and smiling. They were barely speaking to each other at the time. Mroczkowski finally decided to leave First Republic in the spring of 1994.

Some of the $525,000 raised in the second offering was supposed to be used, according to the prospectus, to open a First Republic branch in St. Petersburg, and to place initial orders to lock up exclusive deals with Seagram and Hiram Walker. All those growth plans were put on hold, however. Some of the money raised from the prospectus was used to buy out Mroczkowski's shares. Much of it went to buy beer from Miller. The lion's share of the new offering was taken up by friends of Harken from Wisconsin. One of the Wisconsin group, as Grajirena came to think of them, put in far more money than the other new investors. That investor took a seat on the board. When the dust cleared, the Wisconsin group controlled a majority of the stock in First Republic. While they had been researching the company and considering whether to invest, some of the individual investors from Wisconsin had asked Grajirena lots of questions. After they made their investments, some of the Wisconsin group continued to ask questions about the company in general, along with specific questions about how and why certain decisions were made. At first Grajirena appreciated their interest and suggestions. Soon, however, he did not.

CHAPTER 17

Customs

Getting beer through Russian customs always presented problems for First Republic. The rules and regulations seemed to change from shipment to shipment. At one point, for example, the excise taxes on imported beer were raised overnight from 20 percent to 40 percent. The tax remained at 20 percent, however, for "malt beverages." First Republic quickly had its Miller beer reclassified as a "malt beverage," and its excise taxes went back to 20 percent. In its first several months of operations, First Republic typically paid Miller Brewing about $12,000, including shipping, for a container of beer: 1,240 cases, 24 bottles to the case, or roughly $10 per case. First Republic budgeted the duties paid to customs at an average of around $6,000, but that was only a goal—sometimes a distant goal. If the customs bill was what First Republic budgeted, it cost the company about $18,000 to have a container of Miller Genuine Draft delivered to Russia—about 60 cents a bottle. The company typically sold the beer for about 95 cents a bottle to retailers, which added up to sales of roughly $28,000 for a container. (Beer drinkers then paid anywhere from $1.25 at a kiosk for a bottle of Miller Genuine Draft, to $3 or $4 in a Westernized hotel.) If the duty was $6,000 on a container, First Republic made a gross profit of about $10,000 per container, a tidy margin of close to 40 percent. But the duties changed, from shipment to shipment and sometimes from container to container. As the duty climbed, of course, the gross margin went down: a duty of $9,000, for example, lowered the margin on a container to 25 percent. Any duty in five figures effectively meant that, with overhead, First Republic would lose money unless it raised its prices.

First Republic never knew in advance exactly what duties would be charged on a container, however. Loopholes opened and closed, rates went up and down. Customs agents at the border might charge less—but usually more—than the published duty rate. In the first few months, First Republic was asked to pay as little as $2,000 for a container and as much as $18,000. Later the official demand climbed as high as $28,000 per container. If the customs demand was for more than $6,000, First Republic would appeal. This appeal, however, was typically not a formal process. It usually went through the same customs agent who had made the original demand. He would check with his supervisors—supposedly—and return with a lower duty demand, sometimes the same day, always within a few days. First Republic would pay it and take its beer. Neither Rick Grajirena, nor anyone else at First Republic, knew exactly what was happening, or where the money was going. Customs agents told First Republic how much to pay, and First Republic either paid it or appealed it and then paid whatever the demand was after the appeal. Did customs agents inflate the duty sometimes? Certainly. Were they keeping some of the money that First Republic paid in duties? Probably. Was First Republic knowingly paying bribes? No. Was there any other way for a small company such as First Republic to do business in Russia and survive? Definitely not.

As a result, Grajirena and First Republic spent an extraordinary amount of time on customs issues. They fought a constant battle to keep their costs down in order to compete not only with other legitimate beer importers but with black-market and gray-market importers. On the black market, beer was smuggled in illegally, without going through customs at all. Black-market beer could be sold for half of what First Republic charged, and the smugglers would make the same profit margin as First Republic did when it paid its usual $6,000 in duties per container. Fortunately for First Republic, there was little beer on the black market. Smugglers preferred smaller shipments that were easier to spirit into the country, particularly those that yielded bigger profits. Liquor was more appealing to black-market smugglers than beer. But liquor was bulky, too. The black market's absolute favorite product of choice was cigarettes. Easy to find and cheap to buy in other countries, cigarettes were relatively light and easy to disguise in large shipments. There was an almost unlimited market for Western cigarettes, and they offered smugglers absolutely huge profit margins. Cigarettes were what the *mafiya* smugglers really wanted, and what formed the backbone of Russia's black market.

The gray market was a different story. The gray market included many consumer items that were brought into Russia not completely legally, but not totally by the rules, either. The Miller beer from Puerto Rico that flooded the Moscow market and cut into First Republic's business in the summer of 1993 was an example of the gray market. Somebody had bought the beer from Miller legally. But somewhere along the line, official forms were erased or altered and destinations were switched. Bribes were probably paid to get customs inspectors to look the other way. First Republic survived that first brush with the gray market and the flood of Miller beer from Puerto Rico. But there were many subsequent problems with the gray market. In several instances Miller again sold overstocks of beer to wildcatters, or independent exporters, who said they were sending the beer to a territory where Miller did not have a distributor but instead brought it into Russia. The beer was usually not Miller Genuine Draft or any other American premium beer, but that did not matter on the gray market. Most Russian drinkers didn't know a premium label such as Miller Genuine Draft from a cheaper Miller label such as Milwaukee's Best. To them, it was all American beer, and they were often willing to pay the same for Milwaukee's Best as for Miller Genuine Draft.

Even if the wildcatters paid the same as First Republic for beer—which they rarely did, since they were buying marked-down overstocks on a one-time basis—they could sell it for less than First Republic by paying outright bribes to customs officers or trying to sneak the beer into the country disguised as something else that carried lower duties, such as soda pop or fruit juice. One common ploy among the gray marketeers was to arrange for beer to be shipped to some other former Soviet republic, such as Kazakhstan. The beer would arrive in a duty-free warehouse in Moscow for transshipping. But instead of taking it to Kazakhstan, the trucks carrying the beer might just drive around the corner to a private warehouse in Moscow. The importers would have forged papers, perhaps acquired and approved through bribes, to show that the beer had indeed arrived in Kazakhstan. They saved not only the duties but also the cost of trucking the beer across Russia, and they would sell the beer for 50 cents per bottle compared with First Republic's 95 cents. Rick Grajirena at one point told his board of directors that 40 percent of the beer being imported to Moscow was coming in via the gray market and being offered at cut-rate prices because the importers had not been required to pay the full duties the way First Republic had. Corruption and bribery were a way of life—*the* way of doing business—in Russia. The World Bank did a study rating the world's fifty largest countries according to how corrupt they were. Russia was not the most corrupt: Colombia, Bolivia, and Nigeria were worse. Despite the widespread corruption in Russia, and in many cases the widespread acceptance of corruption, Grajirena did not want First Republic to pay bribes or fudge the paperwork or bend the rules or flirt with the gray market. "We are going to prove that a private American company can make a profit in Russia playing by the rules," he insisted.

Beer was shipped in across the Baltic Sea, but First Republic experimented with different ways to clear customs into Russia. Sometimes it was shipped to St. Petersburg, which is in Russia, and cleared customs there. Sometimes it was shipped into Latvia, a former Soviet republic that had become an independent nation again, and then trucked across the Russian border. Sometimes the trucks took main highways, and sometimes they took circuitous routes looking for smaller customs stations where perhaps the inspectors would impose smaller customs demands. But that could backfire, too. Once Grajirena got a call from Moscow saying that a shipment of thirteen containers of beer was stalled at a small border crossing between Latvia and Russia. No one could figure out why the beer couldn't get through. In repeated calls to the customs station, the only answer was the typical Russian response when something was not getting done: "It is not possible." Why isn't it possible? Grajirena demanded. He told the Moscow staff to find out what the problem was and resolve it. The problem, he was told after the beer had been at the crossing for five days, was that the electricity was out at the border station. The customs inspectors at the border station did not have the money to pay their electricity bill, and they had no idea when—or whether—their superiors in Moscow might send them the money. Their superiors had told them there was no money. The inspectors also said that the First Republic beer could not be released to be taken to another crossing. It had entered the formal inspection process, and once that happened, it could not be released. Those were the rules. If a truck drove away and tried to cross into Russia somewhere else, it would be turned away. The beer had to cross at this particular darkened station or nowhere. Grajirena told Misha, the general manager of the Moscow operation, to find out how much it would cost to get the electricity turned back on at the inspection station. He wasn't surprised that Misha was able to come back quickly with a figure: $3,000. In dollars. Grajirena did not bother asking why American dollars, not rubles, were needed for a Russian government agency to pay its bills to a Russian utility company. There was no point. He told Misha to take $3,000 in cash, get in one of the company cars, and drive all night to the border crossing. Grajirena figured that even if the

$3,000 was a complete scam by the inspectors, for thirteen containers that worked out to a mere $230 per container. He just wished they had come up with the figure immediately because he would have paid it immediately instead of wasting over a week. Misha paid the $3,000, the lights came back on—within minutes, he reported—and the thirteen containers of Miller beer made it to Moscow without further incident.

Once when a shipment of beer arrived, Grajirena was told that it was being delayed because of a new Russian law that required a special stamp on alcoholic beverages. But the customs inspectors did not seem to know whether the alcohol stamp applied to beer—or if it did, whether each and every bottle of beer had to be stamped. Maybe it was just each case. Or maybe one stamp covered the whole container. The law was so new, the customs inspectors explained, that they had not yet seen a stamp. They had received a directive that a stamp was required, but that was all they knew. They wanted to wait for details. It took several days to sort out the confusion. Meanwhile the beer sat on the docks. First Republic's drivers sat around with no beer to deliver. First Republic's customers served some other beer if they had it, or no beer at all if they didn't. Finally, after paying a chief inspector several hundred dollars to "expedite" the information, First Republic was told that the stamp did not, after all, cover beer. It was for wine and spirits. The shipment was released, but when it arrived, several pallets of beer were missing. Pilferage was a normal cost of doing business with Russian customs. But in this case more beer than usual was stolen, perhaps because so many different customs officers had been in and out of the containers to inspect the beer for the elusive stamps.

In another instance a trucking company hired to deliver beer from a port had unpacked the beer from a container and repacked it into a truck. Rather than an enclosed freight compartment, the bed of the truck had a metal framework covered by heavy canvas that could be rolled up for unloading. Grajirena told the trucking company that the beer would never make it to Moscow, but the company promised there would be no problem. Grajirena happened to be at the warehouse the day the truck arrived. The canvas was rolled up, and all the beer was there—until it was partly unloaded and it was discovered that thieves had cut open the canvas covering on top of the truck and taken out several dozen cases from the very middle of the shipment.

Grajirena himself made what turned out to be a big customs mistake.

One of First Republic's investors in Florida sold popcorn machines for bars. Grajirena shipped one machine over to Moscow and installed it in one of First Republic's accounts to see how it would go over. American customers loved it, of course, and so did Russian customers—they had never seen anything like it. Free popcorn was in itself a reason to go to a bar and pay four dollars for a beer. The First Republic salesman showed the bar manager how to salt the popcorn to make customers thirstier and get them to order more four-dollar beers. Other Moscow bar owners and managers were soon asking First Republic if they could have popcorn machines, too.

Grajirena loaded up a half-size container with twenty popcorn machines from the investor. There was some extra room on the container, and Grajirena hated to waste it. He decided to toss on some odds and ends from First Republic's duty-free warehouse in Tampa—several cases of liqueurs that had been acquired with the inventory when First Republic bought the duty-free business. The liqueurs were odd brands and styles from around the world—flavored schnapps from somewhere in Africa, an odd kind of local brandy from somewhere in Asia—that cruise ships did not want to buy. Grajirena figured he could find someone, some bar owner, in Russia who would unload the stuff. At customs in Russia there was no problem with the popcorn machines. All the paperwork, including technical specifications on how the machines worked, was in order.

But there was a problem with the liqueurs. The import rules on spirits had changed while the shipment was at sea. Because so little good, affordable booze was available in Russia, some people were peddling dangerous substitutes and fakes made with kerosene or industrial alcohol. Someone might find an empty whiskey bottle, fill it with a mixture of grain alcohol and Coke, and pass it off as scotch. Some people made whole batches of such poison, complete with fake labels. The government decided to crack down by requiring special certificates for every brand of liquor that was imported. The certificate, which had to be from the country where the liquor was made, would prove that the liquor was authentic and would list its contents.

Grajirena's liqueurs did not have the necessary certificates. It would be impossible to round up that information from around the world. "Look, I just want the popcorn machines," Grajirena pleaded. "We'll pour the goddamned liqueurs down the drain right there in customs, right in front of them, if they'll just release our popcorn machines." The customs officers said no. After weeks of back and forth with customs officials, Grajirena finally told the Moscow office of First Republic to forget it. Years later he said that that container with twenty popcorn machines and a few pallets of off-brand liqueurs could still be sitting somewhere on the docks in St. Petersburg. If only he hadn't had the bright idea of getting rid of those old liqueurs by shipping them off to Moscow. He blamed himself for doing exactly the same thing that he was accusing Miller of doing: using Russia as a dumping ground for anything and everything that no one else wanted.

———————

First Republic's worst shipping debacle had nothing to do with customs but with problems between Miller and First Republic's shipping agent. By the end of 1993, First Republic was able to sell all the Miller beer it could get. The problem was creating enough cash flow to order enough beer to keep up with the demand. First Republic was ordering ten or more containers at a time. If it had been able to order ten more containers while it was selling the first shipment, it would have had no cash-flow problem. Instead, it had to wait until it had collected much of the money from the first shipment before it could order the second shipment. Consequently, it was essential to get every shipment of beer cleared through customs and into the warehouse in Moscow as quickly as possible. In December 1993, a shipment of fourteen containers was on the way and was anticipated with near desperation. The previous Christmas and New Year's—when First Republic's very first shipment of Miller beer had been delayed because the ship broke down— had been the biggest holiday celebration in Moscow in decades. This year, welcoming 1994, promised to be even bigger. First Republic had enough beer to get through the holidays, barely, but by mid-January the cupboard would be bare. The fourteen containers ordered in December were critical to restocking Moscow with Miller beer in January.

Just before Christmas, Grajirena got another one of those emergency phone calls that he had come to dread. Five of the fourteen containers had been delivered to Moscow, but much of the beer was frozen. There had been a bitter cold snap, severe even by Russian standards, with several days of temperatures well below zero. The other nine containers were still sitting on the docks in St. Petersburg, and presumably all or most of the beer in them was frozen, too. What should the Moscow office do? Working the phone, giving instructions and asking questions—Moscow, St. Petersburg, Milwaukee, London, Lausanne, Rotterdam—Grajirena pieced together the story over the next few days. Miller, he was told, had not shipped the beer in insulated containers. Miller said it had shipped beer to Russia and elsewhere in colder temperatures in noninsulated containers, and they had not frozen. Miller blamed the shipping agent. The shipping agent blamed Miller, even though Grajirena was told that the shipping agent could have moved the beer earlier, perhaps in time to avoid freezing. The reports to First Republic from the docks indicated that the shipping agent, perhaps in response to bribes or threats or both from the *mafiya*, supposedly had moved a shipment of cigarettes off the docks instead of the beer. The shipping agent denied it, and its insurance carrier refused to pay for the spoiled beer because the containers were not insulated.

Grajirena wanted to reject the nine containers still on the docks, but to ship them back he would first have to pay more than $50,000 to get them out of customs. He didn't want to pay the money, and neither did Miller. Grajirena said he would ship back the five containers that had already cleared customs, but Miller talked him out of it. The beer in the five containers was a mixture of bottles and kegs. Miller suggested that First Republic salvage as much of the unfrozen bottled beer as possible. It made sense, since First Republic was desperate for inventory. Miller also suggested that the beer frozen in kegs be thawed out and dumped because it would be much cheaper to ship back empty kegs. Miller said that despite the arguments over who was at fault and whether the beer should have been in insulated containers, Miller and First Republic would work things out. Grajirena went along with it. Not all the beer was frozen in the five containers in Moscow. At least First Republic would have something to deliver in January. But without any beer First Republic's accounts would go straight to the gray market to buy their beer. Grajirena decided to worry later about compensation for the nine containers still on the docks.

Dealing with the five containers already in the Moscow warehouse was an incredible mess. Thousands of bottles had been broken by the frozen beer. Then the frozen beer had melted. Not only were the floors of the containers awash in rank beer and broken glass, but thousands of cardboard cases were sopping and in tatters. It was impossible to lift up a case of beer and haul it out. The soaked cardboard collapsed, and the bottles fell out. Each bottle had to be lifted out, one by one. Some of the kegs had blown their stoppers, so even more beer was draining out as it melted. Grajirena called Miller and ordered an emergency shipment of new cardboard cases so the beer bottles that survived could be repacked. Every bottle from the five containers had to be lifted out, one at a time, and inspected to see if it was still frozen, or had been frozen. First Republic employees—virtually everyone got involved, from salesmen and clerks to warehouse workers—learned to glance at a bottle and tell whether it had been frozen. A few of them, just to satisfy their curiosity, sampled bottles that had been frozen and then thawed. The experts were right. Freezing ruined the taste of beer, even if it was thawed out again. Bottles that had been frozen were uncapped, and the contents poured down the drains in the gutters in the street outside the First Republic warehouse. Sopping cardboard cases were piled high. Broken bottles were swept into small mountains of jagged brown glass. Kegs were rolled outside to the gutters, positioned over the drains, and uncapped, letting what had been $300 worth of beer flow away into the sewers of Moscow. In each container some beer, packed away snugly in the middle, had been insulated by the hundreds of other cases around them and had not frozen. Out of the five containers, First Republic salvaged enough bottles of unfrozen beer to assemble close to a thousand cases—less than one container.

The nearly one thousand cases salvaged from the five containers in Moscow was gone quickly. Customers snapped it up. Grajirena begged Miller for credit and an emergency shipment to make up for the frozen beer. Miller said the terms had not changed and insisted on payment up front, in cash. Moreover, it threatened to sue for nonpayment of the frozen beer. If First Republic wanted compensation, Miller said, then First Republic should sue the shipping agent. It was weeks before First Republic collected enough receivables to order more beer. During that time, its accounts restocked by buying on the gray market—and so did First Republic. Grajirena always had resisted the gray market, but now it had become necessary. Chris Mitchell and other salesmen scoured the city. When they found a kiosk selling Miller beer for 85 cents a bottle, they bought out the kiosk's supply. Then they drove it over to one of their accounts and sold it for 95 cents a bottle. The salesmen paid the kiosks cash for the beer. The account would pay for the beer in a week or two or three, after selling it to the public. It was a thin margin for a long cash-flow lag. Miller and First Republic argued for years over the nine containers left on the docks. First Republic asked Miller for compensation of close to $400,000 in damages, including lost future sales. Then $164,000. Then $100,000. Then $75,000. First Republic never got any compensation from Miller, from the shipping agent, or from any insurance company. Grajirena never found out what happened to the nine containers left on the docks. "They might still be there," he said years later.

CHAPTER 18

Summer 1994

Frustrated by the frozen beer debacle and other problems in dealing with Miller Brewing, Rick Grajirena began searching for another beer to complement—or if it came to that, to replace—Miller as First Republic's main product line. Heineken, the Netherlands brewering concern, had long been a popular beer in Moscow. But it never had an exclusive distribution agreement with any single company. Anyone and everyone who wanted to import Heineken did so on a cash-and-carry basis. Grajirena thought that First Republic's strong distribution network might appeal to Heineken. He was right. Heineken had been watching First Republic for some time, and it welcomed Grajirena's approach. The Dutchman in charge of finding a distributor for Russia hit it off with Grajirena. They both liked to have a beer or three, and they both loved to tell jokes. They were raconteurs. One late-afternoon business meeting turned into a beer-swilling festival of each man's greatest hits of dirty jokes. They bonded in mutual admiration.

A few days later the Dutchman also liked what he saw when Grajirena showed him around First Republic's accounts in Moscow. Grajirena carefully laid out the day's itinerary for Chris Mitchell, who had become First Republic's Moscow sales manager after Misha was promoted to general manager. From account to account, from store to restaurant to bar to nightclub, Mitchell raced around Moscow one step ahead of Grajirena and the Dutchman, who cut a trim, dapper figure in his tailored double-breasted suits. Every account they walked into was ready for them. Miller beer displays were prominently positioned in the grocery stores and supermarkets. Shelves and coolers were fully stocked, with bottles facing out. In the bars and clubs,

Miller signs and posters greeted them. There was Miller point-of-sale material on every table. The store managers and clerks and bartenders wore Miller shirts, hats, buttons, and badges. The managers, who had been promised free beer by Mitchell if they talked up First Republic, were positively enthusiastic about the American company and its level of service.

The Dutchman was duly impressed. That evening Grajirena took him out for dinner with a couple of First Republic staff members from Tampa and a First Republic investor. As usual Grajirena headed off to bed after dinner. The staffers and the investor said they would take the Dutchman out on the town. The next morning Grajirena got all the sordid details. They had gone to several places and had a lot to drink, then gone back to the company apartment and had more to drink. At some point during the predawn hours, the Dutchman apparently roused himself from the couch and tried to get into bed with one of the First Republic staffers. She eventually kicked him out the room, after some shouting and the tearing of her nightshirt. This tale was related to Grajirena, without emotion, at six A.M. by the investor, who appeared to have either wet his pants or thrown up on himself or both. Grajirena did not want to ask for the details, and the investor might not have been able to provide them anyway. It was a small comfort to know that Dutchmen, and not just Americans, could be afflicted with Moscow Madness.

But Grajirena was upset with his own people. He got the two staffers and the investor together that afternoon and gave them an old-fashioned scolding for their unprofessional behavior. "All this partying on these trips is Moscow Madness, and it has got to stop," he said. He told them they were making fools of themselves and hurting the company. What if the Dutchman decided that Heineken wanted no part of the deal? True, he was at fault for trying to get into bed with the First Republic staffer, but she and the other First Republic people could also be accused of creating the situation for it to happen in the first place. Why did they allow things get so out of hand by letting everyone get so drunk?

Grajirena fretted all day about the meeting he was supposed to have over beers with the Dutchman at the end of the workday. But he shouldn't have worried—the Dutchman was all smiles. He drank beer and told jokes with his usual gusto and never mentioned the night before. He told Grajirena he had reported back to the headquarters in Amsterdam, and First Republic had the green light. The papers were being drawn up for a one-year distribution arrangement in Moscow for First Republic. If things went well the first year, Heineken would give First Republic a distributorship for all of Russia and perhaps other parts of the former Soviet Union. They shook on it and celebrated with one more Heineken toast, and then Grajirena went off to tell his board that First Republic was cleared to order and distribute Heineken beer as well as Miller. All they needed was the money to do it. One of the Wisconsin investors stepped up and loaned First Republic the money to place its first order for several containers of Heineken.

———————

Rick Grajirena had always disliked the idea of consultants. First Republic had hired a major accounting firm to do regular audits and make recommendations, but that was less because he wanted its advice than because he wanted to build a corporate record in anticipation of taking the company public someday. First Republic's lawyer, Karen, who had joined the company with Mark Mroczkowski and stayed after the CFO departed, came to Grajirena with a suggestion. She had a childhood friend who had been in military intelligence—she hinted CIA, but was not specific—and was now a specialist in international business. He was serving as a consultant to major corporations doing business in the Soviet Union, and she could get him relatively cheap. She suggested that Grajirena hire her friend for a few months to go over to Moscow, look around, get to know the people and the company, find out if anyone was stealing or cheating, and make recommendations about how to clean things up and get First Republic back on track.

The man's fee didn't seem cheap to Grajirena, especially since he would be staying in the company apartment in Moscow. But he was under pressure from the board of directors and other investors. He got one or more calls or faxes from Wisconsin almost every day, always with questions. What was he doing about the frozen beer? How much money did the company make last month? How much beer did it sell? How much was in the warehouse? Several members of the Wisconsin group were pressuring Grajirena himself to move to Moscow. He was the president of First Republic, after all. Wasn't it his job to run the company? How could he run it from Tampa? If Moscow was where he was needed, why wasn't he in Moscow? Grajirena still had no intention of moving to Moscow. But he knew he needed help. It seemed like First Republic was spinning out of control. He bounced the idea about the consultant off the other directors, and they agreed that it might help. Grajirena hired the consultant, who became known to the First Republic staffers in Moscow—in a joking or smirking manner—as the Spy.

The Spy was hired on a month-to-month basis. He moved to Moscow and was introduced to the staff as a consultant who would be observing the Moscow office and warehouse and asking questions about every aspect of the operation. The staff was instructed to cooperate with him fully. The Spy began faxing reports almost immediately back to Grajirena. The reports were breathtaking in their simplicity. The Spy cited a lack of communication between Tampa and Moscow and said something should be done about it. His recommendation was that the Russians should try to learn more English, and the Americans should try to learn more Russian. "More time should be spent getting to know each other. . . . Everyone needs a better understanding of other First Republic jobs." It was grade school stuff, Grajirena thought.

The Spy said staffers needed to be more polite to each other. "Consideration and courtesy breed respect and loyalty," he said in one report. One of his first recommendations was for Grajirena to purchase Miller lapel pins for the salesmen. Another was for Grajirena and other First Republic visitors from the States to stop arriving in Moscow on weekends because the drivers who picked them up had to be paid overtime. Yet another recommendation was for Misha to take a vacation; the Spy thought he was working too hard. The Spy singled out Grajirena for criticism, telling him that he was being impolite by not riding in the front seat of First Republic vehicles whenever a company driver took him somewhere. He said Grajirena insulted Russian staffers by not eating Russian food at company parties. He urged Grajirena to make friends with the staff. And he said that Grajirena should trust Misha, because Misha was a great natural leader. The Spy said he had become personal friends with Misha in a short time and admired him very much. He said all Misha's accounting problems were just misunderstandings.

Grajirena told the Spy he didn't feel safe in the front seat of Russian cars, not with any Russian driver. He told the Spy he didn't like Russian food, and that he didn't think the CEO needed to go out drinking with the staff. And he told the Spy that the Spy's job was not to speak about how likable Misha was; everyone knew that. The Spy's job was to find out what was wrong and fix it. Maybe Misha's problems were indeed the result of misunderstandings. So, Grajirena told the Spy, straighten out the misunderstandings. Grajirena realized that hiring the Spy had been a mistake. The Spy didn't seem to be the sharpest knife in the drawer. Grajirena wished he had taken the time to check out the Spy more carefully, to check his references, to look more closely at his experience. If he had, he found out later, he would have learned that the Spy's only real hands-on management experience in private business was half-ownership of a Taco Bell franchise in Tennessee. But when he hired the Spy, Grajirena hadn't had time to do a lot of background checks. He had needed help, and Karen, the corporate attorney, had spoken highly of the Spy. He began to wonder about Karen's judgment. Grajirena decided he would get rid of the Spy in due time—after resolving a bigger pesonnel problem, the problem with the Moscow general manager.

Misha, who had done so well in taking charge and getting the beer out of the collapsed warehouse a year earlier, had not done as well since then as general manager of the Moscow office. After the departure earlier in the year of Mark Mroczkowski, the CFO, who had been spending two to three weeks a month in Moscow, Misha was the senior First Republic staff member in the Moscow operation. There was no American on the ground and in charge, and Grajirena thought it showed. There was tension between Tampa and Moscow. The staff in Moscow had grown from fewer than twenty to nearly forty. Many of them were Misha's friends. Grajirena had been told that some of them were Misha's relatives. Many of them had small clerical or warehouse or driver jobs. Some of them earned $200 a month, some as little as $50 or $60. The Russian bookkeeper hired by Misha turned out to be Misha's girlfriend. Misha did not send in reports often enough to suit Grajirena. The reports he did send were vague or incomplete. When he noticed Moscow staff members and their friends wearing Miller hats, T-shirts, shoes, jackets, and other point-of-sale and promotional material, Grajirena checked into how much the Mocow office was ordering from Miller. He found orders as high as $20,000. He wrote a memo: No point-of-sale purchases from Miller for more than $1,500 at a time. He later found that the office simply started ordering $1,300 or $1,400 worth of POS material almost every day. None of this added up to evidence that Misha was doing anything illegal, and Grajirena never accused him of doing anything wrong—other than being a poor manager. He had been a good sales manager, but the company was not doing well with him as the general manager in Moscow.

July 1, 1994, was a critical date for two reasons. Misha had told Grajirena in May that First Republic's landlord—the American who had rented them office space and a warehouse after Arkady An's warehouse collapsed the previous year—was not going to renew the lease. Grajirena wanted to find new space as soon as possible, but Misha seemed in no hurry. Grajirena kept asking him if he had been looking at places, if he had some possibilities. Misha's answer was always "No problem. Don't worry. We'll find something." When he finally did find something, the company had to move hurriedly in late June. Grajirena was not happy about the tumult of a sudden move that he believed could have been more orderly. Nor was he happy about the new space. Instead of having its own warehouse, First Republic was subletting space in a giant warehouse complex that was managed by another company. First Republic didn't even have its own key, and the new warehouse closed at 4:30 every afternoon, which meant a much shorter day in terms of beer deliveries. In addition, the warehouse workers locked the doors during their ninety-minute lunch breaks, which meant no deliveries could come in or out during the middle of the day. The space was much larger than First Republic needed, and the rent was more than Grajirena thought the company should be paying. Grajirena felt that First Republic needed to get the keys to a smaller, less-expensive warehouse that it controlled. The warehouse, he felt, was another major example of Misha's poor management.

But it wasn't Grajirena's foremost example of Misha's poor management. The other reason July 1, 1994, was important was that new customs regulations were coming into effect. The new rules supposedly meant it would cost up to $28,000 per container to clear beer through customs—a more than 230 percent tax on the cost of the beer. First Republic would have to raise its prices considerably. But that was not Grajirena's immediate worry. His immediate worry was seven containers of Miller beer that had arrived on the docks in Riga in May. Customs officers had set the duty on them at $8,000 per container. Grajirena wanted to get those seven containers through customs at the $8,000 rate before July 1, when the duties went up. The savings to First Republic would be $140,000. But First Republic's cash flow was so choked that the company didn't have the money—$56,000 —to pay the duties on the seven containers. Grajirena ordered Misha to sell as much beer in Moscow as he could for cash, to clear out the existing inventory as quickly as possible, so the company would have the money to bring in as many of the seven containers as it could before July 1, at the lower rate. Cut deals, Grajirena told Misha. Sell for discounts. Just get cash.

A couple of weeks before the the July deadline, Misha reported that he had found a new customer willing to buy $65,000 worth of beer for cash. Grajirena was suspicious. Who had that kind of cash? The *mafiya* was the only obvious answer. But no matter—the money would allow all seven containers in Riga to clear customs at the lower rate before July 1. "Good work," Grajirena told Misha. There was just one problem, Misha said. The buyer, a company named Slade, had not put up the cash immediately. The money was coming in a couple of days, three at most. In the meantime, Misha said, Slade was delivering collateral to First Republic—several pallets of vodka and other booze that was worth more than $65,000. When Slade paid the $65,000 cash, Misha promised, it would reclaim its booze. Grajirena didn't like it, but Misha had already done the deal and allowed Slade to pick up the beer. Grajirena's fears grew when Misha kept making excuses for the money not coming through from Slade after two days, three days, four days. Then Grajirena learned that the booze from Slade, the collateral, had never been delivered. Misha had no explanation.

Grajirena told Misha to get the money or the beer back from Slade—or else. When Grajirena got nothing more than excuses for several more days, he flew to Moscow. "Call up Slade," Grajirena instructed. Misha didn't have a phone number. "Let's drive to their office," Grajirena insisted. Misha said he didn't have an address. Misha finally admitted that he may have been cheated. He said he would keep trying to get First Republic's money or beer back, but he didn't really know whether he could. He said the people he had been dealing with from Slade had disappeared and he had no way of tracing them. A new nightclub suddenly began offering Miller beer at bargain prices. Grajirena got a bottle and ran the batch number past the Milwaukee headquarters of Miller. The bottle was indeed part of the delivery Misha had made to Slade. "There's our beer," Grajirena told Misha. "Go find out who sold it to that nightclub, and get it back." Nothing happened. For a brief time the Moscow police showed mild interest in the case, but they seemed to think it was more akin to a bad debt than a theft. They said they would check it out, but the detective working on it did not have a way to get around town. First Republic loaned the detective a car and a driver, but after several days he came up with nothing about Slade or where the beer had gone. First Republic withdrew the driver and the car and heard nothing more from the police.

Grajirena returned to the States, knowing that First Republic was in deeper financial trouble than ever. He also knew that he had to fire Misha. But given the second-guessing by investors who had been looking over his shoulder, Grajirena wanted to run it past his fellow board members first. He had a series of phone conversations with other board members and explained his case against Misha—especially the $65,000 sale to Slade that now appeared to be a total write-off. "Was Misha in on it?" more than one board member asked. It was a natural question, given the business climate in Russia at the time, when *mafiya* gangs stole and bribed and threatened and murdered their way to whatever they wanted. Perhaps Misha or his family had been threatened, and he had been forced to do what the gangsters wanted. Grajirena said he didn't know. He didn't know whether Slade was *mafiya*. But it certainly seemed suspicious. Nor did Grajirena have any evidence that Misha was in cahoots with the *mafiya* or Slade or anyone else. The worst he could say about the Slade deal was that it looked suspicious. The best he could say was that it was a terrible business decision by Misha—

bad enough that he should be fired for it. The board agreed. The Spy weighed in with his evaluation. He thought that Misha was a good and honest employee who had been trying to do the right thing, but had been duped by some very shrewd con men. It could have happened to anyone, the Spy said. He said Misha should not suffer from one mistake. No one paid any attention to the Spy's opinion, especially after Grajirena discovered that in April Misha had borrowed $15,000 on behalf of First Republic from a "friend in private banking." The note Misha had signed for First Republic promised 20 percent interest—per month. Grajirena paid off the loan for $26,000: $15,000 principal plus $11,000 interest for four months.

Grajirena began laying plans for Misha's dismissal. He had First Republic's Moscow lawyers draw up papers that gave Misha a modest severance in return for his promise that he would not sue or file a government complaint. Given what had happened to their partner, Jack Robinson, Grajirena didn't blame First Republic's lawyers for refusing to allow him to use their offices for the meeting with Misha. Grajirena went back to an old friend in the Canadian-Russian Trade Council who agreed, reluctantly, to allow him to use a room there. He contacted Viktor Potapov, the first Russian whom Grajirena ever met, and who had become a close friend since getting the Russian national and Olympic yachting teams to buy their sails from Grajirena in the 1970s. Potapov, who had gone on to become an Olympic medalist and one of the yachting heroes of the Soviet Union, was happy to help out his old sailing buddy when Grajirena said he was worried about his own safety. Potapov helped find the two bodyguards to accompany Grajirena to the meeting where he would fire Misha, and for a few days afterward.

Even if things went well, Grajirena had to think about what would happen after Misha left. He needed a steady hand in Moscow. Chris Mitchell, the sales manager, was the senior American in the Moscow office, both in terms of title and length of service. But Grajirena didn't think Mitchell was ready to be the general manager. Grajirena wanted an American. He couldn't find one quickly, so he needed someone to step in temporarily. He asked Potapov to do it. Potapov quickly agreed. He looked the part of a senior manager—middle-aged, strong, and sturdy, with an erect bearing and leonine gray hair swept back. He had an air of importance about him. He and Grajirena quickly agreed to terms for what Grajirena thought they both understood would be a temporary arrangement. Potapov would preside over the Moscow office and keep order and make sure everyone did his or her job. He would be a steadying influence, with no far-reaching management responsibilities, until Grajirena could find an American manager. There was no written contract. The two men shook hands.

When Grajirena flew into Moscow to fire Misha in late July, he thought everything was in place. The only problem was that Misha, sensing he was about to be fired, had taken the Spy's suggestion and gone on vacation to Greece. Grajirena had to wait for several days in Moscow while Misha was lying on a beach. Moving around town with his bodyguards, he recalled with grim humor the way Gadgi's bodyguard had run away at the first sign of trouble a couple of years earlier. He wondered if his guys would do the same. When Misha finally returned, he showed up at the meeting only a few minutes late. He didn't raise a fuss. There wasn't a lot of discussion. Grajirena laid out his complaints about Misha's management and said, "Resign or be fired." Misha said he had not done anything wrong. Yes, perhaps he had made mistakes, but he had not done anything wrong. "I'll resign," he said. He shook hands with Grajirena and walked away. It was the last Grajirena saw of him, but not the last he heard of him.

Grajirena went straight to the First Republic office, where he had called a meeting of the entire staff. He met Potapov there, along with Peter Harken. Harken, also an old friend of Potapov, had taken time off from his yacht equipment business in Wisconsin to come over to Moscow. As a First Republic board member, he wanted to support Grajirena during this stressful time. Being on the scene would also allow Harken to report back to First Republic's other Wisconsin investors, all of whom had made their investments after hearing about the company from Harken. Grajirena told the assembled staff that Misha had been fired. He introduced Potapov as the new general manager and said there would be some changes. The first change would be to trim the staff back down to an appropriate size. Grajirena held in his hand two lists, one of nineteen people being fired, the other of sixteen people being asked to stay on. The people who were being fired were expected to leave immediately. Grajirena read the lists quickly, and then he and Potapov went into the general manager's office while the room outside disintegrated into a tumult of crying, hugging, backslapping, handshaking, commiserations, and muted congratulations. Everyone seemed to be saying good-bye. Several people came in to say good-bye to Grajirena, or to thank him for keeping them on. A few wanted to shake hands with Potapov and introduce themselves.

Grajirena stayed around Moscow for a few days to let the dust settle. The Spy, who had lurked in the background during the meeting when more than half the staff was dismissed, stayed out of Grajirena's way except to say that he would have his weekly report as usual. When he presented his report, it was in the form of a fax signed by the Spy and his old friend Karen, the First Republic lawyer who had recommended him. The fax, which had been sent to all the First Republic board members, recommended that Grajirena be fired for mismanagement. Reading between the lines, the fax seemed to suggest that the Spy and Karen were ready, willing, and able to step in and turn First Republic around. Grajirena read the fax while the Spy sat watching, waiting for his reaction. Grajirena's reaction was to read it through, then think about it for a moment, then look at parts of it again. He finally looked at the Spy and spoke. "You're fired," he said. "Get out of the office. Get your stuff out of the company apartment by tonight." The Spy started to insist that Grajirena could not fire him. "I hired you," Grajirena reminded him. "I can fire you." The Spy sullenly left. Grajirena spent the rest of the day and much of the evening on the telephone talking to directors and investors back in the States, stamping out the fires created by the fax from the Spy and Karen recommending his own dismissal. Within a few days, when it became clear that the attempted coup was going to fail, Karen resigned as First Republic's attorney.

One bit of good news for investors was that the Moscow payroll, which had swollen to $250,000 a year under Misha, had been trimmed to under $150,000 a year. Investors back home still needed reassurances and had a million questions for him, but Grajirena stayed on in Moscow for a few days to help Potapov settle in. Harken was still supporting him, Grajirena knew, but other investors in the Wisconsin group had made it clear they wanted to see First Republic turn around soon. No one told Grajirena, "Or else," but no one needed to. When he got home to Clearwater, a number of messages were waiting for him from investors. One investor wanted to know why Grajirena had moved into a hotel for part of his time in Moscow. Sure, there might have been some threats and some security problems with the company apartment, the investor suggested, but were they really worth spending all that company money on an expensive hotel? A few days later Grajirena announced that he would voluntarily take a 10 percent cut in his salary, which recently had been increased by the board to $80,000 a year.

CHAPTER 19

Roofs

In the early era of *perestroika* in the late 1980s and early 1990s, when many Western companies were just starting to poke their noses into Russia, they were often prey to the *mafiya*. In those early days the *mafiya* were gangs, often hardened criminals from the Republic of Georgia or from Chechnya, the region of Russia where dissidents who opposed rule from Moscow had triggered a bloody uprising. The gangs used strongarm tactics to get hard currency—U.S. dollars, primarily. They operated like 1920s Chicago mobsters. They would focus on people who did business with Westerners and had access to hard currency, either dollars or money that could easily be exchanged for dollars—English pounds, German marks, Italian lire, Japanese yen. The *mafiya* targets included restaurants and bars frequented by Westerners, and high-class prostitutes who serviced visiting Western businessmen. If a target would not cooperate with a *mafiya* gang, that person—or someone close to that person—was at great risk. There were literally thousands of execution-style murders by the *mafiya*. In one year alone, 1995, the Russian government reported the existence of an astounding 8,000 separate *mafiya* organizations. The same year, the government reported 560 contract killings—and there were probably many more that were not reported. Over one two-year period, twenty-seven Russian bankers were gunned down. Russia's relatively low murder rate rose to more than twice that of the United States, which always had been condemned by the Soviet leadership for its violent society. Remarkably, a country known for corruption became even more corrupt as *mafiya* payoffs to police and judicial officers led the public to believe that the gangs could do whatever they wanted. At one point in 1996, the police chief of Moscow estimated that 95 percent of his officers accepted bribes. Some gangs got their guns from the police. Prosecutors and judges were on the take, too. A survey by *U.S. News & World Report* found that Russians were more likely to say that the *mafiya* controlled the country rather than President Yeltsin. A Russian study found that one in four businesses was paying protection money. The *mafiya* controlled more than 40,000 businesses, a Russian newspaper reported, along with more than 500 Russian banks and more than 500 joint ventures involving foreigners. Kroll and Associates, an international consultancy specializing in business intelligence and risk assessment, rated Moscow as one of the ten most dangerous cities in the world for business travelers, along with, in alphabetical order, Algiers, Bogotá, Caracas, Johannesburg, Karachi, Lagos, Medellín, Mexico City, and Rio de Janeiro.

Virtually all Russians whom an American would encounter—in business, while traveling, in school, anywhere—said they hated the *mafiya*. But many disaffected young men saw it as their only way to a better life. They saw the *mafiya* sweeping through town in big imported cars, taking over nightclubs, and spending more in an evening just on booze than most Russians could earn in a year of honest work. The gangsters wore sleek Italian suits, often with wide lapels, dark shirts, and wide ties. They wore lots of gold jewelry. It was as if they were dressing the part of Capone-era gangsters, as depicted in the old American movies that had occasionally been shown on Soviet television as evidence of the corruption of American society. For many young men, becoming *mafiya* was the way to get rich, the only way. The number of gangs and gangsters increased. As competition among the gangs increased—there was never any single *mafiya* superstructure, no meetings of families, no boss of bosses—the gangsters increasingly gunned each other down in turf wars. The competition also led them to demand protection money, not only from Russians doing business with Westerners, but from anyone—Russian or Western—making any kind of money, rubles or dollars, in Russia. The gangs promised to provide a "roof" that would protect the business from anything: from arson, from tax inspectors, from competitors, from other *mafiya* gangs.

Gradually through the 1990s, as the Russian economy improved, the *mafiya* influence waned. No doubt part of the reason was that political leaders responded to the wishes of the vast majority of the Russian people who wanted to live safely and securely and pursue a livelihood without the threat of it being taken from them by crooks with guns. But another part of the reason was that the corruption became institutionalized. Police officials realized that there was no reason they should be getting payoffs that represented a small portion of the extortion that the gangs were collecting—not when the police themselves could be collecting the extortion. Across Russia, *mafiya* gangsters were killed off or thrown into jail, and "security" firms took their place. These firms were relatively legitimate. They were often started by former policemen, or policemen who were moonlighting, and they promised the full support of the police. Some were local, as most of the *mafiya* gangs had been. Some, however, grew in scope and formed alliances with other police departments and other government agencies. By the late 1990s, most American businesspeople in Russia who had a roof knew that the roof's authority probably extended far beyond the police. "The government has become the roof, and the roof has become the government," one American businessman said. "It's hard to know where one stops and the other begins." As organizations, roofs became much more sophisticated. In the early 1990s, a few *mafiya* gangs went so far as to produce crude little brochures that might include a picture of a machine gun on the front. By the mid-to-late-1990s, the security firms offering themselves as roofs had nice offices, slick four-color brochures, multimedia sales presentations by their marketing people, and an array of services that included business consulting. Some went so far as to offer financing, either loans or investment capital.

Only one American was known as a *mafiya* murder victim. Paul Tatum, an Oklahoma lawyer and professional fundraiser for the Republican Party, came to Moscow in 1989 and set up a Westernized business center in one of the first Westernized hotels, the Radisson Slavjanskaya. The center offered good clean direct-dial lines for international phone or fax connections, temporary office or conference space for an hour or a day or a week, and all the standard clerical and administrative services, such as photocopying, transcribing, translating, interpreting, and temporary staffing. The business center was a huge success. For many Westerners coming to Moscow, it was the first stop, the base from which they found their own business space, hired their own staff, and made their own business contacts. For several years Tatum was one of the most visible Americans in town, a champagne-swilling symbol to the West that Moscow was open for business. Part of his legend was that during the standoff at the besieged Russian Parliament building, he had climbed over the barricades to offer Boris Yeltsin the use of his cell phone. But then there were problems. The Slav, as local expats called the hotel, was at first a joint venture between the Radisson chain and Intourist, the old Soviet tourism agency. After the collapse of the Soviet Union, President Yeltsin gave control over all private property in Moscow to the city of Moscow—in effect, to Mayor Yuri Luzhkov. This is what *Forbes* magazine reported in 1995: "The freehold on most Moscow property is owned by the Moscow city government, which in turn is run as a personal proprietorship by the mayor of Moscow, Yuri Luzhkov. The mayor is a big player in the property market: he makes land and buildings available at artificially low prices to favored developers. Are there kickbacks involved? How could there not be? We do know that developers kick back money to the Moscow city government, which Luzhkov controls like a personal bank account."

Conflicts arose between Tatum and the managers appointed by the city to oversee its portion of the joint venture. Some observers saw the conflict as part of a familiar pattern: Westerners came into joint ventures with their money and expertise, and then when the venture was up and running successfully, either the *mafiya* or the government or both forced them out. By the mid-1990s, the office space that Tatum claimed to control at the hotel—indeed, all prime office space in central Moscow—was among the most expensive commercial space in the world, with average rents of $70 to $80 per square foot. Some of the most sought-after space topped $100 per square foot, provided renters would pay up to six years' rent in advance. The issues surrounding Tatum's dispute with the city of Moscow were murky—who said what, who did what, who owed what to whom. No American who was in Moscow then would pretend to know all the details of what happened. But every American would say that Tatum acted foolishly and brazenly. For example, he publicly accused the city officials involved in the joint venture of being connected to the *mafiya*, and he all but accused Mayor Luzhkov of being a crook. Tatum refused to pay the rent for the business center and sued the city for $35 million. At one point he barricaded himself in his office inside the hotel so he would not be evicted. While other American businesspeople in Moscow were keeping low profiles and moving around the city with chauffeurs and bodyguards, Tatum walked the streets and even took the Moscow subway alone. He told friends that by keeping such a high profile, he was safe. He was wrong. In November 1996, he was gunned down at the entrance to the subway just outside the hotel. He was hit by twelve bullets fired from a Kalashnikov assault rifle at short range. Five of them hit Tatum in the neck, above the bulletproof vest he was wearing. "No one was surprised," one American recalled. "We were only surprised that it hadn't happened sooner."

First Republic never had a roof. Rick Grajirena never sought one out. He heard, indirectly, from First Republic staffers in Moscow about quiet approaches from a security firm managed by a former KGB agent. The security firm offered to protect First Republic from the *mafiya*. But First Republic never followed up, in part because the company had never known it was a target of the *mafiya*, in part because Grajirena was determined that First Republic should operate as aboveboard as possible. Early on, he issued an edict: First Republic will operate strictly legally, with everything done by the book. It quickly became clear, however, that operating strictly legally was not possible if the company wanted to stay in business. In Russia there was the strictly legal way to do things, there was the obviously illegal way to do things, and there was a large gray area in between. That was where most companies operated. Sticking by the book was too costly. Companies that stuck by the book went out of business in competition with companies that did not. Besides, it was difficult to stick to the book when the book had not been written yet, or was being rewritten every day. Under Grajirena, First Republic tried to tread the middle ground. The company never smuggled in beer or anything else. It never paid a bribe under the table. It did, however, pay many extra fees and assessments and costs that seemed to be bribes, whether to customs agents who stopped containers of beer or to police officers who pulled over First Republic trucks on their way to make deliveries. "If it's something official, if it's a formal document, if we can get a recognizable receipt for it, we can pay it," Grajirena told his troops. "If the police come to us and ask us if we've paid a bribe, we can say no, it was a formal fee demanded by a government official, and here's the receipt to prove it. If there's a problem, we want it to be a problem for the official who demanded the payment, not for us."

If Russians did not seem particularly concerned about business ethics to Rick Grajirena, it was because they weren't. In the United States, business law and ethics grew out of common law dating back to the Middle Ages. Centuries of commerce helped principles evolve, backed up by thousands of examples of case law. Certain behavior and conduct in business became not only accepted but expected. That never really happened in Russia, which had no tradition of free enterprise. When First Republic and other American companies came to Russia, they found little business law: No law of contracts. No law of bankruptcy. No commercial law. Those laws were never developed because they had never been needed.

For most of its history, Russia was a feudal country. Until the middle of the nineteenth century, two of every three Russians were serfs—basically, peasant slaves to aristocrats who managed the land for princes and czars. (The word *czar* is the Russian version of "caesar," though some of the Russian czars were apparently less than noble in bearing, such as Ivan the Meek and Basil the Squint-Eyed.) The serfs were freed in 1861, only two years before the Emancipation Proclamation in the United States. The imperial era of Russia lasted two centuries and saw the beginning of a merchant or business class, but it ended abruptly with the 1917 revolutions. (There were actually two Russian revolutions in 1917: The first brought down the czar in February and the second—the one that brought the Bolsheviks to power—in October.) After the October revolution the new Communist government estimated that businessmen, the so-called *bourgeoisie*, constituted 15.9 percent of the Russian population. A decade later, at the start of the first of the infamous five-year plans, the number of estimated Russian businessmen officially had dropped to 5 percent. By 1937, it had dropped to zero, and that's where it stayed, officially, until the end of the Soviet Union in 1991.

Some people were nonetheless enriched during the Soviet era, particularly the class known as the *nomenklatura*, people privileged by their Communist Party connections or their high-ranking bureaucratic jobs. Among the sprawling bureaucracy, it became normal to expect bribes and kickbacks: small bribes for minor bureaucrats, big bribes for major bureaucrats. The bureaucracy was not new to Russia with the Soviets. "I do not rule Russia," Czar Nicholas I said. "Ten thousand clerks do." Under the Soviets, the *nomenklatura* had higher salaries, bigger apartments, cars, *dachas*, and seaside vacations. This was in a society where each person was supposed to work to the best of his or her ability and take no more than required for his or her needs. "Under capitalism, man exploits man," Russians used to say. "Under communism, it's exactly the opposite."

Some private business was conducted during the Soviet era, of course, but it was virtually all illegal. It was illegal to own property. It was illegal to charge interest. It was illegal to buy or sell for profit. Yet there was a "shadow economy" of buying and selling. This shadow economy ranged from hardcore criminals, such as drug dealers and smugglers, to common citizens who might want to sell a neighbor a used sofa. A Russian who wanted to go out in the woods and pick wild berries and sell them to a food shop was breaking the law—and so was the owner of the shop who bought the berries and then sold them to customers. A Russian who hired kids to go out in the woods and pick the berries for him to sell to the shop—thereby benefiting personally from the labor of others—could be subject to heavy fines. He could also be punished by exile to Siberia or prison or both. Many economic crimes were punishable not just by fines or prison but by death.

Despite the risks of getting caught, most Soviet citizens broke the country's economic laws, usually in small ways. Say an artist painted a set of *matryoshka* nesting dolls. Then her boyfriend sold them for her at a street market (also illegal), and they split the money. Technically, they were breaking the law and could go to jail. As a practical matter, however, the authorities would not bother with them—unless they sold the dolls to a tourist who paid for them in dollars. Doing things that were technically illegal became accepted in Russia. "On the left" or "from the side" was the phrase for it. Getting around the system. Putting one over on the government. It was not unusual, for example, for Russians with access to a government car to use the vehicle to run personal errands. By the mid-1970s, when the Soviet Union was presumably at the height of its power and influence, only one family in seventy in Moscow had a car. Government employees, on business or moonlighting during a slow time, often stopped to pick up people who flagged them down on the streets of Moscow and charged them a few rubles to take them wherever they wanted to go. After all, taxis were scarce. This was the atmosphere and attitude in which most Russians grew up. There was little or no respect for the law or the government. It was okay to lie and cheat and steal—a little, within reason. Business was illegal, so there was no consideration of ethics in business.

Ironically, those operating in the shadow economy were the only Russian workers showing enterprise, initiative, and efficiency. Therefore, to be enterprising, to take initiative, to be efficient at work—those were all characteristics that Russians came to associate with illegal behavior. It was presumed that anyone who had more than his neighbor was doing something illegal. When private enterprise was suddenly legalized, even in limited form under Gorbachev's *perestroika,* the people operating in the shadow economy, technically illegally, were best equipped to take advantage of it.

In the first years of *perestroika,* even before the end of the Soviet Union, anyone in private business was presumed by his neighbors to be at least a little bit crooked. Anyone who was rich was presumed to be a criminal. After the fall of the Soviet Union, it was of course legal, even desirable, to be rich. But many Russians still regarded anyone in private business as "on the left." Enterprising Russians who started their own businesses often hid the fact from the neighbors, assuming their neighbors would think they were crooked. Before private business could become accepted or expected, before a Western style of "normal" business could evolve, private business became dominated by the *mafiya* and by bureaucrats who demanded bribes and kickbacks. The old privileged Soviet *nomenklatura* retained and in some cases greatly expanded their relatively high standards of living by becoming involved in organized crime or exploiting their government positions—or both. Some of the sons and daughters of the *nomenklatura* who had used their connections to do private business "on the side" during the Soviet era became *mafiya* after 1991. Perhaps even more damaging to Russia, the new duties of the *nomenklatura* who remained in government positions often included overseeing privatization. They decided who would buy what state enterprises, and how much they would pay. A bureaucrat who stayed in government might arrange for a state enterprise to be sold to his friend—and he might get a kickback, or become the friend's silent partner. In effect, the *nomenklatura* sold the country to one another. Many of them became rich, and some became super-rich. They put billions into overseas bank accounts and sent their children to school in London or Paris. They created what George Soros, the financier who channeled hundreds of millions of dollars to Russia for economic and social development programs, called a "financial oligarchy." The "oligarchs," as the Russian media and industry barons became known, used their wealth to wield tremendous political influence. They used that influence to line their own pockets at the cost of slower growth and democratization for the rest of Russian society.

Ruben G. Apressyan, head of the ethics department at the Russian Academy of Science's Institute of Philosophy in Moscow, did a study of ethics—or the lack thereof—in Russia's evolving capitalism. This is what he said about business in Russia in the mid-1990s, when Rick Grajirena was trying to keep First Republic alive: "All forms of economic activity are self-seeking and illegally controlled by a corrupted bureaucracy from the top and by *mafiya*, quasi-*mafiya*, or legal social and state structures 'from the side.' Because of an undeveloped legal system, the state is unable to guarantee businesspersons' personal and material security. Moreover, the most complicated and sharp conflicts in business are usually resolved by a criminal 'mediator.' From their own side, criminals are interested in preserving contradictions and conflicts in business, and they provoke or manufacture conflicts to turn them to their advantage and to redistribute income for their own benefit. It is almost impossible for small businesses to survive the pressure of contradictory laws and regulations, bureaucracy, and criminals. By the summer of 1996, the share of the shadow economy in Russian gross internal output was about 40 percent." Apressyan said business ethics—a right way and a wrong way of doing business—was commonly regarded in Russia as a luxury for rich countries. He noted that in 1993 a handful of Russian *biznesmen* formed a round table, a club, devoted to sharing knowledge and helping to promote the spread of good business practices in Russia. In 1995, they adopted a "Charter of Russian Business" that presented an elementary ethical code. The *biznesmen* who signed it said they rejected and condemned "violence and fraud in competition, collaboration with criminals, and engagement in or the support of 'laundering' dirty money." They vowed to promote the "maintenance of law in the sphere of business." Nothing much ever came of the charter, Apressyan noted, because it was so widely criticized both in business circles and in the news media. It was viewed as too impractical, too pie-in-the-sky for Russia. "Critics were concerned about its purely ethical character," Apressyan said.

Robert Greco became an entrepreneur in the third grade. He helped one of his brothers, Thom, make chocolate-covered pretzels, then sell them at school for 39 cents a bag—a roughly 300 percent profit. They were part of a large, noisy, happy family of overachievers—two daughters, four sons—who grew up in Drums, Pennsylvania, near Wilkes-Barre. Robert was the youngest, the baby of the family. Four of his older siblings went into some aspect of medicine, and young Robert expected to become a doctor. But he was intrigued by his brother Thom's many entertainment-related business ventures, and he began launching his own businesses while still in grade school. By seventh grade he was promoting dances for high school kids. By age fifteen he had his own teen nightclub, Robby Greco's Rock Palace. He was a good student and a jock in high school—basketball, track, and wrestling. He was captain of the wrestling team and good enough to be invited to the Junior Olympics. At Kings College in Wilkes-Barre, he concentrated more on helping at his brother Thom's nightclubs than on his studies. While he never did drugs and rarely drank, he loved being part of the nightclub scene, everything from booking bands to doing advertisements to handling cash at the door. "Rob doesn't have much fun himself, but he provides the fun for everybody else," his friends said.

At the end of Greco's freshman year, he was put on academic probation. He lacked focus, but he knew he wanted to be in business and work for himself. Fine, his parents said. They didn't care what he studied. But they wanted him to apply himself and do his best. Before she went to medical school, his sister Joan had graduated from the Wharton School of Business at the University of Pennsylvania. She urged Robert to get away from the distractions of his brother's nightclubs in Wilkes-Barre. She thought Wharton and Philadelphia offered the kind of challenge he needed. That sounded good to Greco, but he didn't think he had a prayer of getting into a prestigious school like Wharton. His sister was friendly with the dean, however, and the dean agreed to admit Greco on probation. He would get only one chance. It turned out that was all Greco needed. He did well at Wharton. He still traveled to help at Thom's nightclubs back in Wilkes-Barre, but only on weekends and not every weekend. In 1985, at age twenty-one, during the spring of his senior year, while his classmates were interviewing with big corporations, Greco was making trips on his motorcycle back and forth to Wildwood, New Jersey, a touristy summer town on the Jersey shore. He still didn't want to work for anyone else.

After graduating, he rented a shop on the boardwalk and announced that he was in the T-shirt business. He had his T-shirt shop on the boardwalk for several summers, and it was better training for the world of international business than any of his courses at Wharton. The other merchants on the boardwalk were a United Nations of retailers: Indians, Israelis, Koreans, Chinese, all with their individual ways of doing things, yet with a common interest. He got to test out many of the Wharton theories, and he developed his own views on inventory, pricing, supply and demand, marketing, and managing money and people. One important lesson was that Wharton had been wrong about underfinancing. It *was* possible to build up a business without much money in the beginning, but only with great difficulty, risk, and hard work. Starting with a few thousand dollars of his own savings and a line of credit arranged by his father—the total he brought in was less than half what his Wharton textbook models said was needed for the size business he was doing—Greco worked intensely. He quickly began making good money. The selling season was essentially two months, July and August. In a typical year on the Wildwood boardwalk, Greco took home $30,000 to $40,000 after taxes. He spent the rest of the year working with brother Thom in nightclubs and concert promotions in Pennsylvania. Life was good. He bought a Porsche and some real estate. But he wanted more. He needed a long-range goal. He decided to go to law school.

He took the LSAT and was admitted to Duquesne University Law School for the autumn of 1994. With a few months to kill before law school, he put his Harley on a trailer, hitched it to the back of his Cadillac, and drove from Pennsylvania down to Georgia to visit his brother Richard, a plastic surgeon

154 / Moscow Madness

in Savannah. Robert spent a couple of weeks exploring the South on his bike, using Richard's place as a base. In the evenings the two brothers talked often about business. Robert asked about Richard's investment—not a lot of money, but enough to pay attention to—in a small startup that distributed Miller beer in Moscow. Richard Greco, who had met Rick Grajirena through Ron Finger, another Savannah surgeon who was a yachtie, knew that Robert was fascinated with his investment. Every time they got together, Robert would ask about the company and what Richard thought his original investment was worth. On this trip Richard told Robert he thought his investment was worth perhaps four times what he had invested. But he also told Robert that First Republic was having its difficulties with Miller, and with middle management. He said that Grajirena was firing Misha, the Russian general manager, and was looking for an American to go over and head up the Moscow operation. Richard told Robert that Grajirena was looking for some young guy who was more of an entrepreneur than a corporate type, more of a solve-the-problem guy than a go-by-the-book guy. He was looking for someone who knew the beer business or could learn it. International experience could be a plus but wasn't necessary, because doing business in Russia was so different from the usual international experience for most American businesspeople working abroad. Flexibility and aggressiveness were tantamount. Personality was more important than experience. It could be a great opportunity for some young guy, Richard told his brother. Richard suggested that his brother go down to Tampa and see Grajirena. If it didn't work out, all he had wasted was a day of vacation. If it did work out, well, law school would always be there. An opportunity like this wouldn't. At about the same time, Richard Greco's surgeon friend, Ron Finger, the one who introduced him to Grajirena in the first place, called Grajirena and said perhaps First Republic should talk to Richard Greco about his brother. Finger had met Robert, been impressed by him, and thought perhaps he could be a candidate to run the Moscow operation. The day after that, Grajirena got a call from Richard Greco saying his brother wanted to talk about the job. Grajirena invited Robert Greco to come to Tampa, and a couple of days later Robert put on a suit and pointed the Cadillac farther south.

Robert Greco and Rick Grajirena liked each other immediately. They could talk. By the time they shook hands and sat down with a cup of coffee, both men had loosened their ties. Looking at Rick Grajirena, Greco saw a graying middle-aged athlete, a man with a quick smile and an eagerness to embrace new ideas, whether his or someone else's. He saw a man who was passionate about what he was doing, a man who was a natural optimist. Looking at Robert Greco, Grajirena saw a short, stocky young man with curly brown hair pulled into a neat ponytail. He was well-mannered and soft-spoken, and he had a serious demeanor. He was a listener and thought before he spoke. The two men told each other their life stories. Grajirena also told Greco the story of First Republic. Greco was impressed with all the headaches Grajirena had, but he was also impressed with Grajirena's unflagging faith in the company. Grajirena told Greco about all the people who had not worked out for First Republic in the company's brief history, and why. He talked a lot about culture shock, and how Moscow Madness affects Americans. He talked about the business culture, or lack of one, in Russia. He talked about doing business in a climate where no rule of law underpins the entire structure, where ethics and morality have different definitions—or constantly changing definitions. He told Greco that the company was bleeding money, that the investors were on his back, and that the Moscow staff morale was so low that he and Harken had sent an open letter to be read aloud to the entire office. In the letter they tried to dampen the growing resentment from Moscow, where staffers openly complained about "their" hard-earned revenues being siphoned off to fat-cat investors back in the States. The three-page letter told how no one, least of all the investors, had made any money from First Republic. It also said that while the Moscow office had wired $120,000 back to Tampa between April and August 1994, the Tampa office during that same period had paid out nearly $360,000, including more than $250,000 to buy beer and more than $60,000 sent to Moscow to pay salaries and rents. Grajirena painted as grim a picture for Greco as he could. Yet he could not hide his enthusiasm for First Republic, and for the opportunities to make money in Russia.

Greco talked about how Russia and China loomed as the big potential golden frontiers of business for American entrepreneurs in the twenty-first century. His only real international experience, he said, was when he was ten and his parents had arranged an extended-family tour of Europe: fifteen people in a forty-five-person bus for three weeks, traveling from country to country seeing the sights. The Greco Grand Tour. He talked about how he had gone to Wharton not to end up in a corporate job but to learn what he needed to learn about business to become a successful entrepreneur. He talked about how he had never worked for anyone else and was afraid that he might disappoint any employer who expected him to be what he called a "corporate" kind of employee, writing memos and making presentations and working through committees to get things done. Greco said he preferred to work out problems himself. He didn't want supervisors second-guessing him or micromanaging him. He wanted the responsibility, and at the end of the day he wanted the credit—or blame—to be his. He wanted to be trusted.

Many of First Republic's problems had grown out of Grajirena's trust for people whom he shouldn't have trusted. Now he found himself trusting Robert Greco. Why? He didn't know. The board of directors of First Republic would probably hate this young guy and his ponytail. The board was looking for experience, for discipline, for someone who was accountable, for someone who was responsible, for someone who would file reports and take recommendations, and for someone who would protect their investments above all else. Robert Greco did not appear to be that type of person. Greco and Grajirena spent a day together in Tampa, and Grajirena asked him to stay over and talk more the next day. Grajirena knew that he would draw the ire of some board members and investors if he hired a new general manager without first presenting him before a board meeting. But if he did that, Greco probably wouldn't be hired. Grajirena would be staking the company's future, indeed his own future, on this young guy he just met.

They had dinner, and Greco went off to a hotel. Grajirena went home and talked it over with Valerie for hours. Then he got up before dawn the next day to sit alone in his kitchen and think about it some more. When they got together that day, Grajirena offered Greco the job in Moscow. On paper, it wasn't much of a job: $25,000 a year, and one share of First Republic, ostensibly worth $21,000. It was less money than Greco made selling T-shirts for a couple of months on the boardwalk in Wildwood. There was also a vague promise of a raise later and maybe points in the company—if things worked out. Grajirena suggested that Greco go to Moscow for a few weeks, see how things went, and then both sides would decide if they wanted to continue. There were no handcuffs, there was no parachute. If he had checked with them first, Greco's professors at Wharton no doubt would have disapproved of a deal like that. The same with Grajirena and his board of directors. Indeed, when he told them about it, several major investors objected. Why hadn't they been consulted? What were this Greco kid's qualifications? To some of them, it was yet another example of Grajirena's mismanagement, putting First Republic—and their money—at risk. A few investors, however, shrugged and said maybe, just maybe, this young guy was what First Republic needed. Certainly nothing else was working. And there was no way that First Republic could ever attract the kind of manager that some of the investors wanted: a high-powered American with lots of Russian experience. At that point nobody had lots of Russian experience. And any high-powered candidates with international experience had been snapped up long ago by much bigger companies for much bigger salaries. In a market where experienced people could pretty much name their terms with the multinationals, a shaky little company such as First Republic held no great attraction.

Robert Greco called Duquesne Law School to postpone his admission and spent several weeks learning as much about Russia as he could. Even when he got on the plane to fly to Moscow for the first time, however, he didn't know what to expect. He thought he might see people picking potatoes in the fields. He thought he might find a totally broken political and economic system, with poverty everywhere. At Sheremetevo airport, the plane bounced down hard. Greco looked out the window and saw potholes, real potholes, in the runway. It took an hour to get his two bags. He had committed to a four-month tryout. If he was going to stay, he would go back to the States and get the rest of his things. It took another hour to clear customs and immigration. Greco, not used to jet lag, was exhausted. He felt disoriented. It was late autumn, gray and dark. In the taxi from the airport, he strained out the window to see as much as he could. There was little color. There seemed to be a lot of construction under way, but much of it had been abandoned. The infrastructure seemed to be crumbling. At one point, on the approach to a bridge, traffic slowed down. The taxi carefully made its way around a gaping hole in the bridge roadway. There was a forty-foot drop.

Closer to the center of the city, he saw some signs of life and color. There were a few billboards, mostly for big international corporations and their consumer products. But there didn't seem to be anywhere to actually buy the soda pop or cell phones or sweaters in the ads. Grajirena took Greco straight from the airport to the First Republic office and introduced him to the staff. Greco shook hands stiffly with Viktor Potapov, the old sailing buddy of Grajirena who was the "caretaker" general manager until Grajirena found someone else. Grajirena explained to the staff that Greco was there to look and listen and learn and, for now, to act as Potapov's deputy. Grajirena did not say anything about Greco's future role. He had to wait to see how Greco fit in and whether Greco wanted the job. And he had to wait to see how Greco would be affected by Moscow Madness.

By the time Robert Greco arrived in Moscow, he had a clear, if grim, view of how First Republic was doing. Figures for the first nine months of 1994, through September, showed that the Moscow office had bought just over $600,000 of beer and sold it for about $900,000—a gross profit of nearly

$300,000. But the company had spent $1.4 million, for a net loss of more than $500,000. That did not include nearly $200,000 the company was writing off for the frozen beer and currency-exchange losses. Besides the beer it had purchased, the company's expenditures included $320,000 for salaries and payroll taxes, nearly $100,000 for accounting and legal services, $85,000 for advertising and promotion, $83,000 for rents, $25,000 for telephone, and nearly $70,000 in travel and meals.

Greco started slowly and carefully in Moscow. No big or fast moves. Everything was so unfamiliar, so unfriendly, from the architecture to the people. For the first time in his life, he was unsure of himself. He was not in control. He was lonely. He was homesick. He also never considered going home. Life and work were difficult, but he was fascinated with how much he had to learn, and what possibilities Russia held for someone like himself, someone who was willing to make commitments and take chances. But he wanted to be careful before he plunged in. He didn't try to tell anyone what to do. He didn't say, "This is how we do it back in the States." He tried to watch and learn. He moved into one bedroom of the company apartment. The other room was used by First Republic visitors from Tampa—most often Grajirena or Ellen, the controller. The apartment had nice polished parquet floors, but there was not much else to redeem it. The furniture was large and heavy and uncomfortable. The heat would come on in occasional blasts, but otherwise the apartment was usually cold. He got used to taking cold showers since there was almost never any hot water. The refrigerator often didn't work. His bed was so old and creaky that if he rolled over in the night, the noise would wake him up. It took him weeks to get rid of all the roaches in the kitchen. He consoled himself by thinking that this must have been the way his parents were raised during the Great Depression, minus the roaches.

He spent nearly all his time at work. When he wasn't in the office, he would wander the snowy streets in his boots, peering into windows, making mental notes on what he saw in the shops. If he saw something he thought he could take home to eat, he went in and bought it. Mostly it was just cheese, bread, and milk. He couldn't believe that to buy something, customers went to the cashier, announced what they wanted to buy, paid for their prospective purchase with the exact change, got a receipt from the cashier, took the receipt to the respective display area, and exchanged the receipt for the purchase. Sometimes a guard at the door would have to match up the receipts with the purchases before customers could leave. Even in an uncrowded shop, it could take twenty minutes and dealings with four or five different people to buy toothpaste and a comb. Greco often sat alone in the cold little apartment, eating his cheese and bread and wondering, "What am I doing here?" He would try to psych himself up, telling himself this was a great opportunity, a learning experience, a test of his ability, of his entrepreneurial flair. He was afraid sometimes, but not physically fearful. His only real fear was that he might fail.

It was obvious to Greco that Viktor Potapov didn't want to be considered a caretaker. Potapov liked his dollar salary, his big office, his nice title, and his perks. But he was not a businessman, even in the old Soviet sense. He didn't speak much English, and even the Americans in the office who spoke fluent Russian were often not quite sure what he meant or what he was talking about. One of his big decisions was that new hangers were needed in the closet in the conference room, and he spent an inordinate amount of time deciding what kind of hangers. Guests who come to see him should be able to hang their coats up on good hangers, he decreed. When friends and acquaintances heard about his new job, they asked him for free beer. Sometimes he tried to accommodate. Sometimes Grajirena stepped in and turned down the giveaways, but sometimes he wasn't around, such as the time Potapov made a commitment to provide free beer for his health club. At one point Potapov inquired whether First Republic could afford to buy him an apartment for $100,000. The Americans in the office were incredulous. "If we had that kind of money," one wondered, "wouldn't it occur to him that we might want to buy some beer with it?" The Americans in the office tried to keep Grajirena informed, but if Potapov issued an order, what could they do? He was the boss. "He's a good man, but he's clueless," Greco told Grajirena. "He's getting paid a good salary for not doing much. Giving product to his friends may not seem like a big deal, but for a small company that's struggling, it is a big deal."

Three weeks after he arrived in Moscow, Greco told Grajirena he would commit for a year and was ready to take over. Grajirena agreed, then sat down with Potapov and told him that Greco was replacing him. Potapov seemed surprised and tried to tell Grajirena that he had been promised a pension, and that First Republic had promised to buy an apartment for him. They talked, they reviewed who had said what, they negotiated. In the end, Grajirena offered to fly Potapov to a regatta in Florida, put him in a hotel for a few days, and let him borrow a sailboat for the races. Potapov accepted, and that was his severance package. Potapov and Grajirena remained good friends.

Greco took over in November 1994. Morale at First Republic was terrible. The employees looked at him with suspicion. They had liked Misha but had been told he was not a good manager. They had been told to respect Viktor Potapov, but it was clear to them that he was not a manager. Now came this young American, with less Russian experience than any of them, with less experience in the beer business, who couldn't even speak Russian. There was little to suggest that he could turn around First Republic. "The company is operating in survival mode," Greco said in a pleading note to Grajirena. "We need immediate cash for product and operations."

Greco tried to hold things together until the company had more money to order more beer. To him, Moscow Madness was not just the stupid things Americans did in Russia. To him, Moscow Madness was the craziness of trying to do business in Russia at all. "Business should make sense," he told his family back home. "Things just don't make sense in Moscow." For example, he came in one day, and the office phones would not work. First Republic's landlord, the institute that owned the building, had not paid its phone bill. So the phones to the entire building were cut off, even though First Republic had paid its bill. Greco tried to set himself up as an island of sanity amid the madness. After an argument with Chris Mitchell, the senior American on the staff and the sales manager, he began to earn the staff's respect and trust. In many ways Mitchell set the tone for Greco's relations with the rest of the staff. Greco told Mitchell that the shortage of beer from Miller was hurting some of First Republic's customers as much as it was hurting First Republic. Think about supply and demand, he urged. The big hotels knew how tough it was for First Republic to get Miller beer in, he said, so they would be willing to pay more for it. When supply was down and demand went up, so did prices. Greco didn't need a Wharton education to teach him that.

Mitchell disagreed, vehemently. He had good relationships with the hotels. He had always charged them 95 cents a bottle, and he didn't want to charge more because that would harm the long-term relationship. He insisted that they would never pay more. With Mitchell sitting in front of him, Greco picked up the phone, dialed the number of the beverage manager at one of the biggest hotels, and said, "Hi, this is Rob Greco from First Republic. Listen, I've got fifty cases of Miller Genuine Draft that just came in, but I'm afraid I have to charge a little more for it, $1.25 a bottle. That's okay? Great. When do you want it delivered? Good. We'll have it there tomorrow afternoon." He hung up the phone and looked at Mitchell. But he didn't say, "I told you so." Instead he talked about how they needed to work together, learn from each other, try new things, be aggressive, take chances. Some things might not work, but they had to try them, and they had to stick together and support each other. From that moment on, Chris Mitchell's trust and respect for Robert Greco grew.

CHAPTER 21

Winter 1994–95

First Republic's losses ended up totaling more than $1 million for 1994, and more than $2 million for its first two years of operation. In Moscow, Robert Greco tried to figure out what he needed to do to get into the black. The overhead was lower since the staff purge after the firing of Misha the previous summer, and Greco had cracked down on other expenses. But he couldn't make a profit without product to sell. He figured that First Republic needed to sell $150,000 worth of beer in Moscow each month to break even. In January 1995, sales totaled $62,000, barely half the $120,000 in sales for January 1993. In February 1995, sales were a mere $23,000—a decline of 85 percent from February the previous year. The company was in serious trouble. The cash flow became a trickle, which in turn meant that the company could not order enough beer from either Miller or Heineken to keep its accounts happy.

There was a glimmer of hope, however, in the form of a customs loophole. The Russian government, strapped for cash, had no money for worthwhile charities, foundations, and sports organizations. So it decided to grant import privileges to certain nonprofit organizations: the Afghan war disabled veterans' organization; the fund for the children who were victims of fallout from the Chernobyl nuclear accident; and various foundations supporting different sports. These organizations were granted exemptions that allowed them to import goods and products from abroad without paying the usual duties. These "customs privileges" not only allowed the nonprofit organizations to raise money but boosted imports that were in demand. Under the customs privileges, instead of paying up to $28,000 in duties for each container of beer, First Republic might pay a foundation half that, or less—it was negotiable—to bring in the beer under its customs privileges. Other companies importing to Russia, including some bringing in beer, made deals with charities and foundations to import as much of their products as they wanted, whenever they wanted. First Republic was slow to look for such an arrangement, perhaps because of the turmoil in management under Misha, then Potapov, then Greco; or perhaps First Republic did not have the cash to commit to enough large shipments to lock up a foundation or charity as a partner. Perhaps its failure to take quick advantage of the customs privileges was at least partly due to Grajirena's wariness of the loophole. There were reports of some *mafiya* groups putting themselves forward as qualified charities and foundations. They would bring products through customs, but through intimidation and bribery rather than through any legal privileges. And even among some of the legitimate charities and foundations, it was common knowledge that the *mafiya*, through violence or the threat of violence, had moved in and taken over the customs privileges. Customs privileges meant hard currency, and wherever there was hard currency in Russia, the *mafiya* was not far behind.

Grajirena didn't want First Republic to get unwittingly caught in a *mafiya* web. "Russian law being what it is, being certain that the methods and/or entity of the group clearing our goods is totally legal may not be possible," Grajirena noted in a memo. So instead of finding a charity or foundation to import all its beer all the time, First Republic tried to make deals on a shipment-by-shipment basis. But all too often First Republic would order beer, then not be able to find a charity or foundation that had slots available for the beer. "We can import your shipment under our privileges," they would tell First Republic. "But we cannot do it until three months from now." Arranging the import privileges in advance did not work any better. First Republic would line up slots for shipment, but all too often Miller or Heineken would say it could not get beer to Moscow at that time. Chris Mitchell complained to Grajirena that at one point he had secured a good sale to a new account, one of the big hotels. The hotel placed an order, paid for it within two days, and then reordered four days after that. Mitchell said the hotel looked like it would be an eight-hundred-case-a-month account, which would make it one of First Republic's best customers. But when he couldn't fill two orders in a row because First Republic had no beer, the hotel dropped Miller and looked elsewhere for its beer.

When he arrived on the scene, Robert Greco quickly realized that First Republic needed a reliable, ongoing relationship with someone—legal or not—who could clear beer through customs. Greco was impatient with

First Republic's insistence on doing business the American way, the "theoretical" way that it should be conducted. In a note to the board of directors he wrote: "The practical approach is to recognize that First Republic Moscow is a foreign-owned company. We are not in the loop. Secondly, we need to realize that to move forward profitably, a new set of rules have to be followed. We need to become part of the influence establishing the agenda rather than the victims of it. . . . I believe we should all wake up to the realities of the way business is presently done in Russia." Grajirena gave Greco the go-ahead to try to find someone to bring in First Republic's beer—with the caution that he do whatever he could to make sure the foundation or charity was legitimate and not connected to the *mafiya*. Greco talked to fourteen different charities and foundations, but actually ended up finding a partner in a more circuitous way. A container of Heineken beer shipped in by First Republic was misdelivered to the federation overseeing the Russian ice hockey program. Hockey was one of the sports known to be plagued by the *mafiya*, which reputedly used threats to extort large sums of hard currency from Russian athletes in the National Hockey League. When the beer was misdelivered, the ice hockey federation paid the customs bill and accepted delivery. The customs inspectors said they were sorry if there was a mistake, but there was nothing they could do about it. Legally the beer now belonged to the ice hockey federation. It said so right there on the official customs paperwork. The inspectors said all Greco could do was take his own paperwork to the ice hockey federation and try to get the beer back.

It was a daunting assignment for someone who had been in Moscow only a few weeks and still spoke only a few words of Russian. But Greco made an appointment and took along one of First Republic's best interpreters. He was ushered into the large, plush office of one of the federation's executives and made his pitch. He told the interpreter to keep the tone humble. "Thank you for seeing me," Greco began. "I know you are very busy. But I have a problem that only you can help with. There has been a mistake, a complication, some confusion. I need your favor, your understanding, your assistance. This was strictly a paperwork foul-up. It wasn't our fault, it wasn't your fault. Somehow our container of beer was shuffled in with your shipments. I hope we can straighten this out." Greco half-expected to be thrown out of the office. He wasn't. The executive at the ice hockey federation seemed to like him. He seemed to think Greco was a young guy who was out to make a buck but was willing to play by the rules as they existed in Moscow. Greco said he could appreciate that the ice hockey federation must have incurred some unexpected expense in taking delivery of a shipment of beer it had not ordered. Certainly, Greco said, he would compensate the executive for his federation's time and trouble. It was only fair. And if possible, Greco added, he would be eager to do business with the ice hockey federation in the future. Perhaps the federation could extend its customs privileges to First Republic on a regular basis. For a modest payoff to the executive—for the federation's "expenses"—Greco got the beer back. He also got First Republic into a reliable relationship with the federation that allowed the company to import beer for less than $10,000 per container, barely a third of the official cost.

––––––––

In theory First Republic could import as much beer as it could sell through the ice hockey federation. In practice it could not afford to import much beer. The company simply did not have the cash flow. The biggest problem was the seven containers of Miller beer in Riga that Misha was supposed to get into Russia months earlier, before the tax laws changed in mid-1994. Those seven containers of beer arrived at the docks in Riga in May, and Misha had promised for weeks that they would clear customs before the rules changed on July 1. But he never raised enough cash to pay the $8,000 per container that the customs inspectors were demanding. Then the customs officials started demanding storage fees for the containers. At first they said they wanted $1,000. Sometimes they wanted $1,000 per week. Sometimes it was $1,000 per container per week. The demand kept changing. Week after week, through the summer of 1994, Misha kept telling Grajirena that he was about to work something out with the customs inspectors and the containers were about to be delivered to Moscow. They never were. When Misha was fired in August, the beer was still there. Viktor Potapov was unable to get them in. The weeks turned into months, and the inspectors' demands kept adding up. The investors back in the States could not believe that Grajirena was allowing so much inventory and so much capital—First Republic already had paid Miller more than $80,000 for the beer—to be tied up. By the autumn, depending on which inspector in Riga was talking to First Republic, the duties on the beer added up to more than the beer was worth.

In Moscow, Robert Greco believed he could easily sell a dozen containers a month, and maybe more. But until he got those containers to Moscow and began selling them, he would have no money to buy more beer. He couldn't get the beer off the docks, either. Not by any legal means, anyway. He checked with the ice hockey federation, which said it could not help with beer that had arrived before its customs privileges went into effect. Greco said he could try some other group offering cut-rate customs clearance, but Grajirena was still wary of *mafiya* involvement. He continued to insist that First Republic should not knowingly break any Russian laws—nor commit any violation of the U.S. Federal Corrupt Practices Act. His reasoning was that even if the company got away with successfully bribing enough Russian officials to avoid prosecution there, he could still end up in Allentown or some other federal white-collar prison. And, he conceded privately, he was concerned that knowingly violating any law or business ethic would open him up to a lawsuit by First Republic investors. In a note to the board, Grajirena wrote: "We were led to believe that there are 'legal' methods to bring product through customs at a reduced rate. This is not entirely correct. Many of these groups that claim immunity from customs laws simply do not have this right. Through their contacts in the government and in customs they have the ability to bring product through at reduced rates while the officials 'wink and nod' and certainly share in the revenues." He sent a note to an attorney consulting for First Republic, asking for an opinion. Grajirena wanted to know whether he or the company would be violating U.S. law by paying a lump sum to have beer brought through customs if he knew that some of the money was "probably" going to bribes. The attorney never replied.

Nonetheless, Grajirena was convinced there must be some way to get the beer off the docks. He couldn't just walk away from that much inventory. The First Republic controller, Ellen, had been spending a lot of time during her trips to Moscow in casinos—more time than Grajirena thought was healthy, either for the company or for her personally. But one day she came into the First Republic office with a suggestion. She had met two men in a casino who seemed to be well-connected *biznesmen*. They had some ideas about how to get the beer off the docks in Riga. Grajirena was willing to listen to anything. He told her to hear them out. She came back and said that the two men, known only to the people at First Republic as Shakespeare and Palmi, knew people who knew people who could get the duties reduced—legally. They promised that what they wanted to do might be outside the law, but it would not be against the law. Extralegal, rather than illegal. Fair enough, Grajirena said. That was the way a lot of business was done in Russia, where the laws often lagged behind what businesspeople wanted or needed to do.

There was no doubt that Shakespeare and Palmi were mysterious, shadowy figures. Shakespeare was an Israeli citizen of Russian descent. No one at First Republic knew what he did for a living. No one at First Republic ever determined Palmi's nationality or his line of work. But no matter. Shakespeare and Palmi promised that they could get all seven containers in for $30,000—a real bargain, by Grajirena's measure, especially since the customs inspectors were asking for four to six times that. Shakespeare and Palmi wanted the money up front. Grajirena was reluctant but felt he had no choice. He authorized the $30,000 payment. For weeks Shakespeare and Palmi, through Ellen, kept telling First Republic that they were about to get the seven containers of beer off the docks. Time after time nothing happened. Finally, two months after he paid them the money, Grajirena said he wanted to meet Shakespeare and Palmi face to face. They met in one of the Westernized hotels. They sat down in a small arrangement of chairs and a sofa near the bar. But before they could order drinks, Grajirena got down to business. What were they doing to get the beer in, and when were they going to do it? If he wasn't satisfied, he wanted First Republic's money back.

Shakespeare and Palmi were uneasy. Taking turns, they explained how one plan after another had failed, how one contact after another led to a dead end. But now they had a plan that was almost sure to work. It was a little risky, but it would work. They told Grajirena to pay the money the tax inspectors were demanding, which was by then more than $120,000. They said that when First Republic's drivers were trucking the beer to Moscow, they—Shakespeare and Palmi—would arrange to have the entire shipment hijacked. First Republic could then collect on its insurance policy for the value of the beer. Shakespeare and Palmi, meanwhile, would hide the beer for a while, and then deliver it to the First Republic warehouse. The sale of the beer would offset the duties that First Republic had paid. It wasn't a perfect plan, they conceded, but it would get the beer off the docks and get First Republic back into a better cash-flow position. "You guys are nuts," Grajirena said. "We're not going to do that. It's crazy. We'd all end up in jail. Fraud. Tax cheating. Hijacking. Forget about it. You guys are finished. Give us our money back."

To Grajirena's relief, Shakespeare and Palmi actually gave back most of the money, more than $20,000. He had been afraid it was all lost. He decided they were amateurs, would-be high rollers who wanted to be *mafiya* but weren't. That was not the case with another offer to help get the beer off the docks in Riga. Grajirena met an American of Russian descent in Florida, and the man was interested in knowing everything about First Republic. Grajirena for a time thought the man might be interested in investing. Instead, the man came back to Grajirena and said his Russian cousin who still lived in Moscow wanted to meet Grajirena the next time he visited the First Republic operation there. Grajirena said sure and gave the man the dates of his next trip. A few days into that trip, a shiny red BMW pulled up in front of the First Republic office. A very large and very tough-looking guy got out, displaying all the trappings of a *mafiya* henchman: black jeans, Italian sweater, short crew cut, gold chains around his neck, and cashmere sports jacket with a bulge that could have been a gun or a cell phone or both. He pushed his way into the office, stood in front of the receptionist, and announced that he was here to take Rick Grajirena to see his boss.

He gave his boss's name. The receptionist's eyes opened wide. She had heard of the boss. He was one of Moscow's most notorious *mafiya* figures. A couple of First Republic's Russian salesmen heard the bodyguard give his boss's name, too. They retreated into a back room. The receptionist found Grajirena working in the conference room. He knew the name, too. It was the cousin of the man he met in Florida.

Despite the receptionist's misgivings, Grajirena grabbed his coat and followed the driver out to the red BMW. There was no one else in the car. The driver never spoke during the harrowing ride across Moscow into one of the quieter areas of town, away from the center. When they stopped in a small parking lot, the driver grunted and motioned for Grajirena to follow him. They walked through a pretty little garden and into a small mansion. In the marble entry hall was a pool in which swam dozens of fat decorative carp. Grajirena had never seen anything like it in Moscow. It was a private club with six dining rooms.

In one of the rooms sat Nicky. He was finishing what obviously had been an elaborate and expensive late lunch. Caviar. Steak. Lobster. Champagne— the real stuff, from France. Wine and liquor glasses covered the table. Someone had been dining with Nicky but had departed, probably as Grajirena was walking in the front door. Grajirena was invited to sit down and was offered lunch. Just coffee, he said. Cognac? No, he said, just coffee. The two men chatted a bit about Nicky's Florida cousin, about the weather in Tampa and Moscow, and about the nice garden outside the club. "I am told you are having problems with your business," Nicky said finally. "I would like to be able to help you if I can. Please tell me about your problems." Grajirena told him about the seven containers of beer stuck in Riga for months, and about the $65,000 worth of beer that Misha had lost in the deal with Slade.

Nicky listened intently, nodding but not interrupting. He looked like a movie star, a clean-cut young guy, in his early thirties. His hair, his cashmere sports coat, his turtleneck sweater, his manicure—everything was perfect. If not a movie star, at least he looked like a rich yuppie banker or broker from

New York. He certainly didn't fit Grajirena's notion of a gangster from Moscow.

Nicky spoke good English. "I think we can do a lot of business together in the future," Nicky said. "I think we can help each other. We can be partners. But first, as a show of good faith, let me get your money back from Slade. I will do this for 30 percent of whatever I recover." Grajirena asked Nicky not to do anything yet. He said he needed to think about it. Nicky asked Grajirena to also think about selling him cigarettes. He knew First Republic had a duty-free warehouse in Tampa, and that the company sold cigarettes to cruise ships. He suggested that First Republic sell him three or four containers of cigarettes—to start. Nicky said that First Republic could arrange for the cigarettes to be transshipped somewhere else—anywhere else—as long as they were routed through Moscow, but not for ultimate delivery to Moscow. "The manifest must not say Moscow," he said. When the shipment of cigarettes made their supposedly temporary stop in Moscow, his people would arrange for "taking delivery," as he called it. If this first trial shipment went well, he said, First Republic could count on selling him five to ten containers more—every month. Grajirena asked Nicky to let him think about that, too.

Grajirena was driven back to the First Republic office. He got on the phone and started calling American expatriates in Moscow who knew more about the *mafiya* than he did, including one man who was a security specialist for a major U.S. corporation. "Do not get involved with this guy in any way," the security specialist warned. "Yes, he can get you your money back. But the guys he gets it back from won't like it. They won't come after him. And they won't come after you. But none of your employees in Moscow will be safe. Something will happen to one of them."

———

Grajirena wanted no part of this. He telephoned Nicky immediately. He thanked Nicky but said he wanted to hold off on both of Nicky's offers. He said First Republic still had hopes of getting its money back from Slade on its own—which wasn't true—and didn't want Nicky's help. He also said that First Republic did not deal in the volume of cigarettes that Nicky was looking for—which was true. First Republic typically ordered three or four pallets of cigarettes at a time, not three or four containers. And they were never shipped out of Tampa. If he suddenly ordered cigarettes in that kind of volume and started shipping them elsewhere, customs officials would be watching him like a hawk. He was sorry, Grajirena told Nicky. Maybe they could do business in the future. But not right now. No problem, Nicky said. He promised to make no further inquiries regarding Misha and the beer. He wished Grajirena luck and urged him to get in touch if he had any other problems. Grajirena had plenty of other problems. But he didn't want Nicky's kind of help.

CHAPTER 22

Out of Business

O ver the winter of 1994–95 and into the spring, the turmoil deepened at First Republic. The duty-free operation in Tampa was being sold off. In the last few months, the CFO had quit. The corporate attorney had quit. The company was on its fourth Moscow general manager in less than a year. Several other key personnel in Moscow, including a sharp young Englishman who ran the computer operations, also had quit. The company controller, Ellen, was breaking up with her husband in Tampa and wanted to move to Moscow for a fresh start. Grajirena said the company could not afford to post her to Moscow. She lobbied board members and investors to have First Republic send her there. She suggested to Moscow staffers that she could run the Moscow office better than Greco. Indeed, she as much as told Greco that on her many trips to Moscow. She was ostensibly there to look over the books, but he often went in and found her in his office, looking over papers on his desk and suggesting things that he should be doing differently, or that she would do if she was the general manager. He tried to be patient but finally found her sitting in his chair one time too many. "Someday you might have this job," Greco told her. "But right now that's still my chair and this is still my office. Get out." When it became clear that First Republic was not going to send her to Moscow, and that she was not going to replace Greco anytime soon, Ellen resigned and took a job with the Moscow office of one of the big U.S. accounting firms.

Back in the States, First Republic's investors were unhappier than ever. What had happened to their shiny little company? Some investors were unhappy that Grajirena had hired Greco. When Greco made a deal to import sausages to Moscow, a number of investors telephoned or faxed Grajirena: What are we doing selling sausages? Aren't we supposed to be in the beer business? Grajirena told board members that he supported Greco and thought it was a good idea to look for alternative products, maybe products that weren't as difficult to get through customs. Yes, he told them, First Republic was still in the beer business, but if it didn't have enough beer to sell, he liked Greco's idea of finding other products to run through the company's distribution pipeline. The simple fact was that Greco had spent none of the company's money on sausages. He had talked a German sausage manufacturer into giving him the first shipment on credit. He sold them within two days, repaid the sausage manufacturer, and made a small profit for First Republic. Nonetheless, some investors in Wisconsin saw it as an example of Grajirena letting the company get away from him. Grajirena was instructed to tell Greco not to sell any more sausages. Greco was in the process of negotiating a deal for First Republic to distribute Planters Peanuts in Moscow, and he was ordered to drop that, too.

One major investor, knowing that Grajirena had repeatedly said he would never move to Moscow, insisted that Greco be fired and that Grajirena either move to Moscow or resign. Grajirena estimated that he was spending nearly half of his time dealing with the board of directors and other investors instead of managing the company. One board member was particularly nettlesome. He made no secret of the fact that he wanted Grajirena out of the company. Grajirena had begun faxing board members periodic updates, always upon returning from a Moscow trip and often more frequently, to keep them informed. He hoped the updates would forestall calls asking for personalized, one-on-one debriefings and progress reports. That board member, who had never even been to Russia, began faxing fellow board members "rebuttals" to Grajirena's reports. That board member asked Grajirena for all the details of the frozen beer debacle, and Grajirena felt obliged to put together a report for him. Some of the board members still held out hope of a settlement—any kind of settlement—from Miller for the frozen beer, but the minutes of a First Republic board meeting noted, "Attorneys for Miller have not returned phone calls and are unreachable." A board member demanded to know, dollar for dollar, how the money he put into the company had been spent. Grajirena put together a memo itemizing, dollar for dollar, where the money had gone. An investor asked for an accounting of every dollar that First Republic had spent the previous week. Grajirena gave him a list of expenditures for the week. "I'm either answering questions or preparing for meetings or actually in meetings," Grajirena complained to Peter Harken. Grajirena recognized that Harken, the unofficial leader of the

Wisconsin investors since he had brought many of them to First Republic, was torn between his loyalty to his old sailing buddy and his responsibility to his friends who put up their money on his recommendation. Grajirena appreciated the way Harken stuck by him for so long, but he sensed that even Harken was getting frustrated with First Republic's mounting problems: management turnover, cash flow, customs, beer stuck on docks, and most of all the apparent inability to make any money.

Rick Grajirena had an ironclad employment contract. First Republic couldn't fire him, not without paying him his salary, specified at a minimum of $80,000, for the next three years. But he sensed that the company might be able to move ahead more smoothly without him, if he were not such a target for disgruntled shareholders. First Republic needed a CEO who could concentrate on running the company instead of fending off attacks from investors and board members who wanted him out. He considered his choices. Staying and trying to do the job was becoming less and less of an option. He had to get out one way or another. He could walk away or ask for a buyout, but he thought that would be a waste of all the time and effort he had put into First Republic. Despite all the problems, in early 1995 he still believed the company was going to be successful in the long run. He made a proposal to the board of directors. He would resign as CEO and resign his position on the board. He would continue on with First Republic, but as a half-time marketing consultant. He would be paid $30,000 a year, and his sole responsibility would be to expand the business, both in finding new products to sell and in opening up new places to sell the products that First Republic carried. The board accepted his proposal, and Grajirena was replaced as CEO by Hilliard Eure, a respected accountant who was retired from the Tampa office of one of the leading U.S. management consulting firms.

First Republic's cash-flow problems were dire. The two Savannah plastic surgeons who had invested in First Republic—Grajirena's old sailing buddy Ron Finger and Robert Greco's elder brother Richard—made a proposal. They would put up a $1 million line of credit that would allow First Republic to place big orders and keep both its suppliers and its customers happy. In return, Finger and Richard Greco wanted to hold the Heineken import rights. They would grant the distribution rights to First Republic, which would pay Finger and Richard Greco a small premium for every case of Heineken. To Grajirena, it seemed like a win-win proposition. Finger and Richard Greco would get a return on their investment, and First Republic would get the money it needed to stay in business. There was a flurry of faxes and phone calls among the First Republic board members and other investors, but to no avail. "Robert Greco is using his brother and this other doctor to try to hijack the company," one investor told Grajirena. Grajirena retorted, "There won't be a company if we don't order some beer now." The board rejected the offer from the Savannah doctors.

Working mornings only out of the First Republic office in Tampa, in an office next to Hilliard Eure, who had succeeded him as CEO, Grajirena set about trying to shore up First Republic's existing business and find new business. His top priority was Heineken. First Republic was still doing business with Miller Brewing, but relations never really recovered from the dispute over the beer that froze on the docks in St. Petersburg more than a year earlier. But its relationship with Heineken was still good. Like Miller, Heineken required First Republic to make cash payments in advance. Heineken, however, indicated that it would offer favorable credit terms if, at the end of First Republic's one-year trial, the deal was extended and First Republic was granted the exclusive import rights for all of Russia. Heineken was concerned, however, that First Republic had not sold as much beer as anticipated. Grajirena, and everyone else connected with First Republic, knew that if the Heineken distribution agreement was not renewed, First Republic was probably down the tubes. As the end of the one-year trial approached in the spring of 1995, Heineken executives repeatedly asked First Republic for assurances that its business would increase. The Dutchmen were blunt. They said they were willing to offer credit to a distributor that could demonstrate its ability to grow—but not to a distributor so undercapitalized that any credit advances would be squandered. First Republic was undercapitalized. Unless something happened to change that, Heineken would find another distributor. A meeting between First Republic and Heineken executives was scheduled in Moscow for May 11, 1995.

Rick Grajirena could not sleep the night before. At 2:45 A.M. Moscow time, he called Valerie back in Clearwater. "I think this could be the end," he told her. He wrote in his diary that Heineken would be looking for First Republic to come into the meeting with a big order—he figured well into six figures, maybe as much as half a million dollars. First Republic didn't have that kind of money. Hilliard Eure, the new CEO, suggested to the First Republic board that a bankruptcy attorney should be a part of any considerations of the company's future. Eure was in a tough spot. First Republic's investors told him he had to retain the Heineken deal. But he was never given any assurance by those investors that enough money would be forthcoming. "The overriding issue,"

Grajirena wrote in his diary, "is that the Wisconsin group sent him over here without a clear mandate and no guarantee of funds for beer. I sense a real disaster tomorrow and it makes me sick. . . . I must say that I have never felt lower in my life. All the effort, all the friends investing, but more than anything the great opportunity lost. . . . I only hope I can get some sleep before tomorrow."

At the meeting Grajirena's worst fears were realized. The Heineken people said they were disappointed in First Republic. They said First Republic had been in a privileged position for a year but had failed to exploit it. Point-blank, they told Eure he needed to commit to ordering more beer, then and there. He could not do it. The Heineken executives left it this way: They would still consider First Republic if and when it came in with a big order for beer, but in the meantime Heineken would entertain offers from other potential Moscow distributors. If someone else came to Heineken with a more solid position than First Republic, Heineken would go with it. In effect, this was the death knell for First Republic. Grajirena and Eure flew back to the States and tried to talk First Republic's investors into putting up enough money to save the company. None of them wanted to do it. Instead, Eure was instructed to keep looking for new sources of money. A few days after returning from the disastrous meeting, Eure called the Heineken executives in Amsterdam to ask for a little more time for First Republic to come up with the money to place an order. Heineken told him it was too late. Another distributor had already placed an order.

Grajirena was still on the First Republic payroll as a half-time consultant, and he still came into the office every morning. But there wasn't much to do. No one in the company was talking to him. One morning not long after the disastrous trip to Moscow, Grajirena cleaned out most of his files and took them home. The next morning he came in and the lock on the office door had been changed. He couldn't get in. He went away and had a cup of coffee. When he returned, the secretary was there. "I'm sorry, Rick," she said. Grajirena and the secretary shared a morbid laugh over a bit of irony. A couple of days earlier she had told him she was afraid she was going to be laid off. She asked him, as a friend, to tell her as soon as he heard anything. It turned out that he got bounced before she did. He took his pictures off the wall and emptied the last stuff from his desk into a cardboard box. He went home. Later that day, Grajirena got a message from a lawyer who said he had been retained by First Republic to wind down the company. He said First Republic was broke and could pay neither Grajirena's salary nor his health benefits. Rick Grajirena was out of a job. Robert Greco resigned, and all the other employees who didn't quit first were fired. First Republic was out of business.

CHAPTER 23

Postmortem

Years after the collapse of First Republic, Rick Grajirena admitted he still didn't understand everything that had happened or why. He admitted that he probably never would come to grips with the company's failure, and he was still deeply conflicted about his own role. He felt like the company had been so close to lasting success so many times, but it just never managed to get over the hump. Sitting quietly one evening, in a reflective mood, sipping an expensive single-malt whisky and taking occasional puffs from a Cuban cigar, these were his thoughts:

What went wrong with First Republic? Well, I did a lot of things wrong. The biggest thing I did wrong was absentee management. That kind of business could not be run from the States. In hindsight, I should have hired someone else to run the company, someone over there to be in charge. But at the moment, so much happened so fast, and we needed to get things moving quickly. Having me run things from Tampa was the quickest way to get the company up and running.

In terms of what we did wrong, we were doing something that had never been done before. No one had ever set up a Western-style distribution company in Moscow. I was naive in thinking we could set up a company in Russia as a model of a U.S. company. You could probably do it today because things have changed so much. But not then. I was pretty naive in terms of thinking I could run or at least monitor the company from the States. Business is too different there. That's the real Moscow Madness. Crazy things happen. You can't rely on things in business making sense like they usually do in the States. Maybe my own personal Moscow Madness was in thinking I could overcome all the craziness of trying to do business in Russia. Other people went crazy or got drunk or became deal whores or had affairs or whatever. My Moscow Madness was that I thought we could build an American model for a distribution company and run it from the States.

But Moscow Madness within First Republic was also a big factor. Too many of the Americans who went over there didn't do the job for us. But it wasn't just the Americans. The Russians who worked for First Republic in Moscow sensed the weakness of absentee management and took advantage of it. I didn't have the kind of help I needed in setting up the controls necessary to make sure no one within the company took money. We needed to make sure none of the staff took company funds. But we never managed to have those kinds of controls. I always felt that the Russians—some of them, a few of them— were bleeding the company by stealing, but I could never prove it.

I put way too much trust in some people. It wasn't because I'm a bad manager of people. In the sailing business, I started with $5,000 and ended up with a company that did over a million dollars' worth of business a year and had thirty-some employees. My weaknesses weren't in managing people. My weakness was on the financial side, certainly. I thought we had people onboard who could compensate for it. But what could I do? Our first CFO was a successful accountant who was a big investor in the company. He was my partner. It would have been better to hire people instead of bringing in investors and plugging them into jobs in the company.

My frustration level with the people in Moscow was too high. I shouldn't have put up with so much. When I would ask that something get done, there always seemed to be a reason not to get it done. Here's an example that kind of sums it all up. The drivers would get back from finishing up their week's deliveries about six o'clock on Friday evening. I wanted to have the sales reports to me by Monday morning at the latest. With the eight-hour time difference, that meant the Moscow office had all day on Monday to put them together and send them so that they were on my desk first thing Florida time. But I never seemed to get them until Tuesday, sometimes Wednesday.

If we were going to be successful, if the heart of our business was going to be distributing beer in Moscow, we had to be there. If your warehouse is in Moscow, if your office, your customers are going to be in Moscow, then you have to be in Moscow, too.

Another problem was that from the beginning the company was run by committee. You can't do that. I didn't have the control to do everything a CEO ought to be able to do. Just to hire someone became a big issue. Board members wanted to interview Greco themselves before allowing me to hire him. I was told flat out not to hire him, but I did anyway. When you have the title of CEO but not the power to function as CEO, it doesn't foster respect. People within the company who wanted something began to go to board members to get what they wanted. Instead of just letting me do my job, board members and investors were constantly looking over my shoulder and second-guessing me.

In some respects I was a weak leader. The company's failure was my fault. I was treading in an area I had never been involved in. I was counting on other people for their input, for their help. I did a lot of things wrong, and some of what I did wrong was to leave too much to other people.

You know, though, that First Republic could have survived all that. Despite all those problems, the company was still such a strong idea, such a good concept. The distribution network—there was nothing wrong with it. It was the right idea at the right time, and we did it well. Possibly the biggest reason First Republic went under was that it was undercapitalized. We never had enough money to get going. We tried to set up a beer distributorship in Moscow with between $600,000 and $700,000 total investment. We needed four times that. If we had been able to order more beer in the beginning, if we had been able to get credit terms, we would have been able to survive bad breaks like the frozen beer and the collapsed warehouse. We would have been able to last out some of the customs problems. When we started, we didn't have a handle on the complexities of shipping beer into Russia. Everything cost more than we thought it would—a classic thing with small companies.

I am convinced that First Republic would have survived if we had started with Heineken instead of Miller. Heineken was a true international company. Miller treated us like we were a distributor in Moscow, Idaho, rather than Moscow, Russia. We wouldn't have had the frozen beer on the docks. And we wouldn't have had all the shipping and customs problems. The problems with Miller killed us.

From the very beginning of First Republic, my mission, my strength, was marketing. My prospectus got us the Miller deal. I had a lot to do with getting the Heineken deal for us. In the meantime, while

I was concentrating on marketing, which was what I thought the company really needed and what I was really good at, a lot of the other stuff
wasn't getting done. Like the corporate financial controls that were
never put in place. It just wore me out trying to do everything. I was so
tired by the end, by the spring of '95. I wasn't feeling well and went to
my doctor for my annual checkup. He was shocked. I had lost weight,
my blood pressure was up, I looked like I had aged five years in the last
twelve months. He said I was a textbook case of exhaustion, of burn-
out from stress. It was the best thing that ever happened to me when I
put my key in the lock that day and it wouldn't work. It was a relief. I
could start getting on with my life.

Grajirena went on to talk about the comparisons between his sailing
career and his business career. Not normally an introspective man, he
admitted that he had thought about the analogies. He had many successes
as a sailor. He won some big races, he was a world champion, he made it to
the Olympic trials four times, he was widely regarded as one of the best
yachtsmen in America. But he lost many more races than he won. Second or
third place or among the top finishers in a big race was a good performance,
but to him it was still a loss, a failure. He learned that it was possible to do
well—as well as possible—and still fail. He learned how important preparation was on land, before the race. He prided himself on his preparation.
Sometimes boats were built, rebuilt, or specially fitted out specifically to win
a certain race. There was rarely enough money or time to do everything he
wanted to do to a boat, so he learned to prioritize, to decide what he could
live without.

For any yacht racer, one of the most difficult tasks is putting together a
crew—especially for big ocean races when ten or eleven crew are needed.
Grajirena learned how to pick crew, how to ask them to do the things they
were best at, and not to ask them to do things that he could do better himself. He learned to satisfy egos to eke out maximum commitment and maximum effort by each crew member. His crews respected and trusted him.
With him they could win. Out on the water Grajirena loved the challenge of
the actual race, the tactics, responding to the challenges and opportunities
that arose. He learned to think six and seven steps ahead. What was the
wind going to do? How would shifts in the wind affect his boat? Other
boats? What were the other boats going to do? What strategies and tactics
would other captains pursue in this situation? How could he outmaneuver
them, out-think them? He learned to intuitively read the water, the wind,
the competition, his own crew, and himself. He had a knack for guessing

right, for envisioning what the weather and the competition would do. Yet no matter how well prepared he was, no matter how soundly his strategic and tactical decisions were thought out, no matter how well he and the crew executed, more often than not the unexpected intervened.

Putting First Republic together had been like preparing for a big yacht race: getting sponsors, building and fitting out the structure, finding crew. When the company was up and running, it was as if he was at the wheel, watching everything at once: the wind, the water, the crew, the competition, his own boat's performance. What went wrong with First Republic was comparable to the things that can go wrong in a yacht race. The wind shifted. A competitor tacked illegally in front of him, cut off his course, and forced him to change course. Crew members didn't act and react as he expected. Equipment failed. Any one of those things could be a disaster on the ocean. In Russia the equivalent of all those things, and more, happened to First Republic. "I've thought a lot about what happened," Grajirena said. "It was on my watch. There was no reason that company shouldn't have made it. But it turned out there were a lot of reasons, crazy reasons, unforeseen reasons, that it didn't. Moscow Madness. My greatest successes in sailing, in winning races, were due to preparation. In the big ocean races my greatest strength was in putting a crew together, in building a team. I thought that would carry over to First Republic. But it didn't. I didn't do a good job choosing the team. I let the team be chosen, to a certain extent, by other people, by partners, by investors. But it was their money, and I felt like they deserved a say. Losing control of that aspect of the company, picking the crew, meant we were never able to build the kind of team we needed."

Yes, Grajirena said, First Republic was a failure. But he had experienced failure many times before. Failure was an old sailing buddy. When he lost a race that he thought he could have or should have won, he learned from it. Each failure made him stronger. He prepared better the next time. He did not make the same mistakes again. Just because he lost a race did not mean he would not go to sea again. And just because First Republic failed did not mean he would not go to Russia again.

PART 2

HANGOVER HELPERS

[Hangover Helpers]

CHAPTER 24

ORCA

It was not quite two o'clock in the afternoon, but dusk seemed to be settling on Moscow, which is as far north as Hudson's Bay. It was a dark, gloomy midwinter afternoon. That morning's dusting of snow had already turned into an ugly brown slush on top of the previous day's grimy black slush. Nobody was in a good mood, including Rick Grajirena's driver. He was a driver from the Radisson Slavjanskaya, the hotel where Grajirena had been staying regularly for years, so he was a cut above the typical crazy Russian taxi driver. The car was a late-model Mercedes. The driver was clean-shaven and wore a tie beneath a dark V-neck sweater. But he was still a Russian, and he was still muttering about who knows what during the entire drive from the hotel to the government institute where Grajirena had a big meeting.

Grajirena had been out of the beer business for years. With a handful of notable exceptions—including a couple of Americans still working in Moscow—he had little or no idea what had happened to his partners, employees, and associates at First Republic. He was in the pharmaceuticals business, or trying to be. The meeting at the government institute was critical to his latest entrepreneurial effort. If it went well, the little company Grajirena had helped set up could be off to a flying start. It could be making millions within months. He himself could become a millionaire many times over within a few years. Those thoughts were in the back of his mind during the twenty-minute drive from the hotel to the institute.

But foremost in his mind was whether he was going to make it to the meeting alive. The driver was being incredibly aggressive, even by Moscow taxi standards, honking the horn, squealing the tires around corners, slamming on the brakes inches behind cars ahead of him at stoplights, refusing to stop for stop signs at all. Geoffrey Farrar, the Canadian banker who had been advising Grajirena since his first seminar on doing business in Russia years before, groaned alongside him. After First Republic folded, the two of them had formed a consulting group with a handshake agreement to help each other anytime, anywhere they could. They had been on many harrowing taxi rides together, but this one was right up there with the worst. "Remember how the Spy said I was showing disrespect to Russian drivers by not sitting in the front seat? Well, this is why I sit in the back seat," Grajirena murmured as he looked away from yet another close call. Indeed, many world cities claim their share of bad drivers, but Moscow in the late 1990s set new standards. Before the Berlin Wall fell, Moscow was relatively traffic-free: one car for every ten residents. A decade later there was one car for every three residents. Before, they couldn't buy cars. Even if they had the money, Russian would-be drivers waited for years for the state to manufacture and allocate a vehicle. Once they were free to buy anything, Russians bought cars with a vengeance —and as one pundit put it, they drove them that way, too. Moscow had become a city of 10 million people, with no expressways, huge traffic jams, and fewer traffic signals and signs than a medium-size American city. Drivers, many of them novices with little or no instruction in the rules of the road, routinely drove and parked anywhere, including on sidewalks.

When their driver missed a turn on the way to the institute, Grajirena said calmly, as if to no one in particular, "We missed it." It took a couple more seconds for the driver to realize that he had missed the street. He swore and spun the car 180 degrees amid screeching tires and other drivers blaring their horns at him. The driver decided to go down another side street and circle around the block. But the street was one way, the wrong way. No matter—he started *backing* down it, against the traffic, at 40 miles per hour. A woman pushing a baby carriage looked in the direction traffic was supposed to be coming and stepped off the curb—into the path of the taxi coming at her backward from the wrong direction. The driver leaned on the horn, and the woman looked up in surprise and yanked the carriage back onto the curb. The driver swerved only slightly, slammed on the brakes when he came to the side street he was looking for, and roared off down it, forward this time. "Jesus Christ," Farrar said. His eyes met Grajirena's, and they smiled, laughing at themselves. Just another day at the office in Moscow.

In his new pharmaceutical business, Grajirena was trying to avoid the mistakes he had made with First Republic. He didn't want to found any more companies or run them. He wanted to be a facilitator, a middleman who brought two sides together to do deals. "A mouthful o' howdy and a handful o' much-obliged," he said. The meeting that day was with a Russian government official who wanted to do some business on the side with the American company that Grajirena represented. As far as Grajirena knew, he wouldn't be doing anything illegal, and neither would the Russian public official. Grajirena knew the accepted Russian view was that officials deserved a little reward on the side if they brought in business or jobs or foreign products that were good for Russia. If it was good for Russia as a country, the reasoning went, why shouldn't it be good for them as individuals? "We may think it's crazy or on the edge of unethical in America, but we're not in America. It's another part of the Moscow Madness of doing business in Russia. You'll see what I mean during the meeting," Grajirena promised. He stepped out of the cab in front of the institute, avoiding a puddle of nasty-looking water that must have been six inches deep. Grajirena shook his head in wonder. "I love this country," he said.

Dale McElwee and John Hayhurst, the Missouri dentists who had helped Rick Grajirena start First Republic, did not abandon their interest in Russia when they left the company. When First Republic became a corporation in 1992 and they sold their respective interests, they focused their attention not on import-export but on an idealistic project much closer to their hearts: establishing a chain of nonprofit dental teaching clinics throughout Russia. From their homes and offices in Camdenton, Missouri, over the next three years, into 1995, parallel to the rise and fall of First Republic, they worked hard to make it happen. In the States they founded ORCA—Oral-Health Resources Corporation of America. They recruited investors, many of them friends and colleagues in and around Camdenton. They put together a heavyweight board of directors that included the former dean of the Baltimore College of Dental Surgery, and they gathered technical support and information from all over the globe. The head of the World Health Organization's dental program became one of their closest advisers and biggest boosters. In Russia, they worked with Russia's chief dental officer, Valery Leontiev, whom they had met with Grajirena at the Kremlin banquet back when First Republic was little more than an idea scribbled on the back of a cocktail napkin. Leontiev was in charge of Russia's programs for training dentists and overseeing dental practices. He was very interested in the proposal by McElwee and Hayhurst, both as his country's leading dental officer and as a private businessman. He proposed a joint venture.

It was a typical proposal by Russian standards. Leontiev offered to provide a building. McElwee and Hayhurst would pay for renovating the building and for fitting out the offices and dental treatment and training rooms. They would also pay Leontiev rent on the building, and they would pay the costs of training Russian dentists. McElwee and Hayhurst wanted to set a fee schedule that would allow them to meet their expenses and gradually earn back their investment. They figured it would cost close to $1 million to get the first clinic up and running. They were willing to invest some of their own money up front. But they were also looking for grants from governments and NGOs—nongovernmental organizations—concerned with health issues around the globe. McElwee and Hayhurst hoped that when the clinics started generating income, they would be able to use some of the incoming money to open more clinics in Moscow and elsewhere in Russia. The dentists they trained could staff the new clinics. Maybe the Russian dentists would be able to repay the cost of their training to help open new clinics.

Over three years the Missouri dentists and their investors had spent about $300,000 in pursuit of their dream. Much of their time, energy, and money had gone into preparing an exhaustive proposal, thick as a phone book, that they presented to various agencies, government and nongovernment, in the United States and elsewhere. They got high praise from virtually every agency they approached. Their preparations were sound, their principles high, their attitudes enlightened. But not one agency offered them a single dollar, pound, yen, franc, lira, shekel, or any other tiniest bit of money. By the spring of 1995, just as First Republic was foundering, they gave up the idea of creating a nonprofit organization. Perhaps there was another way, McElwee and Hayhurst told each other. Perhaps they could operate their chain of clinics on a for-profit basis. Certainly the economy was getting better in Russia. Certainly dental care was not keeping up. Maybe Russians, who were proving themselves eager to spend as much as they could on other products and services from the West, would be willing to spend a little of their money on caps and fillings and bridges and having their teeth cleaned. McElwee and Hayhurst called the friend who could tell them the most about doing business in Russia.

"You're calling at the perfect time," Rick Grajirena told McElwee and Hayhurst. He was working as a half-time consultant for First Republic, but he knew that wasn't going to last long. First Republic was sinking fast, and he was going to need a job soon. For weeks he and Valerie had been talking about what he would do next, when either First Republic folded completely or he was forced out of the small role he still had in the company. They talked about him going back to making sails or selling yachts, but neither had much appeal. He didn't want to have to kowtow to clients and sail their boats for them, chasing trophies around the world. When the Missouri dentists—the Docs, as he came to call them—asked him to do some consulting work for them, Grajirena jumped at it. They wanted him to evaluate whether and how they could do their chain of dental clinics on a for-profit basis. They wanted to get back the money they and their investors had put into the nonprofit project. Grajirena set about rewriting their nonprofit proposal as a for-profit prospectus and evaluating their prospects. One of his first stops was Moscow, where he renewed his acquaintance with Valery Leontiev. The two men had liked each other from the first time they met, and they became friendly. They went to dinner together. They drank together. They told each other jokes. Remarkably, it was almost all done through interpreters, since Grajirena still spoke very little Russian and Leontiev spoke only a little more English.

The one thing they did not agree upon, however, was Leontiev's version of how McElwee and Hayhurst should participate in a joint venture with him. Leontiev showed Grajirena the building he would contribute for his share. Grajirena never found out how Leontiev came to control the building, but he knew almost immediately that it would not do for a dental clinic. It was on Novy Arbat, one of the busiest—and most expensive—shopping streets in Moscow. Leontiev wanted fair market value in terms of rent. Grajirena thought the Docs would do a lot better with a clinic in a cheaper neighborhood. There was little parking. Leontiev wanted to put the clinic on the fifth floor. Grajirena thought plenty of parking and the ground floor were musts. In addition, the fifth-floor space would require major renovations. Electrical wires and pipes protruded from holes in the walls. Leontiev had it in mind to reorganize the entire space, knocking down some walls and putting up others. He wanted to devote a large part of the floor plan to the office and conference room of the managing director—which he presumed would be himself. The next largest space would go to his assistant, presumably the person who would be in charge of day-to-day operations while Leontiev was in his regular office at the government institute or off traveling and giving speeches. Into the relatively small remaining space would be crammed a dozen dental chairs, some in small private rooms but several others lined up side by side in a common room, more like a barber shop than a dental clinic. Grajirena went over the cost estimates with Leontiev—rent, salaries, overhead, other operating expenses—and found that the clinic would have to charge much more than McElwee and Hayhurst imagined, and operate at near capacity virtually around the clock in order to break even. Would Russians be willing to pay American prices for dental care at midnight or five A.M.? Grajirena didn't see that kind of demand, not in a country where most people were still very poor and were accustomed to free dental care. It would be years, maybe generations, before the average Russian preferred expensive, high-quality dental care to free, not-so-good dental care. He reported back to McElwee and Hayhurst that what Leontiev had come up with so far would not work.

Grajirena's rewritten prospectus for a profit-making chain of clinics received about the same reception from investment banks that the dentists' nonprofit proposal had received from government agencies and NGOs. The bankers liked the idea and said it was righteous stuff, fighting the good fight and all that. They agreed there was a huge need for such a chain of clinics in Russia, and they even conceded that it might make money. But no one wanted to invest in a startup. Grajirena could not counter this argument. Startups, he knew from his First Republic experience, were extremely risky business in Russia. He advised McElwee and Hayhurst to give up the idea of the dental clinics altogether. They did, albeit reluctantly. Leontiev, it should be noted, did not give up on the idea of a private dental clinic. Through one of his side businesses, he opened a small for-profit clinic on the Novy Arbat site. It was probably profitable, but Grajirena assured the Missouri dentists that the profit was not nearly enough to service the debt that McElwee and Hayhurst would have rolled up in opening a more ambitious clinic as a joint venture.

The Russian economy survived the shock therapy of the early reforms and came roaring ahead in the middle 1990s. References to the "boom" in Russia became commonplace in the *Wall Street Journal* and other business publications. The Russian gross domestic product shrank by an estimated 40 percent, then began to recover. After inflation of 2,000 percent a year, the ruble stabilized. By early 1996 more than 70 percent of Russia's economy had been privatized. The Russian stock market increased in value by more than 150 percent that year, and it kept climbing into the autumn of 1997. Dozens of Western financial houses established investment funds in Russia. By 1997 Russia had sold more than $50 billion in treasury bonds. Growth was forecast at 5 to 8 percent, at least through the first decade of the twenty-first century. Russia was not merely an emerging economy, it was blossoming.

Even before getting back in touch with Grajirena, while he was still full time with First Republic, McElwee and Hayhurst had begun looking for other ways to recoup their Russian investment. One of their new ideas was to sell Russians dental equipment and technology produced in North America, like a high-tech dental chair, better than anything most Russian dentists could ever imagine. Leontiev was involved in several private companies—Grajirena never knew the details, but he believed Leontiev was the full owner of one or more companies—and said he might be interested in importing the high-tech chair through one of them. Leontiev could make sure that his government institute bought the chairs from his private company and used them to train Russian dentists. He could also use his influence to persuade Russian dentists to buy the chairs for their own practices and clinics. McElwee and Hayhurst, working with a friend who manufactured the high-tech chairs, helped design and produce a prototype for Russia, a stripped-down version that didn't have all the bells and whistles of the chairs sold to North American dentists but was closer in line with what Leontiev said that he could pay. They named the prototype chair the "Svetlana," after Leontiev's wife, and shipped it over to him for evaluation.

Leontiev said it would take his institute several months to test and ultimately approve the Svetlana. Over the ensuing months, he himself contacted the North American manufacturer of the Svetlana and inquired about buying chairs directly from him, instead of going through the Missouri dentists. The manufacturer turned down Leontiev, saying that he was a friend of the dentists, that he had a deal with them, and that he didn't do business like that anyway. Eventually it became clear to McElwee and Hayhurst that they were going nowhere fast with the plan. That project had cost them tens of thousands of dollars, including several months' worth of salaries after they hired an American salesman in Russia. The salesman not only had nothing to sell at that point—he was waiting for the Svetlana and other dental products to be approved by Leontiev's institute—but he also had considerable expenses, including the salary for his leggy blond assistant, a former star of the Soviet women's basketball team. As the months dragged on at $10,000 to $12,000 a month with no prospect of any cash flow in the near future, McElwee and Hayhurst finally gave up on both the dental clinics and the dental equipment business. But they were not ready to give up on Russia. They still wanted to get their money back somehow. Grajirena, naturally, had another idea for them.

CHAPTER 25

Rexall

In researching the dental clinic idea, Grajirena came in contact with various officials from the World Health Organization and individual countries, not only Russia but also Poland, Latvia, Lithuania, and other former Soviet republics. It became clear to him that the dental clinic idea would not fly— at least not for several years, until more consumers in those countries had the money and were willing to pay for high-quality dental care. Grajirena began asking officials about other health-care needs in Russia and Eastern Europe. "Vitamins," several of them said. Under socialized medicine people had never adopted a tradition of preventive health care. If you got sick, the government treated you for free. But in the future, if you got sick it would cost you money to pay for care. People in Russia and Eastern Europe had never embraced the concept of taking vitamins for preventive health care. But they probably would in the coming years, as it became more expensive to get sick.

Grajirena began thinking seriously about vitamins and other over-the-counter drugs. Not long after First Republic folded, he went to lunch with a semi-retired Tampa management consultant who was one of the original sponsors of the Odessa 200 project. There was nothing in particular on the agenda, but Grajirena was doing all the networking he could. At lunch the man mentioned Rexall. It was a good company, with a good name. Was Rexall selling any of its long list of over-the-counter products in Russia? Grajirena wondered, too. While he was still thinking about it, he happened to run into a close friend, a stock analyst for an investment firm. She brought up Rexall, too, and told him she thought it was a good company. Grajirena did two things. First, he bought as much Rexall stock as he could comfortably afford. Second, he began researching the company. When the Missouri dentists were ready to listen to a new idea, Grajirena had an impressive file on Rexall. "Russians spend very little on health-care products due to unavailability and the perception that Russian products are inferior," Grajirena told them. "Russians spend the least of all Europeans on these products. This is expected to change dramatically as these products become available."

McElwee and Hayhurst gave Grajirena the go-ahead to explore health products in general and Rexall in particular. They said they would listen to anything Grajirena could come up with to keep them from losing the hundreds of thousands of dollars they had invested in Russia. Grajirena called Rexall's headquarters, across Florida in Boca Raton, and asked for an appointment with someone, anyone, in the international division. He wanted to talk about selling Rexall products in Russia. A few days later he was ushered into the office of Barbara Garcia, a smiling, friendly woman who was Rexall's vice-president in charge of international business. Grajirena made a quick pitch, telling her about himself, about his relationship with Hayhurst and McElwee, and about how he thought they could sell Rexall products in Russia and other parts of Eastern Europe. Garcia was interested. She decided to go to a big trade show in Moscow featuring pharmaceuticals and other health-care products. At that trade show, in November 1995, Garcia met and talked with dozens of companies that sold over-the-counter drugs in Russia, Poland, the Czech Republic, Slovakia, Hungary, and other former Soviet republics such as Belarus, Latvia, and Lithuania. She passed out labels and samples and brochures for various Rexall products, particularly vitamins.

Impressed with the interest, Garcia returned to Florida and began working out a distribution agreement with Grajirena. He had contacts in Lithuania and asked for the rights to distribute Rexall products in both Russia and Lithuania. McElwee and Hayhurst created a subsidiary of ORCA called EuroHealth to handle the Rexall business. They gave Grajirena 15 percent of the company, plus a full-time salary and full health benefits for his family. Through his contacts in Moscow, Grajirena found two Russians to undertake marketing studies for him. One was a physician who had been doing studies on the growing Russian pharmaceutical market, and the other was a consultant who had done preliminary research for a number of North American companies considering doing business in Russia. Together they churned out reams and reams of studies, reports, and recommendations. Within a few months Grajirena had a marketing plan showing that Rexall products would do very well in Russia. Rexall was impressed enough to suggest that EuroHealth should have an exclusive licensing agreement for Rexall products, not just in Russia and Lithuania but throughout most of the former Soviet Union and Eastern Europe. It meant that EuroHealth would need more startup cash, but it also raised the earning potential.

Grajirena put together a prospectus for EuroHealth that called for startup costs of $3 million, with offices in Poland, Russia, and Lithuania the first year. Hungary, the Czech Republic, and Slovakia offices would be opened the following year. First-year sales were projected at $2.6 million, with profits of $1 million. Second-year sales would be $7 million, with $2.8 million in profits. Grajirena began looking for investors who could help finance the new company and its licensing and distribution business. A number of international investment firms were interested, but each of them had specific provisions that raised problems. A Polish investment group, for example, might have been willing to put up the $3 million, but the pharmaceuticals had to be manufactured in Poland. Grajirena struggled with that for a while, looking for loopholes—would bringing in pills or tablets from the States be all right if they were then packaged in bottles or containers made in Poland?—and trying to find a Polish manufacturer who could produce the pharmaceuticals to accepted international standards. Grajirena became convinced that manufacturing in Poland was something EuroHealth might well want to do in the future, but at that point it would not work out. The deal with the Polish group fell through.

A Korean group wanted to put up $600,000 cash and a $1.5 million line of credit in exchange for 60 percent of the company. McElwee and Hayhurst were interested, but they wanted a payback for themselves up front. They didn't want to risk losing control and then getting nothing at all if EuroHealth went sour. The Koreans said they did not want to pay off the dentists up front. If and when EuroHealth was successful, McElwee and Hayhurst could get their money out. The dentists said no, and that deal fell apart, too. An American venture capital firm presented a plan to provide $2 million for EuroHealth but wanted 70 percent of the company. McElwee and Hayhurst felt that it was only a matter of time before they would be squeezed out. That deal, like the others, came to nothing. By the middle of 1997, Grajirena was convinced that no major investment group was going to take on EuroHealth. He felt as if he had wasted nearly an entire year. The dentists were discouraged. They had gradually increased Grajirena's compensation from $1,500 a month when he was working as a part-time consultant to $60,000 per year for full-time work as EuroHealth's only employee. He had rolled up $30,000 in telephone and travel expenses over the previous year. McElwee and Hayhurst also paid another $30,000 over that year to the two Russians, the doctor and the marketing man, who had been doing all the market research on how Rexall products would sell. And still the dentists had nothing to show. They were running out of money, and they let Grajirena know it. Sometimes Grajirena's monthly paycheck from Camdenton would be days—a few times, weeks—late. He would call the dentists and not only ask for his money but try to encourage them not to give up. At times they were up, confident, sure that everything was going to work out in the end. Other times they were down in the dumps, depressed, sure that they had wasted a small fortune and years of time and energy. Grajirena knew how they felt. He felt the same way himself many times over, both at First Republic and now on EuroHealth. But he was sure of the potential of EuroHealth and Rexall. At the same time, he more than anyone, including the dentists, knew what could go wrong when Americans tried to do business in Russia. He didn't want EuroHealth to make the same mistakes, and suffer the same fate, as First Republic. Perhaps he and the dentists had been taking the wrong approach.

Their original idea was for EuroHealth to be the importer and master distributor of Rexall products. Under that structure, as master distributor, EuroHealth would receive orders from subdistributors and wholesalers. It would fill the orders through Rexall and ship the pharmaceuticals to the subdistributors and wholesalers, who would then make the deliveries to retailers. It was the way to make the most profit; Grajirena reckoned that the markups would be around 100 percent and the margins around 50 percent. However, it would also be expensive. That was why EuroHealth was seeking $2 million or more from investors. It would mean setting up offices, hiring people, stocking a warehouse, and overseeing from afar a sales and distribution team for each country. The more Grajirena thought about it, the more he thought that the original EuroHealth structure was too ambitious. It was too much like what he had done—or rather had tried to do—with First Republic.

What if he did a new, scaled-down model for the company? He went back to McElwee and Hayhurst with a new plan. Instead of being the master distributor, EuroHealth would operate more like an agent or licensee for Rexall. EuroHealth would find a master distributor for each country. Euro-

Health would receive orders in the States and have Rexall send off the shipments. The master distributor would be the importer in Russia or Lithuania or wherever. The master distributor on the ground, rather than EuroHealth back in the States, would find the subdistributors and wholesalers. Euro-Health would need only a small office in the States to receive orders and arrange shipping from Rexall to the master distributors. EuroHealth would have no warehouse, no inventory, no distribution. The profit margins would be smaller—20 or 30 percent, say, rather than 50 percent—but to Grajirena a smaller cut of the profits was worth avoiding the hassles of financing and actually running a business on the ground in Russia or some other former Soviet republic. He approached several of the biggest potential Rexall distributors in Russia and Eastern Europe, and they liked the idea. After all, they already had offices and warehouses and their own distribution networks in place. They also liked the idea of getting a bigger profit margin for themselves. When Grajirena said part of the deal was that they would have to spend a small but predetermined amount of their margins on advertising Rexall products, no one objected.

Grajirena presented this scaled-down approach to McElwee and Hayhurst. They liked it. Establishing EuroHealth as a master distributor based in the States, rather than a hands-on distributor on the ground in Russia, had great appeal for them. For one thing, they might need only $200,000 to get started, not $2 million. For another, they would no longer need the Russian doctor and marketing man to do research. Grajirena assured the dentists that they already had enough market research. McElwee and Hayhurst asked Grajirena to look around for smaller investors. He floated the scaled-down EuroHealth idea to a number of investors interested in Russia—including some who had lost money in First Republic. Robert Snibbe, a Tampa businessman who was an original First Republic investor, said he represented a group of potential investors. He asked Grajirena for a meeting with the dentists. McElwee flew down to Tampa for a lunch meeting at the airport, and Snibbe's group presented its pitch. They would put up $250,000, but they wanted 50 percent of the company and day-to-day control. It was a good meeting, a cordial meeting, and McElwee seemed interested. He asked and answered lots of questions and shook hands warmly with Snibbe before he flew back to Camdentown after lunch. Grajirena had no idea whether McElwee and Hayhurst would accept the Snibbe group's offer. But he hoped not. He thought the dentists had come too far and expended too much capital—not just financial but emotional, too—to give up control of the company. The next day Grajirena's phone rang. It was McElwee. He said that he and Hayhurst had decided against taking the

Snibbe group's offer. They would get the money together themselves, he told Grajirena. Grajirena relayed the news to Snibbe, who took it with his usual aplomb and thanked Grajirena for giving him the chance to pitch the deal. That night, over dinner, Grajirena told Valerie he was surprised at finding himself so happy the dentists had decided to stick it out themselves. After swearing that he would never again get as emotionally involved in a business in Russia as he had been with First Republic, he was doing it all over again with EuroHealth.

Scaling back EuroHealth's ambitions, aiming to act as Rexall's licensee rather than as an importer and master distributor, Grajirena realized that it would be foolish to try to offer all of Rexall's hundreds of products. He began going through the company's product catalogs, trying to pick out a handful that would be most likely to do well and create a foothold for Euro-Health. If and when those first products sold well and EuroHealth had the money to expand, it could begin offering other Rexall products, too. He picked out four popular vitamin products: a one-a-day vitamin, a women's vitamin, a chewable children's vitamin, and an all-purpose multivitamin supplement. One other product caught his eye: Dr. Seltzer's Hangover Helper. "Russians love home remedies," he told McElwee and Hayhurst. "And they drink like fish. They might really go for this." Rexall no longer made Dr. Seltzer's Hangover Helper, but someone at Rexall managed to find some samples in a warehouse.

By then Grajirena had become a regular at Moscow trade shows relating to health and medicine, so he stuck the samples in his briefcase and took them along on his next trip. As usual, he didn't have a booth. Instead he walked around, talking to whoever would talk to him, sitting down with anyone who wanted to sit down with him. He handed out information about the four vitamin products and parceled out samples of Dr. Seltzer's Hangover Helper. He had about fifty small packets, each holding two tablets—the recommended dose for a serious morning-after sufferer. Grajirena stapled each packet to a brochure about Dr. Seltzer and handed them all out on the first day of the three-day show. After he ran out of his fifty sample packets, he could show potential distributors only the box with its drawing of a bespectacled, mustachioed man—Dr. Seltzer, supposedly—who looked more like a nineteenth-century snake-oil salesman than a country doctor. Even without samples, many wholesalers and retailers were interested. Some who did get tablets on the first day of the show came back to Grajirena on the second or third day. At first they were sheepish. "I over-did it a little last night" was the typical response. Then they smiled. "But I've got to tell you, Dr. Seltzer really works. I'm very interested." A fair number of distributors, wholesalers, and retailers wanted to sit down and talk about possibly distributing the Rexall vitamins. Many more were interested in sell-ing Dr. Seltzer's Hangover Helper. Everybody wanted to try it. Everybody wanted a sample. Everybody thought it would sell.

Before flying to Russia for that trade show, Grajirena had telephoned Valery Leontiev, the chief Russian dental officer. The two of them had not spoken for more than a year, since Grajirena had become a consultant to McElwee and Hayhurst and then torpedoed their deal with Leontiev to create a dental clinic. Grajirena was worried that Leontiev might have hard feelings. He needn't have worried. Leontiev came on the line as soon as his secretary told him that Rick Grajirena was calling. He seemed genuinely glad to hear from him. "He knows I was the one who squashed the dental clinics deal, and he could have blown me off," Grajirena said later. "But he's a businessman. He knew I must be calling for some good reason. He would never let personal issues get in the way of business."

Grajirena explained that he was trying to make a deal with Rexall. He wondered if Leontiev, through one of his private companies, might be inter-ested in importing and distributing Rexall products in Russia. It was a pos-sibility, Leontiev said. But first he wanted Grajirena to meet Vladimir Lazarenko, a doctor and *biznesman* from Belarus, the old White Russia, which had been one of the Soviet republics and then became an indepen-dent nation when the USSR broke up. Grajirena made arrangements to meet Lazarenko early on the first day of the Moscow trade show, when he still had samples of Dr. Seltzer's Hangover Helper. Lazarenko told Grajirena that he represented a major pharmaceutical company based in Minsk, the capital of Belarus. The principals of the company were former Soviet sports stars and current Belarus government officials. The company, Lazarenko said, was looking for American pharmaceutical products to distribute, espe-cially over-the-counter drugs. Grajirena gave him his pitch on the four vita-mins and one of his Dr. Seltzer brochures stapled to a packet of two hangover tablets.

Lazarenko called Grajirena the next day and asked for another meeting. They sat down in the bar of the hall where the trade show was being held, and Lazarenko came right to the point. He had checked with his people in Minsk and faxed them some of the information Grajirena provided about Rexall. Lazarenko's people wanted to be EuroHealth's importer and master distributor for Belarus. They would take care of getting all the products registered. They would pay cash. They wanted to start with Dr. Seltzer. Lazarenko, smiling, said he himself did not drink very much, but a friend who had overindulged the previous evening had taken Dr. Seltzer that morning and had made a sufficient recovery from his hangover to give the product a hearty endorsement. Lazarenko and Grajirena shook hands and agreed to meet again during Grajirena's next trip to Moscow.

During that trip a few weeks later, in November 1997, Grajirena and Lazarenko met in Leontiev's office. Leontiev was not a direct part of their deal, as far as Grajirena knew, but he sat in on their meeting. Leontiev would probably get some sort of fee or commission from the Belarussians if the deal went through, Grajirena figured, so he was providing his office just to keep an eye on things and smooth the way. At that meeting Lazarenko brought along one of the principals of the Minsk pharmaceutical company he represented: a tall, barrel-chested, middle-aged man whom Lazarenko introduced as a former Soviet Olympic gold medalist in rowing. The man said nothing during the meeting but seemed to understand everything, even when Grajirena spoke in English.

At that meeting Lazarenko said the Belarussians wanted to order one million of the two-tablet packets of Dr. Seltzer's Hangover Helper as soon as the regulatory paperwork was ironed out. Grajirena was stunned. "One million?" he asked, looking back and forth between Lazarenko and the interpreter. The interpreter and Lazarenko replied in unison, in English, "Yes, one million units." Grajirena said that would cost $380,000, cash up front. The Belarussians would have to make that amount available in a letter of credit to be drawn on an established U.S. bank—not a Russian bank. When the Dr. Seltzer shipment arrived in Minsk and the Belarussians accepted delivery, the letter of credit would "drop" and EuroHealth would get its $380,000. Lazarenko said he understood. Arranging an LC with an American bank would be no problem. He gave Grajirena a list, in English, of the various documents he would need, including statements and test results from Rexall and reports from the U.S. Food and Drug Administration. Grajirena said it would take several weeks to get the documents together. He and Lazarenko agreed to meet again in Leontiev's office in January 1998.

CHAPTER 26

The Slav

The Russian night was howling black and cold and snowy behind him one evening in late January 1998, when Rick Grajirena blew through the hotel doors into the brightly lighted lobby. Straight in from the airport, he was in travel mode. He wore tennis shoes, jeans, a well-lined tan trench coat, and a big Russian fur hat. As he propelled himself down the lobby across the slick marble floors of the Radisson Slavjanskaya, pulling his luggage behind him, other guests on their way in or out turned to glance at that hat. Few stylish Russians wore those fur hats anymore. They were more likely to go hatless, or to wear berets or loden caps with earflaps. Tourists wore fur hats. But Grajirena's hat wasn't like the cheap, ill-fitting, rabbit-fur hats that most tourists wore—or like the ones that Grajirena bought and wore and ultimately gave away when he first began doing business in Russia years before, back during his First Republic days. This one, a gift from Sergei, a Russian friend, was well made, of fox. It fit him beautifully, but it was a big hat, a look-at-me hat. His luggage was all black: a suitcase on wheels, a smaller carry-on bag, and a briefcase big enough for a laptop computer, a portable printer, stacks of reports and papers about over-the-counter drugs, several small boxes of Jelly Belly candy, pictures of his wife and kids, and a John Grisham thriller. At the front desk he recognized two of the three receptionists on duty, and they recognized him. He spoke a few words of Russian to them to be polite, and they spoke English to him, both to be polite and to make sure he understood them. He gave one of the boxes of Jelly Belly to the Russian receptionist who checked him in. She smiled and slipped the candy into a safe place beneath the counter. He talked to her about a wakeup call, and about reserving a car and driver for later in the week. She promised to take care of everything, and if he needed anything else, he should ring the desk and ask for her by name.

Over the years the 430-room Radisson Slavjanskaya, on the Berezhovskaya Embankment overlooking the Moscow River, had become Rick Grajirena's home away from home. He had been making several trips to Moscow each year for the better part of a decade—dozens of trips in all, so many he lost count—and in the years since First Republic got going, he had stayed almost exclusively at the Radisson Slavjanskaya. It was one of the first of several "Western" hotels that opened in Moscow in the late 1980s and early 1990s, during *perestroika*. Mikhail Gorbachev, then the Soviet leader, wanted to encourage the gradual growth of capitalism, with strict limits and controls. At first, for example, only cooperatives, not individuals, could form for-profit ventures. Gorbachev also wanted to encourage Western investment, and he knew that traditional Soviet hotels, with their lack of creature comforts and particularly communications, kept many Americans from coming to Moscow to do business. If Americans could fly to Moscow and stay in a nice hotel, get a good meal, and call home or send a fax when necessary, they would be much more amenable to the possibilities of doing business in Moscow.

On his first trip, when the mysterious Ludmilla had put Grajirena and the Bass Oil men up in a former Communist Youth hotel, Grajirena tolerated it for several days before asking to be moved to the Metropol, the first of the grand old Soviet hotels to be renovated to Western standards. All those hotel renovations were joint ventures between old Soviet government authorities, which put up the property, and Western corporations, which put up the money, equipment, furnishings, management, and virtually everything else, from the chips for the casino tables to the beef for the cheeseburgers. In the early days of First Republic, Grajirena often stayed at the Penta, which was a joint venture between a Russian government agency and Lufthansa. He flew back and forth to Russia so many times on Lufthansa, which was one of the corporate sponsors of the ill-fated Odessa 200 project, that he was given a discount at the hotel. A discount was vital to many Western travelers, especially those who didn't have big expense accounts with major corporations. Moscow was at or near the top of the list of most expensive cities in the world for business travelers. When First Republic was made the distributor for Miller beer, Grajirena switched to the Radisson Slavjanskaya, a joint venture between the city of Moscow and the Radisson chain, and got the discount that the hotel offered to Miller's corporate parent, the Philip Morris tobacco conglomerate. As a frequent visitor, he managed to keep the corporate discount even after First Republic folded. He paid less than $200 a night, compared with the usual nightly rate that was closer to $300.

The Radisson was geared toward American business travelers. In the early days some Americans worked at the hotel, helping train the Russian staff. By the late 1990s, however, nearly all the staff were Russians. The desk staff spoke fluent English, and many other staffers—down to the maids and room-service waiters—spoke at least some English. There were several restaurants in the hotel, including a coffee shop, a midrange Scandinavian restaurant, an upscale Japanese restaurant, and an American-style chophouse that was widely regarded as having the best steaks in Moscow. Moscow's best American cinema, a multiscreen theater showing mostly first-run movies without dubbing or subtitles, was in the hotel. The Radisson also offered one of the best health clubs in Moscow, complete with pool and saunas and gym, and a number of tony shops featuring designer shoes, apparel, and luggage. Many of the clerks and attendants were young Russian women—typically tall, blond, and beautiful. "Like the women in a James Bond film," Grajirena said. Besides the women with legitimate jobs in the hotel, there were many others in the restaurants, in the bar, in the lobby just sitting around, who were more beautiful—longer legs, more spectacular figures, prettier, more exotic looks, in sleek, sexy designer clothing. Some were the wives or girlfriends of business travelers. More were the girlfriends of *mafiya* guys, or prostitutes, or both. A quick date supposedly started at several hundred dollars, and a night could run a thousand or more, according to what other business travelers told Grajirena. In the early 1990s, it was not unusual for him to be approached in the Radisson bar by women who asked him to buy them drinks. By the late 1990s, whether because the prostitutes had become more sophisticated or the hotel had gotten complaints or the staff was not being bribed as much, things had changed. It was rare for a prostitute to approach a man who did not at least make eye contact and smile at her first.

In the early 1990s, President Bill Clinton and a number of other American politicians, business leaders, and celebrities made highly publicized visits to the Slav. Grajirena guessed that in those days 90 percent of the hotel's guests were Americans. Over the years the clientele changed. Many more European and Asian business travelers, particularly Japanese, frequented the hotel. By the second half of the 1990s, many more guests at the hotel were "new Russians," ranging from legitimate or semilegitimate *biznesmen* to hard-core *mafiya*. Grajirena guessed that fewer than half the guests were Americans. Another big change was that when the old hotels first became joint-venture Westernized hotels, they had stern doormen who kept out ordinary Russians. An American business traveler who met a Russian at a conference could not invite the Russian over for lunch in a hotel coffee shop. The Russian would be stopped at the door unless the American waited outside and escorted the Russian in. The only Russians allowed inside were those who bribed the doormen, usually prostitutes or *mafiya*.

By the late 1990s the prostitutes and *mafiya*, still wearing expensive Italian sweaters and dressy leather jackets, were as much in evidence as ever in hotel lobbies. But so were Russian citizens who had not bribed their way in. As long as they didn't look scruffy, as long as they acted like they had legitimate business there, no one bothered them—the same as in any nice hotel in America. Indeed, the bank branch inside the hotel allowed anyone, not just guests, to change rubles for dollars and vice versa. In addition, many Russians who lived in Moscow used the hotel's business center in the same way as visiting Americans, for meetings with foreign businesspeople and occasionally with other Russians. These hustling new Russians, eager to meet new people and find new opportunities, were shedding their country's stereotypical fear of foreigners, their cynicism, their gloomy fatalism, and what one Russian writer called "the three strings of the Russian lyre"—sadness, skepticism, and irony. Instead of looking to the past and not trusting what they were told, these new Russians were looking to the future and preparing to write it themselves. "History would be an excellent thing," a Russian scholar observed in 1908, "if only it were true." The Russians browsing in the designer boutiques, laughing around restaurant tables, or crowding up to the bar at the Slav seemed far removed from Russian history. Instead they were visible, reassuring evidence of the emergence of what might turn out to be the first middle class ever in Russia. Someone once said that Russian society historically was like a pie without the filling: all upper crust and lower crust, nothing in between. The American pie, in contrast, always had a thin crust on top, a thin crust on the bottom, and a thick middle that provided substance and flavor.

Much of the Radisson Slavjanskaya's mezzanine level was given over to the Moscow International Business Center, which had been started by Paul Tatum and cost him his life after he came into conflict with his joint-venture partner, the city of Moscow. Years later the center still offered business travelers a full range of services: phone, fax, photocopying, translating, interpreters, transcribers, computers, even temporary office space. Tatum was still the first and only American presumed murdered by the *mafiya*. His death remained unsolved. No one expected it ever to be solved. But that appeared to have little impact on the hotel or the business center. Since Tatum's death the business center had operated smoothly under new management—Russian management. Tatum's name was rarely mentioned, except when one veteran American traveler would quietly tell a newcomer Tatum's story. It was ancient history, not pertinent to the deals spread out on the coffee tables. Much of the attention paid to Tatum during his life at the Slav was focused on the message that Moscow was open for business. The relative lack of attention to his death carried the same message.

Geoffrey Farrar initially named his consulting company Trans-Russia. When Grajirena came aboard, he persuaded Farrar that the name might put off potential contacts outside Russia, in former Soviet republics and other Eastern European countries, where Russians were not everyone's favorite people. They settled on the CEER Group, for Central and Eastern Europe and Russia. It seemed like a good match. Farrar had corporate credibility, banking know-how, and government connections. Grajirena was the marketing man, the salesman, with a vast and ever-growing network of contacts. "Rick is where the rubber meets the road," Farrar said. Farrar kept a small apartment in central Moscow, and he and Grajirena often had meetings at the Radisson, both with each other and with clients and contacts. They used the hotel's business center occasionally, particularly if they needed a document translated into or out of Russian quickly.

But they spent much more time camped out on the sofas and easy chairs grouped in the wide, open spaces of the second floor of the hotel near the business center, or in the similar groupings of furniture downstairs in the large lobby bar area. This was their temporary office in Moscow. "I'll meet you on the second floor at ten o'clock in the morning," Grajirena would tell a business contact. Grajirena would leave his room at about 9:30 and go down to the second floor in plenty of time to claim an area, usually a small sofa and two easy chairs around a coffee table. When his business contact arrived, Grajirena would welcome him over. If they had their meeting downstairs in the lobby bar area, a waitress would come around and offer coffee or tea, which Grajirena would charge to his room. Grajirena and most other American business travelers preferred to use the second floor, which had fewer furniture groups farther apart, for more serious talks, when they wanted more privacy. It was not unusual for both Grajirena and Farrar to be involved in separate meetings in neighboring furniture group-ings at the hotel, and for one of them to interrupt the other. "Sorry, but I need you just for a minute," they would say. "There's someone over here I want you to meet."

Downstairs, in the cozier lobby bar, people in one business meeting could often overhear neighboring meetings. Once Grajirena was sitting on a couch having a drink with an associate—talking about their business, but not having a meeting as such—when he overheard the men on the couch behind him discussing Russian licensing for a popular over-the-counter medicine for upset stomachs. The men were talking about a certain Russian company they were going to use as a distributor. Grajirena knew the com-pany. He had been involved in a potential deal with that company, but he had backed away when he checked out the Russians who ran it and learned that they had cheated several other potential American partners. These par-ticular Russians typically made a great pitch and signed a deal that commit-ted their American partners to substantial up-front investments. They took the money but didn't keep their part of the bargain. The Americans ended up out of money, out of luck, and out of Russia.

The Americans on the couch behind Grajirena seemed to know nothing about the Russian company's bad reputation. They were going to meet with their American lawyers in Moscow the next day to sign an agreement. Gra-jirena had qualms about eavesdropping. But he got over it quickly. Russia had a great tradition of eavesdropping, dating to the revolution and the czars and further back. If these guys were going to sit here and spill their secrets for anyone to hear, it was their own fault. He also considered inter-rupting them and telling them what he knew about the Russian company. But he decided it literally wasn't any of his business. For one thing, the Americans were his potential competitors in the Russian market. Rexall had a similar stomach-calming over-the-counter medicine that Grajirena might eventually want to sell in Russia. If this other product did well first, it could hurt his business later. Another possibility would be that the Americans might hire him someday as a consultant. They would be more likely to do that if their efforts with the shady Russian company turned out badly.

But who were the Americans? What company were they with? Grajirena wanted to know who his competition was. When the Americans departed, he called the waitress over. "I think I know that guy who just left, but I can't remember his name. Can you look on the check he just signed?" It wasn't the first time that one customer had asked her who another customer was. American business travelers often met one another in the bar, and then couldn't remember the details when they ran into each other months later. The waitress showed Grajirena the bill, so he got not only the man's name but also his room number. "Excuse me," Grajirena said to his associate. "I'll be right back." He strolled over to the front desk. One of the desk clerks he knew was on duty. He gave her the man's name and room number and asked if she could look at his registration to see what company he represented. There was no company name on the registration, she said, but there was the name and phone number of the man's travel agent in the Midwest. Grajirena took down the number, went up to his room, and called the travel agent. He said that the American had suggested Grajirena might want to use his travel agent, but he had lost the American's card. Did the travel agent have his office number? And the name of the company he worked for?

The travel agent, eager for potential business, gave Grajirena both the number and the name of the company, which was in Michigan. It was indeed a Rexall competitor. Grajirena went back downstairs with this information, and his colleague was so impressed that for weeks he called Grajirena "007." Grajirena did nothing with the information for about a year. Finally, curious, he called the man to ask whether the Michigan company might be interested in manufacturing some over-the-counter products that Grajirena was considering for the Russian market. They chatted about it for a time, until Grajirena asked, casually, whatever had happened to the deal with that Russian company and the stomach-calming medicine. The man seemed surprised that Grajirena knew anything about it. And he didn't want to talk about it. "Uh, that didn't work out so well," he finally said.

For Grajirena and many other Americans in Moscow, the hotel lobby bar was the living room of their home away from home, their place to unwind, their place to make friends and contacts. But they never really stopped working. They were always on the make for someone who might have a bit of information they could use, a contact who might be valuable, some advice that might come in handy. One typical evening in early 1998 Grajirena stopped at the bank windows just off the Slav's lobby. The Russian government recently had knocked three zeros off its money. A thousand rubles in old money was now worth one new ruble. He changed some money at just over six rubles to the dollar and bantered with the cashier about how the new ruble made it easier to do the math. Grajirena then repaired to the Slav's bar for a nightcap and a smoke. Another man came in by himself and sat in an easy chair next to the furniture grouping where Grajirena was sitting, about fifteen feet away. The man looked over at Grajirena three or four times. "Excuse me, sir," the man finally said in a loud voice. "Would that be a Cuban cigar you're smoking there?" Grajirena exhaled a thick plume of smoke. "Sure is," he said with good-natured satisfaction. "Would you like one?"

And so began yet another ships-in-the-night meeting of American businessmen traveling in Russia. After a couple of minutes of back and forth about cigars, the other man moved over to sit near Grajirena. He was built like a block of ice, with a head that seemed to come right out of his thick torso and only a hint of a neck. He introduced himself as a former Marine who was now the international marketing director for an ice cream company. Most of his work had been in Asia, where he was stationed years ago in the military. "I pretty much grew up in Asia," the Marine said in a thick Mississippi accent. This was his first trip to Moscow, and he had been flying for most of the past twenty-eight hours from Southeast Asia. It had been hot there. Now he couldn't believe how cold it was. "High of eleven degrees today," Grajirena told him. "But that's good. It was only eight degrees yesterday." The Marine asked if it was safe to eat everything in Moscow. "I was in Hong Kong, and with the chicken scare, the fish scare, the vegetable scare, you can't eat anything there," he said. Grajirena told him it was safe to eat anything at the Radisson, and pretty much anything else in any other Western hotel or restaurant. "I can't vouch for the Russian places," he said.

The Marine said he was having doubts about his Moscow distributor, who wasn't selling as much ice cream as the Marine thought he should. "He says we need to spend a lot of money on advertising," the Marine said. "We don't think so. These Russian guys want the ice cream to sell itself. They don't want to go out and sell it. We don't spend a lot of money on advertising in the States, so why should we here? Ice cream is taste, not advertising. You buy it because it tastes good, not because you like the advertising." Grajirena said that if the Marine couldn't get things straightened out, he knew a guy who distributed a range of consumer products in Moscow, including food and beer. "Beer?" the Marine inquired. "He distributes beer? Does he have refrigerated trucks? Our distributor has been making deliveries with coolers strapped onto the back of pickup trucks. Refrigerated trucks would make a big difference."

The Marine had more questions. Should he join the American Chamber of Commerce in Moscow? Did he need to cultivate contacts in the government? Grajirena told him no. He could join the chamber, but in Grajirena's opinion it was more geared toward big operators than toward little guys such as the Marine and his ice cream company. And he could spend a lot of time and money getting to know people who said they knew people in the government who could do him some good—but he probably wouldn't get anything out of it, Grajirena said. "At the level you're doing business here, you don't need government connections," Grajirena assured him. "You just need to focus on two things. One, you need a reliable distributor. Two, you need to be sure you're getting your money out." The Marine said his company's policy was "We don't ship, we don't even load, till we have the cash in hand." Grajirena talked about how, in the early 1990s, virtually every American company selling in Moscow had offered products on consignment because no one in Russia had the money to pay in advance. The Marine talked about the difficulty of getting Moscow supermarkets to carry his ice cream. After all those years of having just one example of each product on the shelves—one kind of bread, one kind of toothpaste, one kind of underwear—some Russian retailers still couldn't get used to the idea of having lots of competing brands. Okay, maybe they would have two or three different brands. But a retailer carrying five types of ice cream often didn't see the need for yet another. Grajirena told him how the Cold Patrol had worked for First Republic in introducing Miller beer to the market. The Marine seemed impressed and said he might try something like that. He liked the idea. The Marine said he was interested in opening markets for his ice cream in the former Baltic republics, especially Latvia and Lithuania. Grajirena said he knew people there. The Marine said perhaps they should get together in Florida and talk business the following month. Grajirena asked whether the Marine had considered Sakhalin Island, on Russia's Atlantic coast, eleven time zones to the east. "It's going to boom. There's a lot of oil money pouring in there. They're building a lot of infrastructure. Hotels. Whole new towns for oil workers. It's going to be the biggest oil project in the world when they're finished, bigger than the North Sea fields. It's where Moscow was a few years ago," Grajirena said. The Marine nodded seriously, making a mental note. He had not heard of Sakhalin Island, but he would check it out. It sounded like the sort of place where people would buy ice cream.

The Marine said he wanted to see some of the sights in Moscow over the next few days. "You know, like that Red Center," he said. Grajirena said it was Red Square, and he told the Marine how to walk there from the hotel. He offered him the use of Dennis Batlle, a young Russian who had been doing all sorts of chores for Grajirena in Moscow. "He'll show you all around the town if you like," Grajirena said. "He'll take you on the subway. He'll take you to buy Cuban cigars. He can translate for you, too. He speaks real good

English. You just have to pay him a few bucks." He gave the Marine Batlle's phone number. The Marine asked about changing money. Someone told him that he didn't need to change dollars into rubles, that dollars were better than rubles. "That used to be the way it was, but not anymore," Grajirena said. "The ruble has stabilized a lot, and it's a convertible currency now just like any other. Most places want rubles, if you're paying cash. If you want to keep your expenses in dollars, just use a credit card."

It was the sort of conversation Grajirena had been involved in a hundred times before, with a hundred other Americans visiting Russia. In the early days he was the newcomer, trying to gather as much information and advice as he could. Now, after spending a large part of his recent life in Russia, he was the old sage, the voice of experience. The Marine felt lucky to run into Grajirena and pick his brain, and he said so. They met for breakfast at the hotel the next morning. The Marine had a few more questions and picked up Grajirena's check—$26 for two eggs, two pieces of toast, a couple small slices of bacon, and a cup of coffee. The two men shook hands warmly, agreed to stay in touch, and talked about getting together to talk in the States. Both said they thought they could help each other do business in Russia or Latvia or somewhere else. Most of the time, after chance encounters such as this one, Grajirena and the other American never saw each other again, or talked to each other. But sometimes they did. In this case the Marine called Grajirena several times asking him for advice, information, or contacts. Like so many other fellow travelers, if Grajirena ever ran into the Marine again, they would no doubt shake hands and slap backs and share drinks and swap stories like old friends. Which they were, in the curious manner of the late-twentieth-century international-marketing road warrior.

CHAPTER 27

January 1998

After his meeting with Lazarenko in Leontiev's office in the autumn of 1997, Rick Grajirena had more than two months to get together the documents that the Belarussians needed for regulatory approval of Dr. Seltzer's Hangover Helper. He almost didn't make it. Rexall said it didn't have some of the documents. Then it said it couldn't find some of them. Then there was no one at Rexall to put them together for Grajirena. Finally, the documents were ready. They were supposed to arrive at his house by regular mail. They didn't. Then they were supposed to arrive by Federal Express. They didn't. On the day Grajirena was flying to Moscow for his next meeting with Lazarenko, he had scheduled an airport taxi to pick him up at his house in Clearwater at 12:30 P.M. A FedEx truck pulled up with the documents from Rexall at 12:15.

After a stop in Poland to talk to a potential Rexall master distributor there, Grajirena arrived in Moscow and blew into the Radisson Slavjanskaya on that snowy night at the end of January 1998. The receptionist who got a box of Jelly Belly was the one who had arranged for the taxi to take him from the Radisson to his meeting with Lazarenko and Leontiev in Leontiev's office at the Central Institute of Dentistry. Grajirena made a mental note during that harrowing drive, right after they went the wrong way in reverse and just missed a baby carriage, to mention the crazy driver to the receptionist. She was definitely on Jelly Belly probation. When they finally got out of the taxi safely, though shakily, at Leontiev's institute, Grajirena and Geoffrey Farrar congratulated each other for surviving, as they had during many other taxi rides in Moscow. They loved telling their taxi stories. Sometimes, when they weren't someplace where they could catch a proper taxi, they did what Russians do—held out their arms at the side of the road and waited for any vehicle to stop and pick them up. It was like hitchhiking, except they didn't stick out their thumbs, and the rides were never free. The driver, usually an ordinary Moscovite going to or from work, or on some personal errand, or just out cruising for some extra money from these informal fares, always negotiated the price in advance. Once Farrar was picked up by an ambulance that was between calls. The whole time he kept praying that the ambulance wouldn't get called to an emergency in the opposite direction. Years earlier, before inflation sent prices for consumer goods skyrocketing, Grajirena caught a ride in a private car that was out of windshield-cleaning fluid. The windshield got more and more mud splattered on it and gradually went from transparent to translucent to opaque. The driver, sticking his head out his window so he could see, steered over to the curb in front of a kiosk. He jumped out, went to the kiosk, forked over some crumpled rubles, and came back with a bottle of vodka. He popped the hood, poured the vodka into the container where the windshield-cleaning fluid was supposed to go, hopped back in the car, and grinned from ear to ear as he sprayed the vodka onto the windshield. The wipers eventually cleared away the mixture of booze and mud enough for them to resume their journey.

Leontiev's institute was nothing fancy from the outside, but it did have a big iron gate that a guard had to swing open so they could pull into the tiny, puddled courtyard. The inside of the institute was even less impressive. A substantial portion of the slush from the courtyard had migrated into the hallways and soaked through some old newspaper that someone put down on the cracking tile floor. The hallways were narrow. Rather than an office building, the place seemed like an old aristocratic townhouse that probably had been "requisitioned" by the Communists. Everything looked cheap, at least by Western standards, from the fake flowers to the laminated desks to the drab clothing of the women in the clerical area, who greeted Grajirena and Geoffrey Farrar when they walked in from the slush-slippery hallway. Grajirena stated his name but probably didn't need to. They knew him. Within seconds a small, trim, nervous but smiling Russian appeared. "Rimsky!" Grajirena all but bellowed. It looked like they might hug for a moment, but instead they shook hands enthusiastically, each using two hands.

The Russian was Leontiev's right-hand man, his administrative assistant, and his English interpreter. He had translated for Leontiev and Grajirena several times, and since Grajirena got along with Leontiev, he also got along with Rimsky. His real name was not Rimsky, incidentally. His real name was Koysakov. But when he met John Hayhurst, Hayhurst had decided that his name sounded like "Rimsky-Korsakov," the turn-of-the-century Russian composer. So for a brief time Hayhurst and Grajirena called him "Rimsky-Korsakov," but that was soon shortened to plain "Rimsky." Rimsky seemed to like the nickname, in the same way that little guys on a playground like it when big guys give them a nickname, even if the nickname isn't especially complimentary. Rimsky was Leontiev's do-everything, all-purpose aide. He was officially on the institute payroll, but he also took on many different roles for Leontiev's private enterprises, too. Grajirena once jokingly asked Rimsky just how many jobs he had. "I have about four jobs," Rimsky told him cheerfully. "Unfortunately, I only get paid for one."

After greeting Grajirena enthusiastically, Rimsky apologized. His boss, Leontiev, had a conflict. Some bigwigs from the Ministry of Health wanted to see him on short notice, and they were in Leontiev's office. Until he got rid of them, would Grajirena mind waiting in Rimsky's office? As soon as Lazarenko arrived, they could start the meeting right there in Rimsky's office. That was easier said than done. Rimsky's office was perhaps eight by ten feet and was jammed with his desk, computer, printer, a large photocopy machine, a small boom box, filing cabinets, several shelves overflowing with books and reports, and a yellow canary chirping away happily in a cage. For several minutes Rimsky busied himself bringing in chairs, smiling, apologizing, bumping, and thumping back and forth from the hallway, until he had chairs crammed in for six people: Grajirena, Lazarenko, Farrar, the manager of one of Leontiev's companies, a visiting journalist, and Rimsky himself. Lazarenko had just arrived, so while they were waiting for him to take his coat off, Grajirena slipped Rimsky a box of Jelly Belly. "He likes the watermelon best, but it doesn't matter. He's like all Russians. They go nuts for Jelly Belly." Grajirena grinned. Rimsky's eyes lit up, and he quickly put the box of candy into an out-of-the-way desk drawer, presumably to avoid being expected to share if anyone else saw it. According to Grajirena, the United States might have won the Cold War a decade or two earlier if Dwight Eisenhower had known what Rick Grajirena knew about Jelly Belly diplomacy.

Vladimir Lazarenko squeezed into the room, shook hands with everyone, and balanced himself halfway on one of the chairs, next to Grajirena. The six men sat literally elbow to elbow, knee to knee. Grajirena and Lazarenko both juggled stacks of papers on their laps. The setting did not have the feel of an important business meeting, but no one seemed to mind. Lazarenko was a pleasant, soft-looking, middle-aged man, with thinning hair that he combed as if it were all still there. He had a tidy little mustache and wore a houndstooth jacket. Pens jutted out of his shirt pocket. Grajirena was not sure of Lazarenko's role with the Belarus pharmaceutical company, but he knew it was a big company that had dominated the over-the-counter drug business in Belarus during the previous three years. It was possible that Lazarenko was one of the main people in the company. But it seemed unlikely. More likely, Grajirena thought, Lazarenko was an agent or middleman, much like himself. Grajirena was dressed much like Lazarenko: a plaid brown sports jacket, a blue button-down shirt, khaki trousers, and a striped tie. This was not a dark-suit type of meeting. He didn't want to overpower anyone. He wanted to be accessible, approachable, dressed down but still functional and businesslike. If he had been back in Florida, he probably would have worn some soft leather loafers. In Russia his shoes were more like cut-down work boots, chunky and clunky, distinctly unstylish but sturdy. They were Russian shoes, the only Russian-made apparel Grajirena wore. He had started wearing them several years earlier, after wrecking several pairs of good American and English shoes in the Moscow slush.

With Rimsky translating, Grajirena and Lazarenko plunged into their meeting. Everyone else listened. Lazarenko began by saying how eager the Minsk company was to begin distributing Dr. Seltzer's Hangover Helper. But there was some worry that it might be expensive by Belarussian standards. At the very minimum the pharmaceutical company would have to charge 50 cents per packet as the distributor. By the time it went through other wholesalers and retailers, it could cost 75 cents or a dollar to consumers who bought it in drugstores. "You're right, that's expensive for a little home remedy," Grajirena agreed. "But if it cures a hangover, it's worth a dollar or whatever else you have to pay." Lazarenko smiled and reminded Grajirena that he himself did not drink. Grajirena said the pharmaceutical company needed to remember that Dr. Seltzer was an unusual product that could be marketed outside the usual drugstores. Supermarkets would surely want to carry it, and so would bars, liquor stores, restaurants, and any other place that sold alcoholic beverages.

Lazarenko and Grajirena went through the stacks of documents teetering on their laps, then swapped a number of the papers. Grajirena gave Lazarenko the documents from Rexall that Lazarenko had requested for registering Dr. Seltzer in Belarus. Lazarenko said he needed several other documents pertaining to Dr. Seltzer, including its FDA certificate. Grajirena said he could press Rexall to find them if really needed, but Lazarenko said they probably would not be needed. "I think this guy is really connected, and this whole registration thing is going to sail through," Grajirena whispered in an aside. One of the documents he received from Lazarenko was a power of attorney in Russian. Grajirena needed to have it translated into English, and then get Rexall to sign it to authorize the Belarus company to register Dr. Seltzer in Belarus. Lazarenko said that as soon as the registration was complete, the Belarus company would place its first order for one million units of Dr. Seltzer. He said the registration process would take only a few weeks.

They talked a bit about the logistics of the shipping, and Grajirena said he was exploring the possibility of sending the shipment by air freight, instead of by sea. Was that all right? Lazarenko said shipping by air was preferable, because it was easier for the pharmaceutical company to bring imports though customs at the Minsk airport than through any of the seaports. Plus it wouldn't be necessary to arrange transshipping from the port to the company's warehouses in Minsk. Lazarenko, in turn, needed to get information to Grajirena for the Dr. Seltzer labels, so they could be printed in Russian. Since the Belarussians were talking about big orders, Rexall had agreed to print the labels for free. But the labels had to meet the requirements of the Belarus Ministry of Health. Lazarenko could get that information to Grajirena before Grajirena left Moscow. It would be easier if he just took it home with him. Lazarenko and Grajirena agreed to meet at the Radisson at ten o'clock the next morning. Grajirena already had requested shipping information, and he expected it to be waiting for him at the hotel when he returned. He could give it to Lazarenko the next day. He also hoped to have the power of attorney form from Rexall for Lazarenko. He would get it translated at the Radisson business center, fax it to Rexall, and get it back right away so he could give it to Lazarenko to take back to Belarus.

It was a remarkable scene, two men knee to knee in that little room, from such different cultures, each committing so much time and energy to a project that, when it came down to it, depended on whether they could look each other in the eye and find trust. They could not even speak each other's language, but here they were negotiating, making promises and accommodations and compromises. Their adventurous spirit, their willingness to face the unknown, and to work under what many others would consider impossible business hardships—Grajirena and Lazarenko, in a sense, were discovering new cultural and commercial territories for each other, and their countries. But probably they never thought of it that way. They were just trying to make a buck.

A secretary knocked on the door of Rimsky's tiny office, which was becoming noticeably stuffy after an hour of six men doing serious business behind a closed door. The secretary said Leontiev's meeting had ended, and the meeting in Rimsky's office could move to Leontiev's office. As everyone stood up and shuffled out, moving chairs to get around them and out the door, Grajirena wore a big smile. The meeting with Lazarenko was going as well as he hoped it would. "If we get this right the first time, it will be a miracle. But miracles do happen," Grajirena whispered as the group moved into Leontiev's office. Leontiev's office was twice as big as Rimsky's, maybe bigger. It was the odd blend typical to Russia: art deco meets 1950s public library. The door was padded with leatherette upholstery. The walls were pale yellow and needed a fresh coat of paint. The carpet was dark gray and coarse, industrial looking, as if it belonged in the office of a trucking company. The furniture was blond wood, large and heavy. A big conference table formed the stem of a T, with Leontiev's big desk the bar of the T. Along the walls was a series of tall bookshelves and low cabinets, most bearing an assortment of decorations and souvenirs: a ten-inch porcelain model of a molar; porcelain models of dogs; a porcelain owl; a porcelain girl on a swing; a woodcarving of a Chinese junk; a big bouquet of real rather than fake flowers; a toy stuffed tiger. A small refrigerator hummed in one corner.

Leontiev shook hands cordially with Lazarenko and greeted Grajirena warmly, placing an arm partly around Grajirena's shoulders. He was a big man, over six feet, with broad shoulders and a gray brush cut. He looked like a tough colonel or a retired NFL linebacker. His clothing was plain and Russian: dark blue suit, white shirt, sturdy shoes like Grajirena's. Outside his office Grajirena had seen Leontiev wear much more stylish clothes and a Rolex watch. Today Leontiev wore a standard Russian watch. He sat behind his big desk while the others spread out before him at the conference table. He asked if Lazarenko and Grajirena had finished their business. Grajirena started to say yes, but Lazarenko interrupted. There was one more bit of business. He wanted to inquire about other products that Grajirena and EuroHealth might be able to offer. "The managers of his company, many of them are top sportsmen in Belarus, and they are interested in any products relating to sports," Rimsky dutifully reported. Grajirena quickly ticked off several items he remembered from Rexall's catalogs—creams, salves, vitamins, a "hot ice" ointment. Lazarenko nodded. Those things might be good. What he had been asked to look for, however, was a powder that could be used as a dietary supplement for adding muscle. He didn't know the word in

English for it, and neither did Rimsky. Steroids? No, no, no, Lazarenko said, not steroids. Grajirena knew the powder Lazarenko was talking about—creatine, an amino-acid dietary supplement used by athletes to add body mass and muscle. Lazarenko nodded and spoke in Russian. "Yes, for weightlifters, bodybuilders," Rimsky translated. Grajirena said he didn't think Rexall offered creatine, but he knew someone else in Florida who manufactured or distributed it or both, and he was confident that he could get Lazarenko enough creatine to turn every pimply-faced teenager in Belarus into a budding young Schwarzenegger. "I'll get back to you on that," he promised. "Not tomorrow, but soon." Grajirena turned to Rimsky. "If he needs anything else, tell him to let me know," he instructed. Rimsky smiled, nodded, and spoke to Lazarenko, who smiled and nodded, too.

It seemed like an opportune moment for Grajirena to segue into a product that he wanted to show both Lazarenko and Leontiev. He jumped into the pause. "I do have something else we might talk about it," he said, pulling a box out of his briefcase. "It's melatonin." Lazarenko and Leontiev both knew what it was, but Grajirena explained anyway. However, he didn't even mention the reason that many international travelers use melatonin—to fight jet lag. (Nor did he mention that melatonin was blamed for then-President George Bush throwing up in the lap of the Japanese prime minister a few years earlier.) "It's a natural product," Grajirena concluded. "As you get older, it's harder to get a good night's sleep, and this product helps you sleep. Lots of older people will like it." Lazarenko and Leontiev passed the box back and forth, looking at the packaging and examining the Dr. Seltzer–sized packets of tablets from the box. Lazarenko, through Rimsky, said he knew the product and liked it and thought his company back in Belarus might be interested. Leontiev spoke to his own interpreter, Pavel, the manager of his private company. Pavel had been in the meeting in Rimsky's office but had said nothing as Lazarenko and Grajirena talked about Dr. Seltzer. Now Pavel listened intently to Leontiev, then turned to Grajirena. "Yes, he knows this product, this melatonin," Pavel said. "It's a good product. But you have to look at the market. Will it sell here? No matter how good the product is, we don't want to bring it into this country if people won't buy it." Then there was a quick little byplay between Lazarenko and Leontiev. Lazarenko wanted the sample box to take back to Belarus. Leontiev waggled his finger and shook his head, as if mock-scolding a schoolboy. "No, no, no," he said in English. "For me." He put the melatonin in his desk drawer and moved the meeting to the next item on the agenda: mouthwash.

CHAPTER 28

Mouthwash

Some months earlier Grajirena had approached Leontiev with a proposal to set up a joint venture to sell American-style mouthwash in Russia. EuroHealth would contribute the manufacturing equipment and the concentrated powder. Leontiev's company would install the equipment in its factory, add the alcohol and water in the correct proportions, and then bottle the mouthwash. Leontiev's company would handle the management and distribution. The mouthwash was not a Rexall product, so Grajirena told Leontiev he could name it anything he wanted. He could make it seem like an American import, or a local Russian product. For all Grajirena cared, Leontiev could name it Svetlana, after his wife, like the ill-fated high-tech dental chair that was still presumably set up and being used for training somewhere in Leontiev's institute.

Leontiev and Pavel, the manager of his private company, obviously had spoken about the mouthwash at length. Pavel was well briefed. He spoke, and Leontiev listened. First Pavel wanted to make sure Grajirena knew that he was speaking for Leontiev. It would do Grajirena no good to try to sell Pavel on the product. Leontiev was the boss. "Nothing is up to me," Pavel said. "I'm just a soldier. If you and Dr. Leontiev decide to do something together, he'll tell me what I have to do, and I'll start putting it together." He went on, however, to say why it did not appear as if any joint venture for mouthwash was in the offing. "This is a new product for us, a new market," Pavel said, explaining that Leontiev's company manufactured only dental tools and equipment, never consumer products. "Expenses will be higher in the initial period. We're not sure if it is worth it. . . . We would have to create our own market." Besides the manufacturing investment, it would take a lot of advertising to spread the concept of mouthwash. One American mouthwash, Reach, was already in the drugstores and was not doing particularly well, Pavel said. Scope and Listerine were just entering the market, he said, and Leontiev was concerned about his little company competing against the likes of Procter & Gamble.

Grajirena, as usual seeing the cup half full instead of half empty, tried to argue that the lack of an established mouthwash market was an opportunity, not an obstacle. "If no one outside Moscow has heard of Scope or Listerine, then we have just as much chance as they do. Especially if our mouthwash is just as good," Grajirena insisted. "If Professor Leontiev says it is a good product, if he recommends it, if he tells the dentists to recommend it to their patients, then it will be a success." He glanced at Leontiev, who sat passively behind his bushy gray eyebrows. "What we're talking about here is cornering the market," Grajirena continued. "In America the head of the American Dental Association can't say, 'This is the product to use,' and then order everybody to use it. You can do that here. It's a tremendous advantage. It's a major edge for us over those other products." Leontiev ignored the compliment to his influence. Nor did he respond to the suppositions that he could throw his weight behind this mouthwash, or that throwing his weight behind it could make it a success. He did not seem troubled by any ethical questions that might be raised by using his official position to endorse a product he was privately selling. When Leontiev did not react for a full thirty seconds, Grajirena spoke again. "Maybe I'm wrong about this," he said. "But I don't think so."

Leontiev gazed thoughtfully at him for another half a minute before he spoke. "Rick," he said, except with his accent it came out *Reek*. "Reek, you are not right," Leontiev said in English. "We are talking about our population, our people. We know them." Leontiev nodded at Pavel, who continued. "They don't know what mouthwash is," Pavel said. "There are two points. First, we must persuade dentists to use mouthwash, and to recommend it to their patients. We can do that. We can have articles written about mouthwash that will be placed in our scientific journals. We can compile scientific proof that will show the product is very beneficial to everyone. Dentists can tell people they should use mouthwash. But then we come to the second point. Russian people still will not use it without a lot of advertising. Television, magazines, newspapers. And that means a lot of money. Too much money." Leontiev spoke again, in Russian, this time. The only recognizable words to Grajirena were *reklama,* which means "advertising," and *propaganda.* Leontiev used each word several times in talking about persuading both dentists and consumers to embrace mouthwash. Whenever Leontiev mentioned spending large sums of money, he used the universal signal: He held up his hand and rubbed his index and middle fingers vigorously back and forth across his thumb. When Pavel was finished translating, Leontiev seemed ready to dismiss the subject of mouthwash. But Grajirena, selling hard, wasn't finished.

"Okay, but there's one other thing," he said. "Fluoride. This country needs fluoride to help prevent tooth decay. It doesn't look like anybody is going to put fluoride in the water in Russia anytime soon. But dentists all know that fluoride is good. We can put fluoride in the mouthwash. It can be the economical, efficient way to introduce fluoride into Russian households. People will want to use our mouthwash not just because it makes them feel good, but because it is healthy for them. And we can do it very cheaply. This won't be an expensive product." Grajirena mentioned the annual Russian dental conference, where Leontiev was always a main speaker. He said Leontiev could use his speech to promote mouthwash in general, and his own mouthwash in particular. Grajirena said he could have an American scientist write a paper about the benefits of fluoride in mouthwash, and Leontiev could publish it in Russian under his own name, or under the name of some prominent Russian dental researcher. Leontiev's eyes showed a flicker of new interest at the mention of fluoride, but within seconds it was gone. Through Pavel he said yes, his country needed fluoride. But putting fluoride into mouthwash would make it more difficult to gain government approval to sell the mouthwash—especially if the plan was to market it as something that prevents tooth decay. "Maybe someday we will want to make and sell mouthwash. But right now the price is irrelevant," he told Grajirena. He wanted to end the mouthwash discussion.

Grajirena still wasn't ready to let go. He suggested that Leontiev's people get him some preliminary marketing data—"any ballpark estimates"—on how much mouthwash they could sell, if and when they wanted to consider it further. Leontiev nodded yes, his company chairman made a note, and that was finally the end of it. Grajirena was 99 percent sure he would never hear anything from Leontiev about mouthwash again, but he wanted to keep the door open, just in case that changed.

The meeting was winding down. Grajirena and Farrar had been at the institute for three hours. Lazarenko said he had to depart. Everyone stood up, and as he and Grajirena shook hands, they quickly reviewed their deal so far. Lazarenko was still thinking of one million units. He would take care of the regulatory approval with the documents Grajirena had given him, and he would turn over the requirements for the labels at the hotel the next day. Grajirena, in turn, would have more details about shipping for him. They shook hands one last time, and Lazarenko left. Then the atmosphere in Leontiev's office changed. The business day was over. Leontiev began rummaging around on his shelves, bringing out brandy snifters. But Grajirena was not quite finished with business. He told Leontiev that he thought he had a distributor for Dr. Seltzer's Hangover Helper in Russia, but the distributor was not in a position to oversee the application for regulatory approval. Would Leontiev be able to use his influence with the Ministry of Health to get that approval? Yes, Leontiev said, he could help. He knew the people who would be in charge of granting approval for Dr. Seltzer. Some were friends. Some used to work for him. It would take six to eight weeks and cost $12,000 to $16,000. Grajirena seemed pleased. "When Russians tell you something is going to cost $12,000 to $16,000," he said quietly, as Leontiev poured cognac, "it always ends up being $16,000, never $12,000. But that's a fair price. Getting approval usually takes three to four months. If he can get it done in six to eight weeks, it's a bargain." At 5:12 P.M., Leontiev, Grajirena, Pavel, Rimsky, and Geoffrey Farrar raised their glasses.

Leontiev asked after John Hayhurst and Dale McElwee, the Missouri dentists. "They're good people," Pavel translated. Leontiev then said something else, but neither the company chairman nor Rimsky, who had been chipping in to help with the translations now and again, could come up with an interpretation. Leontiev began trying the same word in different languages. Finally, he said *risico*, and someone knew that it meant "risk" in Dutch: Leontiev thought the dentists were too conservative, too reluctant to take risks. As if it had just occurred to him, Grajirena wondered about Leontiev's term in office. How long would he have this job? Leontiev smiled, knowing that Grajirena was really wondering how long he would have this connection. Through Pavel, he said there was no set term. He was appointed for life. "And," he added in English, "I am still young man."

Neither Grajirena nor Farrar was eager to call the hotel and risk having the same driver sent to bring them back, so Leontiev arranged for a car to take them to the hotel. Grajirena seemed exhausted but was upbeat as ever. Mouthwash, hangover helpers—yes, he admitted without any apparent remorse, he was like a modern-day carpetbagger, a flimflam man, a snake-oil salesman, a twenty-first-century Willy Loman traipsing the world with a shoeshine and a smile. Or rather as Grajirena allowed, "A mouthful o' howdy and a handful o' much-obliged." It was becoming his motto. Through the afternoon at Leontiev's institute, Grajirena had been "on"—concentrating, talking, listening, performing—for nearly four hours. "Imagine sitting through four or five straight days of this, six or eight hours a day," Grajirena said. "I've done it many times. Way too often."

He was asked about the relationship between Leontiev and Lazarenko. What was their deal? He said he didn't know and didn't care. Maybe Leontiev had a little piece of the Belarus company. More likely he would get a fee or commission for introducing Lazarenko to Grajirena—if the Dr. Seltzer deal went through. Leontiev was a public official, Grajirena said, but he was also a shrewd businessman. Grajirena was asked about his blunt appeal for Leontiev to use his official influence for private gain—a conflict of interest that would probably be illegal and certainly unethical in the United States. Throughout the afternoon's meetings there had been an unspoken assumption that Leontiev could and would use his influence for private gain. But Leontiev himself had never explicitly said he would do this. No *quid pro quo* was ever spelled out. In the car Grajirena agreed that Leontiev had never indicated he would abuse his influence or position to make money for himself, but he said many Russian officials routinely did so. "Sure, it's a complete conflict of interest," Grajirena said cheerfully. "Absolutely. But Leontiev doesn't look at it that way. In Russia, it's not looked at as a conflict of interest. It's a confirmation of influence. The way they look at it, there's no conflict of interest when a public official uses his power to make money for himself. There's no *conflict* between the competing interests. Instead, the two interests are working together."

Back at the Radisson, Grajirena went to his room to check his messages and make a telephone call. One fax waiting for him had the shipping details he had requested. Yes, air freight was not that much more expensive, and it would speed up delivery—and the payday—by six weeks. The call was to Dale McElwee back in Camdenton, who was waiting for it. Grajirena told him the meeting went well, everything looked good, and it was possible—if everything went perfectly—that Lazarenko's people would place their first order within two months, perhaps as early as March. The order would be for about $380,000. EuroHealth would clear more than $100,000 in profit.

"I told him it looks great. I told him I think we have a good deal," Grajirena said afterward, over a beer in the hotel bar. He paused. "Of course, Dale has heard that before." There were still things that could, and probably would, go wrong. "No matter what, you rarely get it right the first time.

Things always go wrong somewhere along the line, and you have to go back and straighten it out. What's funny, you usually think the screwup is going to be on the Russian side. But just as often it's on the American side. Something we didn't do, or should have done differently," he said. The registration process could get fouled up. The labels might not be exactly right, and they might have to be done again. Rexall might not be able to manufacture one million units of Dr. Seltzer as quickly as Grajirena would like. But the deal seemed solid. Grajirena was tired but exuberant. It looked as if he was finally going to get rich in Russia.

That night he celebrated. Instead of a burger at the coffee shop, he went to the hotel's steak place. He ordered a big porterhouse and washed it down with a good bordeaux. He had brandy afterward, and a Cuban cigar. Yes, he admitted, there was a danger in celebrating too early. Yes, he had done it before. He had celebrated many times during the First Republic years. But this felt different. There wasn't some investor or board member looking over his shoulder. He was able to go out and make deals on his own, and McElwee and Hayhurst—so far—were happy to let him do it. "At the moment, the Docs are satisfied," Grajirena said. "And so am I. This deal looks solid."

The next morning Dennis Batlle arrived at the Radisson around nine thirty. He had met Grajirena a year before, when he began selling him cigars. Batlle was Cuban-Russian. His father was a Russian construction worker sent to Cuba to help on civil engineering projects—"No missile sites," Batlle said—and the family had returned to Moscow to live when he was a teenager. Batlle received a steady supply of Cuban cigars from friends and family in Havana, and he had a nice little business selling them in Moscow. He operated out of his backpack. Grajirena became one of Batlle's cigar customers, and they got to know each other. In recent months Batlle had been helping Grajirena, primarily as an interpreter but also as a general errand-boy and message-taker in Moscow. If papers needed to be delivered somewhere, Grajirena faxed them to Batlle, and he hand-delivered them. Russians who wanted to get in touch with Grajirena called Batlle, and Batlle passed on the message. Batlle and Grajirena e-mailed each other several times a week. Grajirena paid him ten dollars an hour. The money was okay, but Batlle was more interested in the long-term career possibilities. Perhaps EuroHealth would give him a good job someday. Or maybe he would latch on to one of the Russian companies working with Grajirena. He made lots of contacts.

Batlle was only twenty years old, but it was hard to tell. He could have been thirty-five. He was exotic in appearance by Moscow standards. He was of average height but very thin. His skin was light mocha, and his hair was cut just short of shaving it—perhaps to deemphasize the fact that he was going bald at such a young age. His wire-rimmed glasses helped make him look older. On this day he wore jeans and a bulky knit sweater, and he carried a backpack. He sat down with Grajirena in one of the furniture groupings near the Radisson Slavjanskaya bar—it was early, plenty of chairs and sofas were still available—and ordered espresso. Batlle had learned English in school in Cuba, and he was nearly fluent. Grajirena wanted him to translate during the meeting with Lazarenko, so he briefed him on the deal, on the previous day's meeting at Leontiev's office, and on what they were going to talk about that day. Grajirena was going to give Lazarenko the details about shipping the one million units of Dr. Seltzer by air. Grajirena had faxed off the power-of-attorney form to Rexall the previous evening and, remarkably, received it back signed that morning. He would give that to Lazarenko, too, so that the registration process could begin in Belarus. Lazarenko was going to give Grajirena the information needed for Rexall to print labels for Dr. Seltzer in Russian. Once Batlle was briefed, they waited for Lazarenko. And waited. At ten thirty Grajirena called Lazarenko's office. He wasn't there. No one knew where he was. He tried Lazarenko's cell phone. No answer. At eleven o'clock Batlle tried. Same thing. Grajirena and Batlle sat there, saving their furniture grouping, until twelve thirty, when they left for a meeting with Robert Greco.

CHAPTER 29

First Federation

In the way to Moscow in January 1998, Grajirena stopped in Poland to talk to a potential distributor in Warsaw. Changing planes in Frankfurt, he got into an airport waiting-lounge discussion with another American road warrior who did business in Eastern Europe. They were talking about Americans doing business in Moscow, and the other traveler said he had heard some stories—unbelievable to him—about an American who had set up his own Russian company, without any corporate backing from an American company, and was making money hand over fist. The other traveler said it was the damnedest thing he ever heard of, given that there were so many Americans who had gone bust in Russia, even with lots of support from back home. Hell, he said, plenty of Russians had gone bust. But this American, at least according to the stories, was out there on his own, getting rich doing business in Russia the Russians' way—whatever that was. Apparently, the traveler added, the guy was a nutcase. People called this guy "the crazy man." He was so crazy, the traveler said, that he supposedly drove himself around Moscow in a Range Rover, without a single bodyguard. Talk about Moscow Madness. Grajirena shook his head knowingly and sighed. "That guy is real," he told the other traveler. "I know him. He's a friend of mine. His name is Robert Greco."

After Lazarenko failed to show up at the Radisson by midday, Grajirena climbed into another car outside the Radisson Slavjanskaya. This one he knew was safe because it was one of Greco's company cars driven by one of Greco's staff drivers, and Greco knew how much Grajirena hated thrilling taxi rides like the one to Leontiev's office. During the half-hour, relatively sedate drive to Greco's office, well out of central Moscow, Grajirena talked about what had happened to Greco since he had brought him to Moscow to run First Republic years before. Greco had tried to save First Republic. He had tried to get more beer in. He had solved the customs problems by lining up a deal with a sports foundation. He had tried to expand the product line: other beers, sausages, peanuts, anything he could sell. Finally, he had joined with his brother Richard and Ron Finger, the Savannah plastic surgeon, in trying to bail out the company. In each case, what he did was too little too late, or he was shot down by the board of directors. When First Republic failed to keep the Heineken distributorship and the company folded, Heineken offered Greco a job. First Republic was not impressive to the Dutchmen, but Greco was. He accepted the job but figured it would be short-term employment. He was right. It quickly became clear to both Greco and his bosses in Amsterdam that he would be more effective as an importer and distributor if he were working on his own. He told Heineken he was not a corporate guy, and that was all right with Heineken. In some ways it was easier for Heineken not to know what Greco was doing in Moscow.

So Greco set up his own distribution company and called it First Federation. He rounded up the core of the former First Republic employees—the entire staff had been fired—and hired them. Chris Mitchell, First Republic's national sales manager, became First Federation's national sales manager. First Republic's top salespeople became First Federation's top salespeople. First Republic's office manager and many of the clerical staff also followed and joined First Federation in the same jobs. In effect, Greco cannibalized the remains of First Republic. And he proved that First Republic's original concept was a good one. He resurrected its old distribution network and ran it from his office and warehouse in Moscow, rather than from the States. He raised some startup money from private investors back in the States, most of it from a physician friend of the family in Pennsylvania.

He made it clear to the investors, however, that they were investing in Robert Greco more than in First Federation or the concept of an American-style distribution network in Moscow. He would keep them informed, maybe, but he wasn't making any promises. He wouldn't be available to answer detailed questions about how the business was doing. He would pay back their investments, along with shares of the profits, until they were bought out. Looking back, it was the way Grajirena knew First Republic should have been run. Looking at Greco's company, he could see literally what might have been—and how rich he might have become. But he also worried about Greco. He worked too hard. He took too many chances, both personally and professionally. He shouldn't zoom around Moscow alone. He should have bodyguards. He should be cautious when he competed for business, and careful about who he took business away from. "I'm afraid he's going to get whacked one of these days," Grajirena confessed. "I've had nightmares about having to call his parents and tell them something has happened to him. That would be the hardest call I would ever have to make. I would feel responsible. I took him to Russia in the first place."

———————

First Federation's offices were in an upstairs wing of a sprawling building that had once been some sort of technical school. The hallways were wide, the rooms were big, like old classrooms, and the ceilings were high. The neighborhood was drab and plain, just another Moscow neighborhood dominated by characterless institutional buildings and faceless apartment complexes. Greco wanted an out-of-the-way location, Grajirena said as he walked up the wide stairs. Greco wanted to keep a low profile. He didn't want to draw a lot of attention to himself or his business. Greco's offices, aside from the private restrooms, were nothing special even by Russian standards. Functional desks, chairs, and shelves filled the open spaces, where the salesmen worked in one former classroom, the clerical and administrative staff in another, the computer people in yet another. The desks were strewn with papers and file folders. The wall decorations were just as functional—bulletin boards, maps, charts, the occasional poster from Heineken or one of Greco's other products. In the salesmen's office Chris Mitchell sat behind the biggest desk, at the far end of the room, eating a pizza from a nearby shop for his lunch.

Mitchell had become Greco's right-hand man for expanding the beer distribution to other Russian cities. Few Americans had been in Russia as long as Mitchell. Few had seen so many changes, or been part of them. Few had become as Russian as Mitchell. He spoke English to Greco, who was still far from fluent in Russian. But to virtually everyone else, Mitchell spoke in Russian. He could go days without speaking English. He thought in Russian. During a casual conversation, he was telling a story and wanted to say something was chest-high. But he couldn't think of the word for "chest" in English. Patting his upper torso and thinking hard, he finally said, "Breast area." Mitchell lived in one of those nondescript Russian apartment complexes near the office, and he walked to work. He had a Russian girlfriend, a tall, slim, dark-haired woman in her early twenties who could have been a fashion model but was studying for her doctorate in economics. Mitchell apologized that he was in a hurry because he was off to Rostov, a Black Sea port city six hundred miles to the south of Moscow, to see about setting up yet another branch of First Federation there. He would do the preliminary market research and make the early contacts. If it looked like a good move for First Federation, Greco would come in, nail down the details, and close the deal. Mitchell nodded at the pizza. It was good, he said. Even more remarkably, it had been made right there in that nondescript neighborhood, and delivered. He had ordered it by phone. Yes, he said, Moscow was changing. And it was home.

Down the hall, Greco's own office was about twenty feet square and connected to a slightly larger conference room. He greeted Grajirena warmly. He wore a tailored brown-checked sports jacket, with a small Heineken pin in the lapel. His blue denim work shirt was open at the collar, no tie, under a tan cashmere V-neck sweater. He wore dark blue chinos and soft leather boots. He looked like a nine-to-five city guy who had been invited to his rich boss's weekend hunting lodge. A bookkeeper, maybe. Greco's cheeks were pink and clean, as if he had just gotten a really good shave. In his mid-thirties, his hair was starting to thin. It was cut neatly and short. "Hey," Grajirena cried. "The ponytail. What happened?" Greco blushed only slightly. "Ah, I cut it off a few weeks ago," he said, "when I was back in the States for Chrismas. No reason. Just time for a new look." They stood and talked for a few minutes in Greco's office. A good-sized dark wood desk was backed up against a row of shelves. From the desk Greco could easily gaze out the broad window that reached from near the floor almost to the twelve-foot ceiling. But it was a nonview: the tops of more drab buildings just like this one. It did not appear as if Greco had bothered to tell anyone to clean the window in some time. On the desk were a blank yellow legal pad, two calculators, an ashtray with a half-smoked cigar, a desktop computer, and a multiline phone. Greco talked with Grajirena about the new offices where he was moving the company. He would have thirty phone lines, including one of Moscow's first ISDN lines. His employees—he was up to somewhere between seventy and eighty in Moscow, with about fifty more in offices in other Russian cities—often used electronic mail, and a couple of them were setting up a company website. He was looking forward to his Russian customers being able to order beer and check on delivery schedules via the website. The walls and shelves and corners of the office were given over to sample products, brochures, posters, and point-of-sale promotional material from Heineken and companies doing business with First Federation. Cans of pork, turkey, chicken, sausage. Different brands of beer. A Heineken umbrella. A Heineken mirror. There was a world map on one wall, with Russia at the center. The shelves behind the desk held a series of learn-to-speak-Russian tapes and books, Russian-American dictionaries, several volumes on Russian customs and tariff regulations, several boxes of Cuban cigars, and a stack of music CDs by an eclectic range of artists, including Harry Connick, Jr., Gloria Estefan, Frank Sinatra, and Beck.

At one point Grajirena said he had lost the number of a Russian whom he and Greco both knew, an academic who might have some information or advice for Grajirena on marketing Rexall products in Russia. Greco pulled out a palmtop, punched in the man's name, and gave Grajirena the number. On the way to the First Federation offices, Grajirena had talked about how busy Greco was, and how much pressure he was under with his tax problems and a business that was growing rapidly amid competition that could be cutthroat—literally, Grajirena feared. But Greco did not seem stressed. He was calm, relaxed, almost laid back. He seemed to have all the time in the world to talk to Grajirena about anything or nothing for as long as Grajirena wanted to hang around.

When Grajirena finally brought up Dr. Seltzer's Hangover Helper, Greco motioned him into the conference room, and they took two chairs at the nearest end of the long table. Greco had expressed interest in being the exclusive distributor for Russia for Dr. Seltzer. He already delivered beer, food, and snack products to many retail establishments large and small, and he was always looking for new product lines. Plus he figured he could sell Dr. Seltzer to bars and restaurants. They could keep little displays right at the door for people to buy on the way home. Grajirena recapped the negotiations with Lazarenko, never mentioning that Lazarenko stood him up earlier in the day. Grajirena told him that while he had quoted a price of 38 cents per unit for Dr. Seltzer to the Belarussian company, he would charge First Federation only 35 cents per unit. "That's the Greco price, not the Lazarenko price," Grajirena said. Greco nodded and took a few notes but spoke little during the meeting. After Grajirena explained that he hoped to get the product registration for Dr. Seltzer completed within a few weeks with Leontiev's help, the meeting was over. Greco said fine. When Grajirena was ready to ship, he was ready to distribute.

Grajirena went off to make the rounds of the office and say hello to old friends, people he had hired to work for First Republic and who had signed on with Greco afterward. One of his first stops was at the desk of Natasha Volkova, who had started with First Republic as a Cold Patrol girl. Unlike many of the girls, she was never late, never got drunk, and never acted in an unprofessional manner. She was hired full time as a saleswoman and was office manager by the time First Republic folded. Now she was Greco's personal assistant. Grajirena was a very nice man, she said, one of the few First Republic people based in the States whom she liked. But Grajirena "was too far away," she said. She said she loved working for Greco because he was so dynamic yet at the same time he never seemed ruffled. "He is a very good listener," she said.

CHAPTER 30

Greco-Russian

In his conference room Greco was persuaded to talk. An introspective and thoughtful man, Greco nonetheless rarely spoke—seriously, at least—to other Americans about what it was like to do business in Russia. For one thing, he didn't like to talk about himself. For another, few people—in America or in Moscow or anywhere else—could really appreciate what he had done and what he was doing, largely because no one else had ever done it. When friends back in Pennsylvania would ask him about doing business in Russia, he used to dismiss the subject with a crude metaphor.

In his early days with First Republic, what had bothered him the most—what had disgusted him—were the restrooms in Moscow. The building where First Republic had its offices was typical. It was an old building, home to various government business and cultural enterprises. There were two restrooms on each floor, one for women and one for men. Greco couldn't speak for the women's room, but he was sure that no one had cleaned the men's room in years. That wasn't unusual in the Soviet Union, for public or semiprivate restrooms. Even in apartment buildings, where two or more families often shared a bathroom in the hall, neither family would clean it. "Why should we clean it? They just mess it up, and then we have to clean it again," was the common attitude. The Communist theory of everyone doing common work for the common good was noble, but it broke down in practice when it came to cleaning bathrooms. In public buildings the maintenance people had jobs for life, like everyone else. When it became clear that a janitor wouldn't lose his job or get his pay docked or even get told off by his boss for not cleaning a toilet very well, that toilet didn't get cleaned very well. The men's room outside the First Republic office, like many others, had been getting dirtier and dirtier over the years.

Once Greco held his nose and took a camera into the men's room. Back in the States, when he was asked about his job he would pull out the photo and say, "You want to know what it's like doing business in Russia? This is what it's like, except without the smell." When Greco started First Federation, one of the first things he did was build private restrooms strictly for First Federation employees. He also hired maintenance people who understood that they would be fired if they did not keep the restrooms clean.

Doing business in Russia today is still dirty, but in a different way, Greco said. "It's impossible to do business in Russia and be totally legitimate by American standards," he said. "It's comparable to companies in the United States looking for special consideration or a change in legislation. They contribute to campaigns. Well, in Russia it's like everyone is running for office and looking for a contribution. And if that's the way that business is done here, then that's the way you have to do it. Look, giving gifts to people who can help you, to get results, has always been a way of life in Russia. It's part of the culture." First Federation had a "roof," Greco said, but he was reluctant to talk about the people or his relationship with them, for obvious reasons. However, he did say his roof is not made up of what he called "bandits." The bandits, the old *mafiya*, "most of those guys are gone now," he said. Some went legitimate and became *biznesmen* operating aboveboard companies. A few went to jail. Many were killed off, or went back to the provinces to run their gangs or run for public office or both. In Moscow, roofs evolved into all-purpose consultants or fixers, except with the kind of close government connections and influence that American consultants could only dream about. Greco regarded his roof as a necessary cost of doing business, but he always tried to keep the roof at arm's length. He never was tempted, for example, by his roof's financing offers. Yes, the money, at seemingly favorable terms, would have let Greco expand his business faster. But he didn't want to let the roof get so much as a foot in the door in terms of ownership or control of his company. He said companies typically paid their roofs about 10 percent of their gross revenues, but he negotiated a set fee with his roof. Greco said he had no idea what his roof did for him—if anything. Occasionally during his infrequent meetings with his roof, he would be blunt. "So what are you doing for me?" he would demand. The roof would reply, "Have you had any problems with theft or vandalism or inventory disappearing? Have any government inspectors asked for bribes or tried to shut you down? Have any competitors threatened you? No? That's what we're doing for you."

Taxation was the one area in which the roof did not offer any help or protection. And Greco was having huge tax problems. If all the various taxes he was technically required to pay were added up—not counting the many staff hours required to complete all the forms and do all the filings—it came to 115 percent of his profit. One of the problems was that the basic Russian corporate taxes covered gross revenue rather than net profits. Another problem was that many ordinary business expenses were taxed. Advertising, for example, was a normal business expense in the United States, but Greco found that he had to pay an additional 5 percent tax for every ruble he spent on advertising. One Russian study published in 1997 said this: "By the number and volume of taxes, Russia occupies the first place in the world (there are 27 federal taxes and about 70 kinds of local taxes). For instance, the profit-tax reaches the figures of 85–90 percent, which is more than twice as high than the average for the world. The current system of taxation is both unjust and burdensome. It hampers investments and the reconstruction of production. It pushes businesspeople to hide profits and escape taxes. Hence it condemns business to illegitimate existence." So Greco, like pretty much every foreigner who wanted to stay in Russia long term, kept tight books and spent a lot of money on Russian tax advisers. He avoided any and all taxes he could, and he was always looking for new loopholes. But he paid his taxes.

And that grated on him, since so few Russian companies, including his competitors, seemed to pay their taxes. Some Russians opened one company after another, starting over whenever taxes came due. The tax burden was one of the reasons that Russia was having such a hard time rebuilding its infrastructure after all those years of Soviet decline. Neither companies nor individuals paid their taxes. A connection with a roof—openly or surreptitiously—was one way for local officials to raise the money to get things done. Suppose local officials wanted to build a new park or some low-cost housing. If tax revenues had been what they were supposed to be, there would be money for the park or the housing project. But with no tax revenue, there was no money. So when a private business—Russian or foreign, it didn't matter—applied to expand into the district, the officials would insist that the company first build the park or the housing project. The company might not pay its taxes later, but at least the park or housing project would be there.

Even large Russian companies avoided paying taxes. Many of them instead offered to pay through barter—whether or not the products or services they offered could actually be used by the government, or were worth as much as the taxes they owed. In the United States people can go to jail and companies can be closed down for not paying their taxes. In Russia that was impractical. For one thing, Russia needed people to be working and companies to be doing business. It was better to have people working and not paying taxes than have them in jail, where they weren't working and weren't paying their taxes anyway. The same with companies. Closing down a company for failure to pay taxes would cost jobs and hurt the economy, and the taxes still wouldn't be paid. Russian tax authorities made a few exceptions, however. They did go after companies that were rolling up large amounts of cash—especially if a lot of the cash appeared to be leaving Russia.

Robert Greco and First Federation fit the profile. Greco figured he must have been turned in by competitors who were hoping that tax problems would lead him to leave Russia for good. Even if First Federation survived, the competitors apparently felt they would be better off because someone else, not Greco, would be running it. For more than a year Greco had been fighting the tax inspectors. He went through four separate inspections, when officials came to his office, went through records, and interviewed him and his employees. Greco insisted he had paid his taxes. According to him, the inspectors had not proved he had done anything wrong. Instead, they froze some of his bank accounts. Then they started demanding interest on the supposed penalties. His tax bill climbed to more than half a million dollars. Greco's only consolation was that many other American companies had worse tax problems. Even the big companies were not immune. While he was haggling over his $500,000 tax bill, for example, Johnson & Johnson was fighting a staggering $19 million tax bill that had been presented, seemingly out of the blue, by Russian authorities. The Russian Federal Tax Police not only wanted the money, but initiated criminal charges against two of Johnson & Johnson's top American executives in Moscow.

When his own tax problems came up, Greco hired consultants from the Moscow branch of one of America's biggest accounting firms. The consulants charged him $15,000, then advised him to pay whatever the Russian tax inspectors were demanding. Next he hired a firm of Russian accountants, and they seemed to be on the verge of working out a compromise. He would have to pay, but only a fraction of the half million. And he would have some assurances that a major review of his taxes would not become an annual event for the tax inspectors. Greco didn't know how much of what he had to pay was for taxes, how much for penalties, how much for interest, how much for accountants' fees, and how much for "gifts." It didn't matter to him. It was all part of the cost of doing business in Russia.

And business was good. For one thing, the duties for importing beer had been lowered and standardized. The old customs privileges through foundations and charities were abolished after the government realized that the *mafiya* had effectively taken control of them. Many people, including the head of the ice hockey federation, were murdered, often the victims of infighting between *mafiya* gangs competing to control a charity's customs privileges. The low point was the *mafiya* bombing at a cemetery during a memorial service attended by hundreds of Russian veterans of the Afghan war and their families. Fourteen people were killed in the bombing, which apparently was sparked by an intra-*mafiya* war over control of the $200 million a year in customs privileges, mostly for tobacco and alcohol, being collected by the Russian Fund of Invalids of the War in Afghanistan. The violence and corruption led the government to do away with the customs privileges and to crack down on customs bribery and corruption. As a result, by 1998 Robert Greco knew in advance how much he would have to pay to bring in a container of beer. No more bribes. No more electricity mysteriously going out at border crossings. No more Shakespeare and Palmi.

Perhaps even more important, he was getting steady supplies of beer. At First Republic a few years earlier, when he had been lucky to get four containers a month from Miller, Greco had always wondered how much beer he could sell if he could get all he needed. Heineken was selling him all he needed now, and he was importing up to forty containers a month, sometimes more—about the same amount of Miller beer that was being imported by the Russian company that had made a deal with Miller Brewing after First Republic folded. Just as important for Greco's business, in a few short years Russia had become a beer country. Describing a Moscow evening street scene, the American travel writer Jill Schensul wrote, "Streaks of clouds fade to pink behind the gold domes of the Kremlin. People are coming home from work; many are already out for the evening— many toting what seems to be the ubiquitous bottle of beer."

Greco had formed several subsidiaries and sister companies under the First Federation umbrella, and he was using them to expand into other products, like other brands of beer, mineral water, and canned food. He became a partner in several upscale Moscow restaurants and bars that served his Heineken beer exclusively, and he was thinking of promoting some musical events. To Greco, the changes in Russia were all positive. Yes, there were many problems. As he spoke, the Yeltsin government was negotiating for billions in loans from the International Monetary Fund to prop up the sagging economy. Yet he also saw hope. "There's a real consumer economy beginning to develop here," he said. When he first arrived in Moscow, people had lined up to buy whatever goods were available in the shops. They had spent their money as soon as they got it because the rampant inflation would make it worth less tomorrow. In those days, in the mid-1990s, Russia had been a dumping ground for the products the rest of the world didn't want. Greco used to see relatively wealthy Russians wearing ill-fitting, poorly made clothes and shoes, rejects from Third World companies that no other industrialized economy would buy. In Russia that cheap shirt or jacket from Africa or Asia had been a prized possession, to be worn proudly. Over a few short years, tastes had become much more sophisticated. Clothes and shoes that Greco himself wore—from the States, from England, from Germany and Italy—had become widely available in Moscow boutiques and department stores. But he didn't shop in Moscow. "Too expensive," he said. "They charge the manufacturer's suggested price, or more, for designer clothes. When I go back to the States, I shop."

Greco expressed long-term hopes for the Russian economy despite the doom and gloom of the Yeltsin government's official figures and the IMF. "The official figures aren't accurate," Greco said. "So much business is conducted on the black market or the gray market that the real economy is hidden. I see a real middle class developing, but you don't see that in the official figures because those people are not reporting all their income or paying all their taxes. People are saving and acquiring. They're improving their lifestyles. They are realizing that if they work hard, they can get the things they want, they can have a better life." Indeed, Russian sociologists said one of the remarkable transformations of Russia was that after decades of depending on the state to tell them what to do, when to do it, and how to do it, many Russians were beginning to take charge of their own lives. "People are becoming more oriented toward their own personal, professional, financial, social possibilities," one professor observed. He said that conducting commerce—whether becoming an entrepreneur or just going out and buying something—is the kind of social activity that is showing Russian citizens how to be independent from the state. "Stores are popping up everywhere," Greco agreed. "It's a story I've seen many times. A guy sets up a kiosk. Then another. Then another. Pretty soon he gets a storefront. Then another. Pretty soon he has a store. Then another. Then a chain of stores. It's exciting to see that happen, to be part of it in a small way, to feel like you're helping it happen. Those of us doing business in Moscow today are helping to make the rules that this country will live by. Russia is an old country, but in a sense it's a new country, too. It's starting all over, and it's feeling its way, developing a new set of rules. There is no rule of law as we know it in America. Ethics don't matter. Contracts are no good. You operate on trust, with a handshake. I like that part of it, and I'm totally in tune with it. I'm not sitting down in a lot of meetings, looking at a lot of contracts, all tied up in legalese."

Greco told of a twenty-two-year-old Russian who came to him and asked to be his representative on Sakhalin Island, four thousand miles to the east. The kid had no credentials, no experience, no business education. He didn't have "two dimes to rub together," as Greco put it. But the kid explained convincingly to Greco how he could make money for both of them. Remote Sakhalin Island was about to be enveloped in an oil boom, potentially more productive than the North Sea. Tens of thousands of workers would be moving in. Entire towns were being built from the ground up. Greco usually sold kegs of beer for about $75. The kid offered to buy beer from him for $150. The kid would then air-freight the beer to Sakhalin Island and sell it for $300 to $350. There was that kind of demand. Greco believed in the young man. He agreed to finance him, and Greco's new Sakhalin Island outpost boomed. So impressive was the young guy's development as a manager that Greco began promoting him through the ranks of First Federation and eventually put him in charge of the company's operations in St. Petersburg.

Greco was less than impressed with most of the other Americans doing business in Moscow. Many were only occasional visitors, in town for a week or two at a time, a few times a year. "Those are the guys and gals, bankers and lawyers and marketing people, who are like kamikazes when they land in Moscow. In Russia nobody cares if you go mad, so they do. They drink too much and drop all their inhibitions. You see them getting so drunk they take off their shirts, drop trou, and dance on bar tops," he said. Moscow Madness, he said, also claims many Americans who are posted to Moscow by their companies for a few months, two or three years at most. "They're just passing through. They are more interested in being able to say they were here. But while they're here, if they have any character flaws at all, Moscow will find them. You've got a have a lot of backbone in Moscow to remain true to yourself. You've got to stand on your own two feet, and be very sure of who you are." Moscow Madness strikes both the business visitors and those who are living in Russia, Greco said.

He had seen many examples. One involved a young American woman in her twenties, a lawyer, who had been married for just a couple of years to another lawyer. They had a great future, a golden couple. She was sent to Moscow a few times by her firm. She liked it. Greco did some business with a company that she was representing and got to know her—strictly socially. But apparently she felt as if she could confide in him. "I feel like a different person when I'm in Moscow. So wild, so free," she told him. She started coming to Moscow more and more. She got a Russian boyfriend, a *mafiya* guy. "Being naughty was part of the charm of Moscow to her," Greco said. He would see her out at nightclubs drunk, and then friends told him she was hanging around in casinos in revealing leather outfits. He heard she was into cocaine, and that she was being passed from guy to guy. "Then she got into some lesbian stuff because that was what the Russian guys wanted. They wanted to watch," Greco said. The woman left her husband in the States and took a job with the Moscow office of an American law firm. She didn't last long. She got fired but refused to go home. She said she would stay in Moscow. The last Greco heard, she had tried to commit suicide. Some friends raised the money to send her home. "I heard she was getting all sorts of treatment, but I don't know," Greco said. "Such a waste. Moscow Madness."

Greco was interrupted for a phone call. It looked as if the managers of Gorky Park, Moscow's version of Central Park, might go for Greco's proposal to take over the exclusive beer concession for the park. His bid included plans for rock concerts in the summer. It would be a good deal for Greco, a good deal for Gorky Park, and a bad deal for the Russians who had been selling beer in Gorky Park. The competition would not be happy about losing another lucrative deal to Greco. Grajirena, who had returned to Greco's office, listened to Greco's explanation. "Be careful with this one. This could be real trouble," Grajirena cautioned. Greco said he was always careful. Grajirena said if that was true, Greco wouldn't drive himself. He should have drivers and bodyguards. "I have been driving myself for years," Greco said patiently. It was territory that he and Grajirena, like a fretting parent and an independent son, had been over many times. "I didn't like having a driver. It restricted my freedom. I found that driving myself gave me a better feel for the city," Greco explained. He didn't say it in so many words, but Greco had become, in effect, a new Russian himself. A player. He didn't try to do business the old American way, the way that Grajirena and the rest of First Republic tried to do. "There's a whole secret world here I had to pierce to become one of the players, to swim with the sharks," Greco said. "To succeed, I had to take that risk."

Some of his scariest times in Moscow were in the early days with First

Republic, when the combination of customs troubles, cash-flow problems, and difficulties with Miller Brewing kept First Republic from importing and distributing enough beer to keep up with the demand. Miller was the dominant American beer in Moscow. People went to bars that served Miller specifically to drink Miller. Bar owners didn't like it when First Republic couldn't deliver Miller, and their customers started going elsewhere to look for it. Bar owners, themselves often *mafiya* guys or guys who had *mafiya* connections, called Greco at First Republic and demanded, "Where's our beer?" He tried to explain that he was not getting as much beer from Miller as he needed, and he tried to explain why. The Russians weren't interested. Several bar owners threatened violence. One offered to slit Greco's throat. One said, "If the next keg of beer out of your warehouse does not come to me, whoever gets it will open the tap and piss will come out. What do you think that will do for your business?" While he was living with that in Moscow, Greco grimaced, investors back in the States were pressuring him to "hang on" and "work his magic" while they tried to come up with new money that never came. "They did not appreciate what I was dealing with here," he reflected.

Sitting in his own company's conference room years later, Greco said he believed that if and when his personal safety was in jeopardy, he would know where the threat was coming from. He would perhaps ask his roof for help, but he doubted that any roof could save his life. More likely he would try to arrange a compromise, a business solution, with whoever wanted him out of the way. "I feel safest at the office," Greco said. "Maybe that's one of the reasons I work so much." He said he left the office late most nights. Once in a while he stopped at a club or restaurant that was a good customer, or where he was a partner. He said he still rarely took a drink. A few times a week, he stopped to work out at a health club. Once in a while he went to the ballet—a love he discovered when Grajirena sent him to St. Petersburg years before to renegotiate the customs bill for the frozen beer. He used a free night to attend his first ballet. He has been hooked ever since. Unlike Chris Mitchell, Greco never came to regard Moscow as home. It was where he worked, part of another life, a separate reality. Pennsylvania was still home, back with his family. In three to five years, he might be out of Russia. He had no concrete idea what he would do, but he did know where. His parents were retiring and didn't want to take care of their big house. So Greco was buying it, the house where he and his five brothers and sisters grew up. "I just couldn't imagine driving past that house and knowing someone else was living in it," he said.

Grajirena and Greco shook hands and said good-bye. Grajirena invited Greco to come to the Radisson the following evening—Grajirena's last evening in Moscow on this trip—to meet Boris and his family. Boris was important, Grajirena said, but he didn't know exactly who Boris was or what Boris did for a living. But he had met Boris in Tampa through mutual Russian-American friends, and Boris had told him that he had a *dacha* near Yeltsin's own weekend house. "And he'll have his wife and daughters along," Grajirena said. "Real cute girls. They're seventeen and twenty-four. But that's too old for you." Greco laughed and said no thanks, he had to catch up on some paperwork. Back at the hotel, there was a message for Grajirena. Lazarenko was sorry he had missed that day's meeting, but he had car trouble and his cell phone wasn't working. He could come to the hotel the next morning at ten o'clock.

The next morning Grajirena and Dennis Batlle again met and claimed a furniture grouping in the lobby area near the bar at the Radisson Slavjanskaya. They ordered coffee and waited. Lazarenko rushed in, flushed, a few minutes after ten, all apologies and all business. Grajirena introduced Batlle as his translator and his personal assistant in Moscow, who would be Lazarenko's primary contact when Grajirena was in Florida, and who could help Lazarenko with anything that needed to be done. Grajirena turned over the power of attorney he had received from Rexall, and Lazarenko gave him the documents detailing the Belarus requirements for labeling Dr. Seltzer. It was a brief, cordial, and altogether satisfactory meeting. Lazarenko and Grajirena agreed to talk soon, through Batlle, and to get together during Grajirena's next trip to Moscow in six weeks. At that point Lazarenko would have a better idea of exactly when the Belarus company would send the letter of credit for $380,000 and order its one million units, and Grajirena would have a better idea exactly when the first shipment of Dr. Selzter would arrive by air freight in Minsk. The two men shook hands, and Lazarenko left.

It was the last time Grajirena ever saw him.

CHAPTER 31

Fizz and Fizzles

Not long after those meetings with Vladimir Lazarenko in Moscow, the Belarus economy collapsed. The Belarussian ruble crashed, and kept crashing. In the coming weeks it would lose half its value. That meant it would cost twice as much for the company Lazarenko was representing to import Dr. Seltzer. The Belarussian company suddenly was more worried about protecting its domestic business and keeping its doors open than in importing a hangover helper from the States. Across Belarus, business with foreign companies came to a screeching halt. Lazarenko sent word to Grajirena through Dennis Batlle: The deal was off. Lazarenko returned the documents that Grajirena had provided for him. With those documents, to Grajirena's surprise, were the papers that Grajirena had given to Leontiev to register Dr. Seltzer with the Russian Ministry of Health and get the labels approved for the four Rexall vitamin products, which had been registered earlier but did not yet have approved labels. Leontiev apparently had dumped the whole registration process on Lazarenko, probably for half the fee Grajirena was supposed to pay. Leontiev had done nothing, and neither had Lazarenko. "I am so pissed off," Grajirena told Batlle. He seethed for a few days. Then providence intervened. A fax arrived in Grajirena's home office. It was a news release, dated months earlier, from the U.S. Department of Commerce. There was no indication who had sent the fax, or why. It was a notice about a reverse trade mission to be held at UCLA. Among the Russians attending the conference were several of the key people in the Ministry of Health, including the top deputy in charge of registering foreign pharmaceutical products for sale in Russia.

They had only two days before the deadline for registration, but Grajirena called John Hayhurst in Camdenton to ask if he wanted to go along. Hayhurst said sure. The first night of the conference, Grajirena tracked down the deputy, was pleased to find that he was fluent in English, and made a date to chat one-on-one the next afternoon. When they sat down, Grajirena explained what he wanted to do and gave the deputy a sample of Dr. Seltzer's Hangover Helper. Smiling, the deputy said it was, sadly, a product that probably would do well in Russia. "So tell me exactly what I need to do to get it registered," Grajirena said. "I have already registered my four vitamin products, and I have the labels translated into Russian. But I still need approval for the labels from your office. I'll be in Moscow next month. Let's make an appointment. I'll hand-deliver everything I need, and we can get this thing done." The deputy agreed. He laid out the requirements step by step and promised to help. For once, everything went exactly as Grajirena hoped. The registration went smoothly on his next trip to Moscow, and the fees added up to $2,300, not the $12,000 to $16,000 Leontiev had wanted.

But then there was another problem with Dr. Seltzer. Robert Greco no longer wanted to be the master distributor for Russia. He didn't want anything to do with Dr. Seltzer. He discovered that adding pharmaceuticals to his distribution network, even simple over-the-counter remedies, was more complicated than adding another brand of beer or another kind of canned sausages. He would need special permits and licensing to distribute Dr. Seltzer. It simply wasn't worth the trouble, not when the rest of his business was booming. Not when he was already wrapped up in enough red tape with his tax problems. Thanks, but no thanks, Greco told Grajirena. No problem, Grajirena told Greco. He was disappointed. He would have loved to work with Greco again. But he respected Greco's business judgment. If this wasn't the right time or the right deal for them to work on together, Grajirena would be patient. He figured they would both be doing business in Russia for a long time. Grajirena went back to the list of contacts he had compiled, primarily from trade shows, as potential Dr. Seltzer distributors in Russia. He rated the companies according to how he thought they would do, and started at the top of the list with the biggest and best.

He made an appointment with the marketing manager, who greeted him by recalling their meeting at a trade show and saying, "Hey, where have you been for two years? Some of my friends have had some pretty bad hangovers, and I wish I had your stuff to help them out." He and Grajirena went over EuroHealth's proposal for a master distributor, and how the Russian company could market Dr. Seltzer. Grajirena was pleased, however, that the marketing man seemed even more interested in the four Rexall vitamins that EuroHealth already had registered in Russia. Grajirena saw much more long-term growth potential for EuroHealth in vitamins and other over-the-counter pharmaceuticals than in home remedies such as Dr. Seltzer. He saw the Hangover Helper almost as a gimmick, as a novelty item that could get EuroHealth's foot in the door and start a cash flow on which to base further growth. If he could skip the gimmick stage altogether, so much the better.

It was a good thing he had that attitude, because when Grajirena returned to the States in the spring of 1998 and talked to Rexall about what the new Russian distributor wanted in its first order—sometime in the summer of 1998, he hoped—he was told that Rexall might not be able to produce Dr. Seltzer in time to make an initial delivery anytime that year. "They said there were some quality-control problems with production, and then they said they had to find a new manufacturer to actually make the stuff for them," Grajirena mused. "I don't know, maybe they just didn't want Rexall to be associated with a product that would seem to encourage heavy drinking, or at least would tell people it was okay for them to drink a lot because here was this medicine they could take that would make them feel better the next day. I tried to tell them there isn't the same sort of antidrinking stigma in Russia, that the culture is different, but I don't know whether that had any impact." No matter. The Russian distributor wanted the four vitamins to begin with, and he said the first order would be coming as soon as all the paperwork was cleared up. The Lithuanian distributor said the same thing.

EuroHealth gave both master distributors five-year exclusives for its Rexall products, with requirements for certain minimum sales levels. Grajirena concentrated on trying to work out better credit terms for payments from the master distributors. Neither of the master distributors, the Lithuanian company nor the Russian company, was willing to pay cash in advance on a regular basis. They agreed to pay cash up front for two small initial shipments, but after that they wanted to place bigger orders on credit. Rexall agreed to sixty-day credit terms after the first two shipments. But Grajirena was hoping growth prospects would be strong enough that the two master distributors would want to order shipments of vitamins beyond what they could pay for in sixty days. He found a Florida-based, government-backed export finance corporation that was supposed to make export guarantees for products shipped out of Florida. Grajirena began putting together the documentation needed to convince the export financiers that they should extend credit so that the Russian and Lithuanian master distributors could defer their payments beyond sixty days. In Boca Raton, Grajirena convinced Rexall that it needed to support its products in these markets. He suggested that Rexall commit its trade-show booth, with all the corresponding brochures and other presentation materials, to a series of health-themed trade shows throughout Russia and Lithuania in the autumn of 1998. Rexall said yes. In Camdenton, Dale McElwee and John Hayhurst began putting together plans for a small office, staffed by probably one or two clerical people, who would process the orders and payments and schedule the shipments through Rexall. Hayhurst cut back his orthodontics practice to part time and began drawing a salary from EuroHealth to oversee the office.

———

Meanwhile, with little to do concerning Russia and Lithuania except wait for the first orders to actually come in, by the middle of 1998 Grajirena stepped up his efforts to find new master distributors for EuroHealth's Rexall products and to find new product areas for EuroHealth. He returned to Poland, where he had made contact with a pharmaceutical company executive a couple of years earlier, when EuroHealth had a more ambitious business plan and was courting a Polish investment bank in hopes of attracting $2 million or more. The deal with the Poles fell through, but Grajirena kept in touch with the pharmaceutical executive. The executive was interested in trying something new, and Grajirena talked to him about establishing a new company that would serve as a master distributor for EuroHealth's Rexall products in Poland. And there were other leads. In Los Angeles earlier in the spring, at the conference where he met the Russian official in charge of product registration, Grajirena met a young woman named Katya who was serving as an interpreter. They chatted, and she told him her mother was a doctor at a clinic in Moscow providing beauty care for women. Grajirena, as always, made a few mental notes and stuck her card in a file.

A couple of weeks later, Grajirena got a call out of the blue from his old friend Robert Snibbe, who had been one of the original First Republic investors and who had led the group of Tampa investors that made a $250,000 offer for a controlling interest in EuroHealth a few months earlier. McElwee and Hayhurst rejected that offer, but Snibbe's business radar remained up for health-related products that might be transferable to Eastern Europe. He told Grajirena about Key West Aloe, a company that produced expensive skin and face creams for women. Grajirena got in touch with the company, which agreed to send him a catalog and samples of some of the products. When he asked for samples of some other products in the catalog that he thought might sell in Russia, the company said it would take a while. So

Grajirena sent Valerie to the local drugstore, where she spent $164 collecting samples for him. He got in touch with Katya, the interpreter, and set up a meeting with her mother in Moscow on his next trip. Katya's mother turned out to be Dr. Olga Panova, medical director of the Russian Academy of Science's Hospital for Aesthetic Dermatology. The hospital did all manner of cosmetic treatment for women, including surgery: hair implants, breast enhancements, face-lifts, laser surgery for blemishes, liposuction. Panova was very interested in the Key West Aloe products that Grajirena showed her, especially when he told her that the Florida company could private-label them for her. She could be the importer and master distributor of those products in Russia.

"Uh, there's just one thing," Grajirena told the doctor. "I have been through a nightmare with getting other products registered in Russia, and I'm not sure I'm up for going through it again. Do you have any idea what's involved in getting these products registered? What do I have to do? How much will it cost me?" Panova smiled at him and said he didn't have to do anything. She was in charge of registering skin-care products. She would do the clinical testing in her own lab, and then she herself would make sure the registration papers were issued. Grajirena did not have to fill out any papers, stand in any lines, or pay any bribes. Grajirena introduced Panova to Dennis Batlle. Since the meeting with Lazarenko a few months earlier, Batlle steadily had taken on a larger role as EuroHealth's public face in Moscow when Grajirena was back in Florida. Batlle, who had proved himself reliable, had changed in appearance and demeanor. When he met Dr. Panova, he wore a suit and tie, rather than jeans and sweater. He carried a briefcase instead of a backpack. He handed out business cards that listed him as "Assistant to the President" of EuroHealth, and he carried himself not like a student but like an eager but assured young businessman. He had applied to business school in Finland and been accepted. But Grajirena talked him out of it, arguing that Batlle would have many more opportunities to get rich if he stuck with EuroHealth and remained Grajirena's main contact in Moscow. Grajirena offered him a full-time job for $1,000 a month. Batlle thought about it overnight and said he would do it for $1,200 a month. Hayhurst and McElwee gave the thumbs-up.

Things were moving ahead for EuroHealth. There were still no orders by the end of July 1998, and EuroHealth still had not earned a nickel or a ruble. Grajirena remained confident, which was his natural inclination but was made a little more difficult by the uncertainty that marked Russia's worst economic crisis in years. After a period of relative stability, by 1998 it seemed as if the whole economic structure was crumbling. The ruble was crashing, and so was the stock market. Russian bonds were downgraded below investment grade. Foreign investment was drying up. Boris Yeltsin supposedly had recovered from his heart surgery, but he seemed more erratic and at times more detached than ever. He fired and hired government ministers with seemingly little rhyme or reason, shedding known political operators and economic reformers for little-known and unproven assistants and deputies, and then suddenly bringing back people he had fired earlier. The international financial community and the IMF agreed to provide tens of billions of dollars in support, provided Russia met certain conditions. The main thrust of the bailout was to strengthen the ruble, allow the government to balance the budget at least temporarily, and hold down skyrocketing interest rates within Russia. Russian government bonds were restructured, interest rates were raised, foreign-debt payments were delayed, the ruble was devalued, and Yeltsin sacked his government again. The stock market fell even more, and foreign investors took their losses and went home. Banks collapsed. There was speculation that military commanders in the hinterlands, upset that their troops were not being paid and disgruntled with Yeltsin's leadership, were considering mutiny.

Grajirena followed it all, uneasily, from a distance. He sighed and shook his head whenever he came across a report like the one from a London consultancy that rated Russia as the riskiest country in the world for foreign investors, ahead of Venezuela, Mexico, Pakistan, and Brazil. Yes, things looked grim for Russia. Yes, that had to hurt EuroHealth's prospects. But he tried to keep his mind from making a link between the headlines and EuroHealth's prospects. Of course, if the Russian economy collapsed, his Russian master distributor could fold up, just as Lazarenko's company had folded up when the Belarus economy took a dive. Grajirena consoled himself that much of EuroHealth's business would be coming from Lithuania. Of course, if Russia collapsed, Lithuania probably would, too, since so much of its economy was linked to Russia. Even if the bailout ultimately worked and the Russian economy revived, that could mean many smaller headaches for EuroHealth; for instance, one of the demands of the international lenders providing the money to Russia was that the country increase its import fees. Higher duties, naturally, would mean a higher cost of doing business, which would at least cut into EuroHealth's profits and discourage its distributors from ordering Rexall products in the first place. But Grajirena was unable to spend much time thinking about all the bad things that might or could happen. For one thing, it wasn't in his nature. For another, there was too much work to do, too many opportunities that might be missed if he didn't keep working full speed ahead, assuming that everything was going to turn out wonderfully for EuroHealth, that all his deals were doing to work, and that he was going to end up a very rich man.

Grajirena contacted Dr. Ron Finger, the Savannah plastic surgeon who was in practice with Robert Greco's brother and who had been a First Republic investor. Finger had developed a multistep skin-care cream that was particularly useful before and after laser surgery. Grajirena told Finger about Dr. Panova, and Finger was interested. He negotiated a deal with Grajirena for EuroHealth to sell his skin cream in Russia. Grajirena, through Dennis Batlle, told Panova about Finger's skin cream, and she was very interested in it as well as in the Key West Aloe products. She asked for a sample, and Grajirena brought it on his next trip, along with Mariam Howard, the head dermatologist at Finger's clinic in Savannah, to demonstrate and explain how the skin cream should be used. At Sheremetevo airport, however, there was a problem. Customs officers wanted to see the bag Howard was carrying with all the samples. They asked about the jars of skin cream. She told the truth. They were for evaluation at Panova's clinic. But the customs inspectors wanted a commercial invoice, which is required of any sample brought into Russia for a product that might someday be imported for sale. Grajirena didn't have a commercial invoice. Sorry, the inspectors said. They confiscated the samples.

But Howard had sneaked a few jars of the skin cream into a deep pocket in one of her bags. She and Grajirena gave them to Panova, who had them evaluated in her lab and announced that she was satisfied. Panova was going to take care of registration of the postsurgery skin cream, and she wanted to introduce it at a big Moscow conference on dermatology and plastic surgery a few weeks later. Grajirena didn't see how everything could get done in time—shipping the cream, getting Russian labels printed, having brochures printed up. But it was a good problem to have, after so many years of so many bad problems. "I'm thinking of having a sign printed up to carry around that says 'Will work for an easy deal,'" Grajirena told his wife in a phone call home. Just once, he told her, he would like to find a deal that went through easily. But he knew that would never happen. There were no easy deals in Russia.

On his way home from the trip where he and Howard gave Panova the postsurgery skin cream, Grajirena had an afternoon to kill before catching his plane that evening. He told Panova about the samples being confiscated and that she could have them if he could get them out of customs. She gave him two letters to present to the customs inspectors, explaining why the samples were needed for her clinic and why there should be no duty on them. Grajirena went out to the aiport and talked to the chief inspector who had confiscated the samples. The chief inspector looked over Panova's letter and said Grajirena could have the samples back if he gave him $150. It was a bribe. Grajirena said no. The inspector referred him to another supervisor, who referred him to another. Grajirena was bounced around through seven people for over four hours. He finally ended up back with the chief inspector he had talked to first. The inspector said he still wanted $150. Grajirena told him to forget it. He had come this far in Russia without knowingly paying a bribe, and he wasn't going to start now.

CHAPTER 32

At Home

T he years after First Republic folded were the best years of Rick Grajirena's life. He and Val had never been happier. Their sons were growing into polite, considerate, intelligent, capable young men who seemed to have bright futures. The family was close. They had many friends but didn't see them all that often. They rarely socialized. If they went someplace or did something, it was usually as a family. Their house was full of laughter. It was a house where all the people talked to one another, liked one another, and respected one another. One thing they rarely talked about was Grajirena's business, except for his travel schedule. He was gone for a week or ten days every month or six weeks. His highs and lows, his successes and failures, his prospects and problems were not talked about around the table where the family almost always ate dinner together. He and Val often discussed his business when they met for lunch in the kitchen because he valued her opinions, but his work was not a large part of the fabric of family life. Grajirena still went to bed early and got up early. He built a new three-stall garage, and one of the stalls was given over to a small office. The office was crowded but not cluttered: computer, scanner, fax, laptop, in-box, out-box, two chairs, two beige metal filing cabinets, a small bookcase. In the bookcase were various computer and software manuals, a Russian-English dictionary, bottles of sample vitamins, stacks of computers disks, a complete set of *National Geographic* on CD-ROM, a pile of Moscow newspapers and issues of *Foreign Affairs* magazine, a copy of *The Art of Negotiating* by Gerald I. Nierenberg, a world atlas, the Delta Airlines world timetables, and a box of twenty-five Cohiba Robustos. On the bookcase was a piece of the Berlin

Wall and the metal eagle that once adorned the top of the ceremonial flag-pole outside the Kremlin, complete with the gold-braided rope that the guard had thrown in at the banquet years before.

On the desk was a stack of business cards. One well-thumbed card was set to the side. Grajirena had gotten it from a fellow international road warrior on one of his long flights to Moscow. In fact, it was the flight he had taken to Moscow to fire Misha. He had had a nice chat with the guy, pocketed the card, and hadn't looked at it until he returned from that trip, when staffers and board members and investors were sniping at him from all sides. On the back of the card it said this:

It is not the critic who counts, not the man who points out how the strong man stumbled, or where the doer of deeds could have done better.

The credit belongs to the man who is actually in the arena; whose face is marred by dust and sweat and blood; who knows great enthusiasm, great devotion, the triumph of high achievement; and who, at the worse, if he fails, at least fails while daring greatly, so that his place shall never be with those cold and timid souls who know neither victory nor defeat.

You've never lived till you've almost died. For those who have had to fight for it, life has truly a flavor the protected shall never know.

Among the few pictures in Grajirena's office—his boys' school photos, a glamour shot of Val in an off-the-shoulder dress—was a framed copy of the March 1979 cover of *Yacht Racing/Cruising* magazine, showing Grajirena at the helm of the tilted, tacking *Southern Star* in choppy gray seas. There was also a framed embroidery of an English proverb—"A smooth sea never made a skilled mariner"—that Val made for him for Christmas 1994, when First Republic was struggling. Aside from a couple of scrapbooks down in the bottom of one of the filing drawers, there were few other reminders of Grajirena's sailing career. Val said she got rid of more than two hundred trophies, plaques, and awards—including at least one crystal pickle dish—that her husband had won on the water. "I sold them at garage sales over the years," she said. "No, Rick didn't mind. He didn't want them, and he couldn't see why anyone else would want them, either." Out in the garage, the office overflowed in the form of a couple more filing cabinets and shelves. On one shelf, gathering dust, was a thick box marked "The Ultimate Home Study Action Course for Maximum Success in the Consulting Business."

Grajirena was often out in his office at six A.M., checking faxes that had

come in overnight from Russia, doing research on the Internet, writing letters or composing memos or reports. In the afternoon he and Val often went
for a walk or a swim, usually with their chocolate Lab, Murphy. When the
boys came home from school, the family would run errands. Grajirena and
one of his sons occasionally went fishing, walking five minutes to Tampa
Bay or trailering their boat to a nearby marina where they launched it. Grajirena usually made dinner, using recipes only as a starting point. Italian
dishes and grilled meat and seafood were staples. When the boys did their
homework and Val cleaned up the kitchen, he often sneaked back to his
office for another hour, sometimes two. He and Val usually met for an hour
of TV or reading before bedtime. The boys sometimes watched or sat and
read with them, but more often they played video games or did something
on their own computer.

In his mid-fifties, Rick Grajirena had never made as much as $100,000
in a year. He wished he had made more money in his life, but he still
believed he would make enough from his work with the dentists to be well-
off someday, at least by his standards. "I've got a great life," he said. "I'm not
going to be one of those guys on his deathbed who says, 'I wish I'd spent
more time with my family.'" He didn't make a lot of money, but he didn't
have a lavish lifestyle. He had put money away years ago to pay for his boys'
college educations. He had a few small investments, but not enough to retire
on. Maybe he would have enough in a few years, if things went well with
Rexall and some of his other deals in Russia. One afternoon, preparing for a
rare party at their house—it was a summer weekend, and a visitor was in
town whom Grajirena wanted to introduce to some friends—he took a
break from shopping and cooking and setting up tables and chairs and
packing coolers with ice and soda and beer. He sat down under the umbrella by the pool with an icy Heineken and talked about the future.

I can see myself becoming a full-time consultant, working with Geoffrey
Farrar and the CEER Group. That's going to be a good company, a
going business, helping put deals together, helping make things happen for the people who hire us as consultants. Right now, working
with the Docs, I'm on a mission that requires all my time. But it won't
always require all my time. Ultimately this whole EuroHealth deal
belongs in Europe. The headquarters should be there. I learned that
the last time around. The Docs understand that I am not going to
insist on trying to run the whole thing myself. I'm not going to screw it
up. We're going to find the right guy to run the company. The Docs
will step back and be satisfied with that. They're looking to get well,

after all. As soon as this company is on its feet, they'll be happy. They're tired. They want some rest. And I don't blame them.

Eventually I think we might set up the operational headquarters in Poland. Then the Docs can be like the godfathers, just come over once in a while and look around. They're not the types to look over the manager's shoulder, to constantly be asking what's going on, why this, why that. Not like some of the First Republic investors. If I do my job right, they should be in a position where someone, some big company, would come in and want to buy EuroHealth within a few years. I don't think the Docs would want to take it public themselves. That would be pretty expensive. And I don't think they'd want some investment bank to come in and cram them down. I think they'd be better off selling it to a big company that's going to run it as a division, or absorb it into their own operation. I wouldn't want to have a job with the company. No. My share, I'm looking to cash out eventually. So I'm keeping an eye on other opportunities. I'd like to spend my twilight years as a consultant. I can tell people how not to do it in Russia. Not many people know better than I do how not to do business in Russia.

Later that evening, after he grilled porterhouse steaks, Grajirena and his guests sat and talked and drank beer and wine around tables on his deck and in his yard. Night fell, and a soft cool breeze blew in off the bay. Some of the guests were old friends who had invested in First Republic, including Bob Snibbe. Several of them said that if Grajirena asked them, they would invest with him again. Overhearing, Grajirena interrupted, laughing, to promise he would never ask again. Several of the guests were Russians, sailors who had come to Tampa to help raise money for the Odessa 200 project and ended up staying. One of the sailors who had taken over a boatyard dandled his new baby on his knee, while his pretty American wife looked on, smiling. Candles flickered on the checkered tablecloths. Glasses clinked, and occasionally a cork popped. Laughter floating in the breeze collided above the backyard with the squeals and shouts from the pool, where some kids splashed with the dog. Grajirena offered around a box of cigars and lighted one himself. Occasionally his voice was heard above the others, and then there would be peals of laughter.

At one point he told several guests about a new product he might try to market in Russia: a mobile blood bank. And there was another product, packets of prepared meals manufactured by a small company under the brand name Heater Meals. The dehydrated meals, in trays, could be heated up by adding a chemical solution that came in a packet. Scrambled eggs and sausage. Beef stew. Lasagna. Grajirena walked across the lawn to his office, disappeared for a minute, and came back with a cardboard package about the size of a hardbound book. He opened it on the table while a dozen guests gathered around as if they were curious townsfolk come out to see the snake-oil salesman and his medicine show. Grajirena tore open the enclosed packet of chemical solution, poured it onto the dehydrated food, and then stood back as it steamed and smoldered for a minute. The guests *oohed* and *ahhed*. After a minute Grajirena passed out forks, and several guests each took a mouthful or two of scrambled eggs or sausage. It was hot, they marveled. And good. Grajirena said a product like this would do really well in Russia. "There aren't that many restaurants outside the cities," he said. "Soldiers and truck drivers and traveling salesmen, anybody who has a hard time finding a hot meal, will love these things." No, he said, he wasn't involved with the company right now, but he might try to help the manufacturers—"a couple of nice guys who really don't have it all together yet"—try to sell their Heater Meals in Russia and elsewhere in Eastern Europe. The conversation eventually moved on. Voices continued to rise and fall, including Grajirena's. At one point he could be heard above everyone else, his words floating out over the quiet, dark backyards of his neighbors, half a world away from where he did business. "It's all just a mouthful o' howdy and a handful o' much-obliged," he declared. And he laughed.

Epilogue

Much has happened in Russia since this narrative ended in the summer of 1998. The IMF bailout fell apart after Russia devalued the ruble and announced that it was not going to repay its foreign debts on time. The two cornerstones of the Russian economic revival of 1994–97—a stable currency and lowered inflation—disappeared in 1998 as the ruble lost 70 percent of its value and inflation rose 84 percent.

Boris Yeltsin, once the dynamic reformer president, was tired and ill and out of it. By early 1999, his popularity ratings in Russian opinion polls had dropped to 1 percent, about the same as Mikhail Gorbachev's. They had both become yesterday's men. Yeltsin replaced his dynamic young reformer prime minister by bringing back an old conservative he had fired once before, Yevgeny Primakov, who called for a Roosevelt-style New Deal but still had not made any specific proposals after half a year in office.

The country drifted into the first half of 1999 like a giant rudderless ship that was slowly sinking. The Russian government could not reach agreement with foreign governments or foreign banks on restructuring plans either for old debts or for new loans. The gross domestic product fell by 5 percent in 1998 and was expected to drop by another 5 percent in 1999—in some aspects the worst economic depression ever in an industrialized nation.

Russia retreated from free markets, re-nationalizing the largest bank and taking up proposals to return other key industries to the state control of the Soviet era. The *mafiya* took advantage of the economic chaos. Russia's prosecutor general, the equivalent of the U.S. attorney general, reported in late 1998 that nearly half the country's economy was controlled by organized crime, including 40 percent of all state-owned corporations and 50 percent of all commercial banks. Food shortages followed the worst grain harvest since the 1950s, and 30 percent of the population lived below the government's poverty line of $32 a month in income.

Various politicians maneuvered for a run at the presidency during the next scheduled elections in 2000, including a number of nationalist right-wingers, former communists and, probably the front-runner, Moscow Mayor Yuri Luzhkov. The leading liberal contender, a legislator from St. Petersburg, was murdered on the street in an execution-style shooting. The term *demo-*

crat had become "a dirty word" through much of Russia, the *New York Times* noted.

Trade with countries outside the former Soviet Union dwindled by nearly 18 percent, and many American companies stopped doing business in Russia. A few Americans, including Rick Grajirena and Robert Greco, continued to do business as best they could. Greco had a ticket and was ready to fly out at the end of the summer of 1998 during the height of the financial crisis, amid rumors that marauding gangs were going to attack and loot Western-owned businesses, and kidnap, torture, and kill Western businesspeople. But no marauding gangs came, and Greco stayed, though he scaled back his business considerably and lowered his personal profile.

Rick Grajirena kept flying back and forth between Florida and Russia, patiently working on his deals and trying to open up new ones. EuroHealth made its first sales and deliveries of Rexall over-the-counter pharmaceuticals in Lithuania and Russia, and the distributors paid for them on time. The Missouri dentists actually began making back some of the money they had invested in Grajirena and Russia.

Grajirena also reached a tentative deal for EuroHealth to export herbal coffee to Russia, and he began representing Mentor Medical, the leading manufacturer of breast implants, in its efforts to make inroads in the Russian market. As part of that marketing effort, he gave a speech to plastic surgeons at the Russian Academy of Sciences Hospital on Mentor's latest breast-implant procedures, and then opened negotiations for Mentor with a Russian importer.

Grajirena believes the small market for products such as over-the-counter drugs, cosmetics, herbal coffee, and breast implants shows that, despite the widespread poverty of 1999, there is still hope for Russia, and for an American entrepreneur in Russia, in the twenty-first century.

Moscow does not look like it did twenty, ten, even five years ago, and Russians, after this first stunted, unsatisfactory encounter with capitalism, don't think the same way they did in the Soviet era. Russians are coming to understand how they underestimated the time and effort needed to transform their society, whether in changing attitudes or erecting a legal structure or creating the institutions necessary to support a free-market democracy. Moreover, perhaps everyday Russians are coming to the grim realization that they themselves have to help make the changes. Rather than leaving it to Western countries and companies, they must take responsibility for their own future.

Grajirena believes that one way or another, Russia will have another chance to become a free-market democracy, and both Russians and Westerners will profit from their past mistakes.

INDEX

ABOUT THE AUTHOR

Timothy Harper, a journalist and lawyer, writes about international politics, economics, and business for many publications on both sides of the Atlantic. A former Associated Press national writer and London-based special correspondent for several U.S. newspapers, he is a contributing editor for *Sky* magazine, an adjunct member of the faculty at the Columbia University Graduate School of Journalism, and an editorial consultant and writing coach for major corporations. He lives with his wife, Nancy Bobrowitz, and their two children in Ridgewood, New Jersey. This is his tenth book. He can be reached at:

timharper@compuserve.com *or*
harpertim@aol.com